# EMPLOYMENT LAW 1992

## CHRISTOPHER WAUD

of the Middle Temple
Barrister and Chairman of
Industrial Tribunals

**The Practical Guide
for Personnel Managers
Trade Union Officials
Employers, Employees
and Lawyers**

Michael O'Mara Books Limited

Published in 1992 by Michael O'Mara Books Limited, 9 Lion Yard, Tremadoc Road, London SW4 7NQ

**REDUNDANCY & UNFAIR DISMISSAL**

First Edition 1981–1982 ISBN 0 85144 179 3
Second Edition 1982–1983 ISBN 0 85144 183 1
Third Edition 1983–1984 ISBN 0 85144 229 3

**GUIDE TO EMPLOYMENT LAW**

First Edition 1985 ISBN 0 85144 337 0
Second Edition 1986 ISBN 0 85144 337 0
Third Edition 1987 ISBN 0 85144 393 1
Fourth Edition 1988 ISBN 0 85144 426 1
Fifth Edition 1989 ISBN 0 85144 499 7
Sixth Edition 1990 ISBN 0 85144 546 2
Seventh Edition 1991 ISBN 1 85592 706 3

Typeset by Florencetype Limited, Kewstoke, Avon
Printed and Bound in Great Britain by Richard Clay Ltd, Bungay, Suffolk

# HOW TO USE THIS BOOK

THE LAW RELATING to employment and its procedures is ever more complicated and confusing. The purpose of this book is to make it more understandable to personnel managers, trades union officials and as a quick, easy-reference guide to the law.

Subjects are listed in the Contents on Page 7. If the required point cannot be found, consult the index (Page 299). All the text is cross-referenced.

For example, should you be dealing with a claim for unfair dismissal then read Chapter 5. If it appears that there will be a hearing read Chapter 18. And if the question of sex discrimination arises check Chapter 11.

Anyone constantly dealing with employment matters should read the first chapter and then glance through the book to acquire a cursory knowledge of points for future reference.

At the side of the text are references to the cases which decide the point, together with the sections and paragraphs of the various attendant Acts.

The following abbreviations are used:

## Courts

| | |
|---|---|
| HL | *House of Lords* |
| PC | *Privy Council* |
| CA | *Court of Appeal* |
| CS | *Court of Session (Scot)* |
| ChD | *Chancery Division of High Court* |
| QB or QBD | *Queen's Bench Division of High Court* |
| DC | *Divisional Court of High Court* |
| EAT | *Employment Appeal Tribunal* |
| NIRC | *National Industrial Relations Court* |
| ECJ | *European Court of Justice* |
| ECHR | *European Court of Human Rights* |
| IT | *Industrial Tribunal* |

## Law Reports

| | |
|---|---|
| AC | *Appeal Cases* |
| ChD | *Law Reports, Chancery Division* |
| QB or QBD | *Law Reports, Queen's Bench* |
| AER | *All England Reports* |
| ITR | *Industrial Tribunal Reports* |
| IRLR | *Industrial Relations Law Reports* |
| TLR | *Times Law Reports* |
| ICR | *Industrial Cases Reports* |
| LGR | *Local Government Reports* |
| WLR | *Weekly Law Reports* |
| ER | *English Reports* |
| ECR | *European Court Reports* |
| CMLR | *Common Market Law Reports* |

## Acts, Orders, Regulations

| | |
|---|---|
| AMR Act 1988 | *Access to Medical Reports Act 1988* |
| CE Act 1963 | *Contracts of Employment Act 1963* |
| Co Act 1985 | *Companies Act 1985* |
| CL Act 1977 | *Criminal Law Act 1977* |
| DP (E) Act 1944 | *Disabled Persons (Employment) Act 1944* |
| DP (DE) Order 1946 | *Disabled Persons (Designated Employment) Order 1946.* |
| E Act 1980 | *Employment Act 1980* |
| E Act 1982 | *Employment Act 1982* |
| E Act 1988 | *Employment Act 1988* |
| E Act 1989 | *Employment Act 1989* |
| E Act 1990 | *Employment Act 1990* |
| EAT Rules 1980 | *Employment Appeal Tribunal Rules 1980* |
| EAT (A) Rules 1985 | *Employment Appeal Tribunal (Amendment) Rules 1985* |
| EP Act 1975 | *Employment Protection Act 1975* |
| EP(C) Act 1978 | *Employment Protection (Consolidation) Act 1978* |
| EP (H of R) Var Order 1979 | *Employment Protection (Handling of Redundancies) Variation Order 1979* |
| EP (R of UB & SB Reg. 1977 | *Employment Protection (Repayment of Unemployment and Supplementary Benefit) Regulations 1977* |
| EP (V of L) Order 1992 | *Employment Protection (Variation of Limits) Order 1992* |
| EqP Act 1970 (as amended) | *Equal Pay Act 1970 (as amended by the Sex Discrimination Act 1975).* |
| EqP (A) Reg. 1983 | *Equal Pay (Amendment) Regulations 1983* |
| EC Act 1972 | *European Communities Act 1972* |
| HSW Act 1974 | *Health & Safety at Work etc. Act 1974* |
| HS Act 1980 | *Health Services Act 1980* |
| IR Act 1971 | *Industrial Relations Act 1971* |
| IE (IC) Reg. 1983 | *Insolvency of Employer (Excluded Classes) Regulations 1983* |
| IT Act 1982 | *Industrial Training Act 1982* |
| IT (E&W) Reg. 1965 | *Industrial Tribunals (England and Wales) Regulations 1965* |
| IT (IPNA) Reg. 1974 | *Industrial Tribunals (Improvement and Prohibition Notices Appeals) Regulations 1974* |
| IT (R of P) Reg. 1985 | *Industrial Tribunals (Rules of Procedure) Regulations 1985.* |
| LR (C of E) Reg. 1976 | *Labour Relations (Continuity of Employment) Regulations 1976* |
| P of W Act 1960 | *Payment of Wages Act 1960* |
| P Act 1890 | *Partnership Act 1890* |
| RR Act 1976 | *Race Relations Act 1976* |
| RR (Q & R) Order 1977 | *The Race Relations (Questions and Replies) Order 1977* |
| RPP Reg. 1965 | *The Redundancy Payment Pensions Regulation 1965* |
| RP (V of R) Order 1985 | *The Redundancy Payments (Variation of Rebates) Order 1985* |
| RO Act 1974 | *Rehabilitation of Offenders Act 1974* |

| | |
|---|---|
| RO Act 1974 (Exemption) Order 1975 | *Rehabilitation of Offenders Act 1974 (Exemption) Order 1975* |
| RO Act 1974 (Exemption) (Amendment) Order 1986 | *Rehabilitation of Offenders Act 1974 (Exemption) (Amendment) Order 1986* |
| SRSC Reg. 1977 | *The Safety Representatives and Safety Committees Regulations 1977* |
| SD Act 1975 | *Sex Discrimination Act 1975* |
| SD Act 1986 | *Sex Discrimination Act 1986* |
| SD (A) Order 1987 | *Sex Discrimination (Amendment) Order 1987* |
| SD (Q & R) Order 1975 | *The Sex Discrimination (Questions and Replies) Order 1975* |
| TU (P of E) Reg. 1981 | *The Transfer of Undertakings (Protection of Employment) Regulations 1981* |
| TU Act 1913 | *Trade Union Act 1913* |
| TU Act 1984 | *Trade Union Act 1984* |
| TULR Act 1974 | *Trade Union and Labour Relations Act 1974* |
| UD (I of CL) Order 1991 | *The Unfair Dismissal (Increase of Compensation Limit) Order 1991* |
| UD (V of QP) Order 1985 | *The Unfair Dismissal (Variation of Qualifying Period) Order 1985* |
| UD (I of L & B & SA) Order 1992 | *The Unfair Dismissal (Increase of Limits & Basic and Special Awards) Order 1992* |
| W Act 1986 | *Wages Act 1986* |

# CHAMBERS OF MR. MICHAEL BURTON QC
## 2, Crown Office Row,
### Temple
### EC4Y 7HJ

**Specialists in Employment Law:**

- Employer and Employee rights
- transfer of undertakings
- restraint of trade clauses
- collective agreements
- confidentiality
- Industrial Tribunals
- Interlocutory Injuctions

- Anton Pillers
- industrial disputes
- redundancy
- wrongful dismissal
- unfair dismissal
- sex & race discrimination
- Trade Unions

| | | |
|---|---|---|
| Michael Burton QC | Michel Kallipetis QC | Michael Sherrard QC |
| Robert Rhodes QC | Daniel Serota QC | Richard Price |
| Colin Manning | Richard Perkoff | Ian Mayes |
| Philip Bartle | Mark Lomas | Timothy Higginson |
| Clive Freedman | John Bowers | Andrew Clarke |
| Caroline Harry Thomas | John Davies | Shirley Bothroyd |
| Selwyn Bloch | Antony Sendall | Ian Gatt |
| Michael Duggan | Paul Lowenstein | Raoul Downey |
| Martyn Barklem | Charles Samek | Jeffrey Bacon |

Donald Harris (*Door Tenant*)     Mohammed Syed (*Door Tenant*)

*Practice Manager:* David Douglas
*Clerks:* Jeff Cox, Deborah Anderson
*Fees Clerk:* Tony Shaddock
*Accounts Receivable Manager:* Nita Johnston

Telephone: 071 583 2681
Fax: 071 583 2850   DX: 1047   LIX: LON 052

# CONTENTS

# CONTENTS

# CHAPTER ONE

# The Law at work

## GENERAL INFORMATION

**1.1**   The law relating to the rights and duties of employers and employees is derived from three sources: 'common law', our own legislation mostly introduced since 1963, and the Treaty of Rome. It is also influenced by the European Convention for the Protection of Human Rights.

**1.2**   This subject has become extremely complicated, not least because of the flood of decisions, flowing from our own courts, the European Court of Justice and from the European Court of Human Rights.

**1.3**   Faced with this array of law, some of it highly technical and difficult to understand, what is the ordinary employer or worker to do when faced with an employment problem? He may not want to incur the expenses or go to the trouble of consulting a solicitor, and yet if he makes a wrong decision the consequences can be very costly.

**1.4**   This book tries to help by explaining the law simply. Where it is derived from Acts, the intention of Parliament is set out as well as the principles to be applied. Included are summaries of cases to show the general approach, as well as important technicalities that have to be strictly followed.

**1.5**   It is only intended as a guide, as the subject is too comprehensive to be condensed into a volume of this size. Furthermore, it must be borne in mind that this is still a very fluid part of our law, with frequent Acts being passed, supplementing, repealing or amending previous legislation.

**1.6**   The impetus is likely to continue with the European Economic Community [EEC] passing new laws. Under Article 118, the Commission for the EEC is required to promote:

'close co-operation between Member States in the social field, particularly in matters relating to:

- employment;

- labour law and working conditions;
- the right of association, and collective bargaining between employers and employees.'

**1.7**    Lord Denning MR saw the problem in this way:

*H P Bulmer Ltd. v J*
*Bollinger SA [1974] Ch.*
*401, CA*

". . . when we come to matters with a European element, the Treaty is like an incoming tide. It flows into the estuaries and up the rivers. It cannot be held back. Parliament has decreed that the Treaty is henceforward to form part of our law. It is equal in force to any statute."

"The draftsmen of our statutes have striven to express themselves with the utmost exactness. They have tried to foresee all possible consequences and provide for them. They have foregone brevity."

". . . How different is this Treaty! It lays down general principles. It expresses its aims and purposes. All in sentences of moderate length and commendable style. But it lacks precision. . . . All the way through the Treaty there are gaps and lacunae. They have to be filled in by the judges, or by Regulations or Directives. It is the European way."

## POSITION AT PRESENT TIME

**1.8**    Employment law up to 1963 was almost exclusively derived from the 'common law', that which has been made by judges over centuries (see Chapter 8). It came under the heading of 'master and servant' and was archaic; in most respects it was unsuited to the needs of the latter part of the 20th century.

**1.9**    Parliament started to intervene in 1963 when it passed the Contracts of Employment Act. That Act required a minimum period of notice of termination of employment to be given to and by an employee, and laid down what particulars of employment had to be given in writing to an employee.

**1.10**    Since then there has been a deluge of legislation covering every area of employment, from sex discrimination to the rights of employees to have paid time off to undertake some public duties. There is almost no sphere left now that is not affected by one Act or another.

**1.11** The law relating to some of the older 'common law' claims like 'wrongful dismissal' can only, at present, be dealt with in the ordinary courts, (see Chapter 8). 'Common Law' claims have fallen away dramatically in recent years, even though they are not fully covered by the statutory law. It is expected that some common law jurisdiction will be conferred on tribunals shortly (see para. 1.48).

## TRIBUNALS/COURTS – WHICH COURSE TO FOLLOW?

**1.12** Usually a litigant would be better off using the remedies available in the Tribunals under the statutory provisions. The procedures are less cumbersome and quicker. In any event there cannot be duplication of damages. There may be little to gain by taking proceedings in the civil courts, unless the loss is much higher than can be recovered in the tribunals or there is another special factor.

*O'Laoire v. Jackel International Ltd. (No 2) [1991] ICR 718, CA*

**1.13** On a complaint of unfair dismissal a tribunal awarded the maximum under its jurisdiction, having found that the losses were more than that figure. It was held that a civil court, hearing a claim for damages arising out of the same facts, could not reduce its award by the sum given by the tribunal unless the plaintiff would obtain compensation under two heads of damages for the same loss, e.g., obtain double compensation.

### Merits of Each Case

**1.14** When considering the merits of any particular case, it must be realised that a ruling previously given in a similar case may not apply because of some particular facts. That sometimes appear to lead to contradictory decisions. Furthermore there is always a 'grey area' where one tribunal or court will take one view, and another will take the opposite. Badly drafted legislation has been responsible for what seems strange decisions.

**1.15** It should also be borne in mind that one witness may impress whereas another one giving identical evidence may not, and this could affect the outcome of a case.

## RELATIONSHIP BETWEEN 'COMMON LAW' AND STATUTORY LAW

**1.16** When ascertaining the rights and obligations of the employer and employee under a contract of employment, the common law rules have to be used. This has to be done before any of the statutory provisions are applied to them.

**1.17** For instance, if a lorry driver alleges that he has been unfairly dismissed because he had refused to drive on the continent, and he contends that he could only be required to drive within the U.K., then it would be necessary to examine the terms of his contract. The ordinary 'common law' canons of construction would be used to determine what were his duties.

**1.18** Some of the terms in the contract will be express, and they will generally not cause any difficulty. Many will be implied, and this is where there is likely to be a difference of opinion.

**1.19** Where there is ambiguity in the terms of a contract or in a document, the general rule is that it will be construed against the party seeking to rely on it.

**1.20** An employer who dismisses an employee for refusing to move to a different site, relying on a mobility clause that is not wholly clear, is likely to find that it will not provide him with protection should any proceedings arise in consequence of it.

*Litster v. Fram Gerrard Ltd. [1973] IRLR 302, NIRC*

### Effects of Difference

**1.21** At 'common law', an employee who refuses to carry out an important part of his contract may be summarily dismissed and he lacks redress. Under the statutory law, such a breach of contract would be an important factor that would be taken into account in deciding whether a dismissal was fair or unfair (see paras. 5.53–55).

### Interpretation of Words and Phrases

**1.22** Many words and phrases that have particular meanings attached to them at 'common law' are frequently to be found in statutes. Sometimes, the Acts give them definitions, or there may be some slight difference in the wording or phraseology.

**1.23** Generally, the same meaning is given to them as in the 'common law'. Thus, although the word 'employee' is given various definitions under different statutes, the same 'common law' tests are applied to determine whether a person is an 'employee' or not (see paras. 2.1–11).

## Common Concepts

**1.24** Some concepts of 'common law' are also imported into the statutes. For instance, in order to see whether an employee has been 'constructively dismissed' (see para. 3.57) it is necessary to see whether there has been a (common law) fundamental breach of contract (see paras. 8.11–16).

**1.25**

*EP(C) Act 1978, s.74(4) Gallear v. J F Watson & Son Ltd. [1979] IRLR 306, EAT*

Some of the same rules apply in other respects. At 'common law' and under the statutory provisions, an employee is required to 'mitigate any loss' (see paras. 2.76–83) sustained by him, and the same tests would be applied in each case.

**1.26**

*Gunton v. Richmond-upon-Thames BC [1980] ICR 755, CA*

The 'common law' and statutory law do part company in some instances. At 'common law' a purported dismissal, which is in breach of contract, is ineffective to end the contract unless it is accepted by the innocent party (see para. 8.33). However, because the right to receive remuneration and the obligation to render services are mutually dependent, it is rare that the contract can remain alive except for very limited purposes.

**1.27**

*Robt. Cort & Son Ltd. v. Charman [1981] ICR 816, EAT*

*Reg. v. East Berkshire Health Authority, ex p. Walsh [1984] ICR 743, CA*

Under the statutory law the dismissal takes effect on the date specified by the employer. This may be subject to an extension of up to 12 weeks under the deeming provisions that apply for certain purposes (see paras. 3.10–17). It does not need acceptance. Hence the result is that there many be one date for dismissal under the 'common law' and another under the statutes.

# LEGISLATION – HOW EFFECTED

## Parliament

**1.28** The primary source of legislation dealing with employment comes from our own statutes, and from orders and regulations made under them. Some substantial changes in the law are also effected under statutory instruments made pursuant to powers conferred on a Minister under the European Communities Act, 1972.

## Treaty of Rome and laws made under it

**1.29**

*EC Act 1972 s.2(1)*

*Shields v. E. Coombes (Holdings) Ltd. [1978] ITR 473 CA*

The Articles in the Treaty of Rome and regulations made thereunder are binding and directly enforceable in the tribunals and courts of the United Kingdom. They have primacy over our own laws inasmuch as if there is any conflict or inconsistency, then the Community law takes precedence.

**1.30**

*Pickstone & ors. v. Freemans plc [1987] ICR 867, CA (but upheld on appeal by House of Lords on other grounds).*

Further, if the domestic law fails to implement any of the detailed requirements set out in the Treaty of Rome, then a party can rely on an Article (in the Treaty) direct.When it relates to employment law, it can be enforced in the tribunals even though no statutory authority has been expressly conferred on them to do so.

**1.31**

*Livingstone v. Hepworth Refractories Ltd. [1992] IRLR 63, EAT*

Where this occurs, the tribunals have to adopt procedural rules that are not less favourable than similar provisions laid out in similar domestic law. Further they must not be so unreasonable as to render it virtually impossible to exercise rights conferred by the Community Law (see para. 1.33 below).

**1.32**

The Council of European Communities who, after considering (i) proposals from the Commission, and (ii) the opinion of the European Parliament and (iii) the Economic and Social Committee, issues 'Directives' to member States. Each country has to integrate the requirement into their law. There have been several 'Directives' that have been incorporated into our own law, mostly by regulations and orders.

**1.33**

*Marshall v. Southampton & SW Hampshire Area Health Authority (Teaching) [1986] ICR 335, ECJ*

*Emmott v. Minister for Social Welfare & anr. [1991] IRLR 387, ECJ*

If the European law comes via a Directive that requires legislation to be passed and there has been a failure to comply, then a person employed in an 'organ of the State' can rely directly on that Directive, provided it is sufficiently clear and unconditional. Furthermore, any time limits imposed by the general law do *not* apply until there has been compliance by the State with the Directive.

**1.34**

*Foster & ors. v. British Gas plc [1991] ICR 84, ECJ [1991] ICR 463 HL*

The European Court has ruled that an organ of the State extends to any organisation or body whatever its legal form, (a) that is responsible for providing a public service under the control of the State and (b) with special powers for that purpose, and (c) that are not available to the ordinary employer.

**1.35**

*Foster & ors. v. British Gas plc [1991] ICR 463, HL*

It has been held that British Gas, before privatisation, fell within the definition of an 'organ of the State' because (a) it had monopoly powers that had been conferred by Parliament, (b) it was created to provide a public service, (c) it was generally under the control of the State and (d) the Government was entitled to its surplus revenue.

**1.36**

*Worringham v. Lloyds Bank plc [1982] ICR 299, CA*

But in the private sector, employees can *only* rely on the domestic law. They may be able to get the same result, but by a circuitous route. They may be able to persuade our courts to refer a case to the European Court for a declaration of whether the obligations emanate from the Treaty, and if there is a ruling in their favour, then our own courts will enforce it (see paras. 19.48).

**1.37**

*Duke v. GEC Reliance Ltd. [1988] ICR 339, HL*

Some 'Directives' are promulgated to facilitate the practical application of duties imposed by the Articles of the Treaty; and as such they may be relied upon directly in actions against employers.

**1.38**

The European Court tends to adopt a generous approach to the interpretation of the Treaty, especially where it may result in remedying an obvious injustice. But where rights are conferred, they must be clear and precise, and not conditional or qualified, before they can be relied upon.

**1.39**

*Duke v. GEC Reliance Ltd. [1988] ICR 339, HL*

This has led to some enthusiasm by our own courts and tribunals in adopting a similar approach in the interpretation of the very general phrases found in the Treaty. But where there is a direct conflict between our own domestic legislation and any Directive that requires enactments to be passed before it becomes effective, then an employee in the private sector cannot rely on it.

**1.40**

*Pickstone & ors. v. Freemans plc [1988] ICR 697, HL*

In any event, if our own legislation is sufficiently widely drawn to be capable of two (or more) interpretations, then that which accords with the European law must be followed. This means that words and phrases have

*Garland v. British Rail Engineering Ltd [1982] ICR 434, HL*

"to be construed, if they are reasonably capable of bearing such a meaning, as intended to carry out the obligation and not be inconsistent with it" (per Lord Diplock),

*Von Colson & Kamann v. Nordrthein-Westphalia The Times, Apr. 25, 1984, ECJ*

and consequently it is always necessary to consider the European law in many employment problems.

**1.41**

Stevens & Ors. v. Bexley
Health Authority
[1989] ICR 224, EAT
Burra & Ors. v. Belgium
State & City of Liege
The Times, Apr. 4, 1988,
ECJ

An important consequence of a party being able to bring a claim directly under the Community law is that there may be no time limits (see paras. 1.33 & 3.74–91). There is at present a restriction on the amount recoverable (see para. 4.3). Judicial pronouncements have pointed out the desirability of bringing time limits into line. The European Court of Justice has stated that so far as its rulings are concerned, it alone may decide on any time limitation.

### The European Convention for the Protection of Human Rights and Fundamental Freedoms

**1.42**

In 1953 the United Kingdom ratified the Convention. Since 1959 when the European Court of Human Rights was established, it has submitted to its jurisdiction. From 1966, the right of individuals to petition the courtdirect has been recognised.

**1.43**

Secretary of State for the
Home Department, ex p.
Brind
[1991] 2 WLR 588, HL

Although the Articles laid down in the Convention are not directly enforceable in our tribunals and courts, our own legislation has to be construed in the same way as in para. 1.40 above.

**1.44**

New rights and obligations are added to the Articles by way of Protocols. It is up to the British Government, and each signatory to the Treaty, to decide whether to accept them as binding on themselves.

## DIVISION OF WORK

### The Industrial Tribunal

**1.45**

The jurisdiction of the tribunal is limited to those cases where jurisdiction is conferred on it by statute (but see para. 1.30). Most of its work relates to unfair dismissal and redundancy claims. It does cover a wide field, ranging from appeals under the Health and Safety at Work, appeals in respect of levies, awarding compensation for loss of office and other matters.

**1.46**

EP (V of L) Order 1992
UD (I of CL) Order 1991
EqP Act 1970 (as amended)
s.2(5)

In some claims there is a limit on the amount of compensation; for instance £5,940 for redundancy up to April 1, 1992, and thereafter £6,150 (see para. 4.3); for unfair dismissal, £10,000 (in most cases but see para. 5.159(d)(vi)). In equal pay claims the amount is limited to the losses incurred during the period of two years prior to the commencement of proceedings (see para. 11.124(b)).

**1.47**

*EP(C) Act 1978 s.69*

There is power to order reinstatement or re-engagement, and failure by the employer to comply will result in further financial penalties (see paras. 5.147–156 & 5.159(c)).

**1.48**

It has been stated in Parliament that some common law jurisdiction is to be conferred on tribunals shortly, enabling them to determine breaches of contract where a claim is associated with one being brought in the tribunal. This could occur, for instance, if on a dismissal an employer failed to pay money in lieu of notice. Thus it would avoid duplication of actions.

## Representaion

**1.49**

*Clay Cross Ltd. v Fletcher [1979] ICR 1, CA*

It was the intention of the legislature, when tribunals were given powers to deal with the employment law under the various statutes, that they should:

> "provide a quick and cheap remedy for what it had decided were injustices in the employment sphere. The procedure was to be such that both employers and employees could present their cases without having to go to lawyers for help" (per Lawton L.J.).

**1.50**

*Lavery v Plessey Telecommunications Ltd [1982] ICR 373, EAT*

Unfortunately, some of the legislation has become so complicated that even the judiciary has difficulty in understanding it. Browne-Wilkinson J. described the provisions relating to maternity as being "of inordinate complexity exceeding the worst excesses of a taxing statute" and as a "legislative jungle".

## Employment of Lawyers

**1.51**

Over the years there has been a tendency to employ lawyers, especially where the subject-matter is complicated and where a failure in the proceedings may be expensive. Furthermore, procedure plays an ever more important part. A failure to comply with time limits and orders may result in a good claim being lost or a valid defence being debarred (see paras. 3.74–91).

**1.52**

*IT (R of P) Reg 1985 rule 7(6)*

A party is entitled to appear on his own behalf, or alternatively, to be represented by a union, an industrial consultant, or a friend, relative or anyone else.

**1.53**

*Martin v. British Railways*

The risk in using the services of an unqualified person, or one unfamiliar with the law and procedure is that he

Board
[1989] ICR 24, EAT

or she may make a mess of it. In bad cases this may result in the litigant being ordered to pay the costs (see para. 18.95–98). Wood J., emphasised that:

> "It is important that advisers of all kinds, not only lawyers, but those who seek to put themselves forward as advisers or advocates before Tribunals and this court, should appreciate that they are expected to know the law and the procedure; it is perhaps only those acting in person need guidance, that a more lenient approach is justifiable."

**1.54** Legal aid is available for advice but not for representation in the tribunals. The Citizens Advice Bureaux and Legal Advice Centres will provide advice, and very often will either appear for a party or, alternatively, arrange the free services of a legal practitioner. Trade associations or unions will often advise their members and will also appear on their behalf.

### The County Court

**1.55** This court has power to deal with all common law breaches of contract like wrongful dismissal, failure to pay outstanding sums owing to an employee, or give holiday pay and matters of that kind (see Chapter 8).

**1.56** Claims up to £50,000 are now commenced in it, but some may be transferred to the High Court in accordance with statutory requirements or practice directions. A new procedure has been introduced and it will have to be seen how it works. The court has no power to adjudicate on statutory employment law (which is dealt with in the tribunals).

### Representation

**1.57** In any proceedings, only the following have a 'right of audience' to address the court:

(a) any party to the proceedings;

(b) a barrister who is instructed by a solicitor, or, by a solicitor;

(c) any other person allowed by leave to appear instead of that litigant;

(d) an officer of the local authority concerning property relating to the authority where the proceedings are adjudicated upon by the District Judge (see para. 18.99).

**1.58** Legislation is expected that will enlarge the kind of persons who may represent their firms or clients in Court, e.g., accountants, surveyors and other professional persons.

## The Employment Appeal Tribunal ['E.A.T.']

**1.59**

*EP(C) Act 1978*
*sch.11 para.20*

Appeals from Industrial Tribunals lie to this body except those relating to Health and Safety at Work (see paras. 1.64 & 16.28) and levies (see para. 17.23). The composition and powers of this tribunal are dealt with in para. 19.3.

### Representation

**1.60** The same rules about representation apply as in the tribunals. The proceedings are very much more informal than in the High Court, but it does require some expertise to be able to argue a case before it. Appeals from it are heard by the Court of Appeal. Legal Aid is available and should be used wherever possible.

## The High Court

**1.61** This court generally adjudicates in all common law claims where the anticipated damages or award are in excess of £50,000. It may also deal with smaller claims where important points of principle are involved.

**1.62**

*Hill v. C A Parsons & Co.*
*Ltd. [1971] 3 AER 1345, CA*
*Powell v. London Borough*
*of Brent [1988] ICR 176, CA*

Generally the court is limited to making an award of damages for breach of contract and cannot order reinstatement or re-engagement (see paras. 5.147–156). But where there is no loss of confidence and there exists a good working relationship between the parties, then it can make an order of 'specific performance'. This directs the employer to take the employee back into employment, usually for a limited time.

**1.63**

*Alexander & ors v.*
*Standard Telephones &*
*Cables plc. [1990] ICR 291,*
*CD*

Even where the employee's contract has not been finally ended, an injunction cannot be obtained that would have the effect of forcing an employer to retain him in employment where there has been a loss of confidence.

### Judicial Review

**1.64** The court, under powers conferred on it when constituted as a 'Divisional Court', also hears appeals, under a procedure known as 'judicial review'. It considers Health and Safety at Work Act cases, and Levy cases (see paras. 19.35–38) from the tribunals. It also adjudicates on appeals from the Certification Officer (see paras. 1.103–107). Although it has jurisdiction to rule on allegations on misbehaviour by a tribunal, these are invariably dealt with in the EAT (see paras. 1.59–60).

**1.65**

*Reg. v. Dty. Governor of Parkhurst Prison, ex. p Leech*
*The Times, Feb. 5 1988, HL*

Its appellate powers are also exercised under the same procedure to hear cases where any person or body exercises a statutory power that affect the rights or legitimate expectations of citizens and is of a kind that the law requires to be exercised judicially. The Court may review the exercise of that power.

**1.66**

*Calveley & ors. v. Merseyside Police [1986] IRLR 177, CA*

*McLaren v. Home Office [1990] IRLR 338, CA*

*Reg. v. Durham City Council The Times, Jan 31, 1992, DC*

Before a claim can go ahead, leave must be obtained from a High Court judge, who has to be satisfied that there is an arguable case. Further, except where there has been an abuse of natural justice or action has been taken that was in excess of jurisdiction, it is normally only available where all other remedies or avenues of appeal have been exhausted. There is *no* jurisdiction unless there is a sufficient element of public law present. So private disputes have to proceed by an ordinary action. A claim for judicial review *must* be brought within three months of the matter about which the complaint is made.

**1.67**

*Reg. v. Birmingham City Council ex p. Ferrero Ltd. The Times, May 30, 1991, CA*

Where a statute specifically provides a quick and easy means of appealing against an order made against an aggrieved concerning some matter that is alleged to have serious consequences if allowed to continue, that appeal procedure should be followed. This is so even though there might have been grave procedural improprieties in the way the order became made.

**1.68**

*Ridge v. Baldwin [1964] AC 40, HL*

*Reg. v. Lord Chancellor's Department ex p. Nangle [1991] ICR 743, DC*

In employment cases the procedure may generally be used where a person is employed in the public sector and the employment is underpinned by statutory provisions. So where an employer is circumscribed in the manner in which the employee can be disciplined or dismissed, and there has been a breach of those requirements, then the court may intervene.

**1.69**

*Reg. v. Birmingham City Council, ex p. McKenna The Times, May 16, 1991, DC*

Even where an aggrieved is able to show that *prima facie* there has been a breach of *statutory* procedure in the interviewing process, nevertheless leave to proceed may be refused on the grounds that there has been no injustice.

**1.70**

Reg. v. Secretary of State for the Home Department, ex p. Attard, The Times, June 29, 1989, DC

A woman prison officer was able to invoke the procedure by alleging that the Secretary of State had acted in excess of his power. He had suspended her from duty without pay under his statutory powers. At the time disciplinary proceedings by the governor were taking place against her. In the event, it was held that the Secretary of State had residuary powers to take that action, and so the claim was dismissed.

**1.71**

Reg. v. CRE ex p. Westminster C.C. [1985] IRLR 426, CA Reg. v. East Berkshire H.A. ex p Walsh [1984] ICR 743, CA

The issuing of a non-discrimination notice by the Commission of Racial Equality comes within this jurisdiction, but not the dismissal of a nursing officer. In the latter case a breach of contract of employment was not a matter of public law.

**1.72**

Roy v. Kensington Chelsea & Westminster Family Practitioners' Committee The Times, Feb. 10, 1992, HL

On the other hand where a doctor complained about a reduction in his allowances by the Family Practitioners' Committee, payable pursuant to an Act of Parliament, it was held that he could use the process of judicial review if the Committee had (wrongly) refused to include him on their list. Once there, his only remedy for breach of any of his rights lay under private law, e.g., a claim for breach of contract by way of an ordinary action.

**1.73**

Jones v. Lee & Anr [1980] ICR 310, CA

The power to intervene can also be exercised where proceedings are commenced by ordinary writ for a 'declaration' and an injunction (to prevent someone from doing something). This could arise where an employer has a discretionary power to terminate employment that is conditional upon certain procedural steps, and he defaults on them. The court may declare a purported dismissal to be void with the consequence that the employment continues until it is validly ended.

**1.74**

Reg. v. B.B.C., ex p Lavelle [1982] IRLR 404, DC

There is also a discretionary power to halt domestic hearing, if there are criminal proceedings taking place against an employee at the same time. But there must be a real danger of a miscarriage of justice occuring in those criminal proceedings as a result.

**1.75**

Reg. v. Secretary of State for Health & Anr., ex. p. Guirguis [1990] IRLR 30, CA

In determining whether there has been a default by an oficial body under an agreement, the Court applies the strict contractual test. The Secretary of State for Health refused to consider representations made to him by a medical consultant over his *summary* dismissal on the grounds of lack of jurisdiction. It was held that the minister had acted correctly. The conditions of service only gave him power where the dismissal was *'on notice'*. No implied terms could be read into the conditions to confer on him the right to intervene.

**1.76**

*Reg. v. Salford Area Health Authority ex. p. Janaway, The Times, Dec. 2, 1988, HL*

The procedure was used where a person was dismissed for refusing to comply with an instruction to type a letter relating to abortions. She had a conscientious objection to abortions and a statutory right of refusal to act. But her action failed because there was not sufficient proximity between her duties and the exception granted by the legislation.

### Representation

**1.77** Litigants in person are entitled to appear, but they should be wary of doing so, as considerable expertise is required. There are very strict rules of procedure. Legal aid is available and should be used where possible.

**1.78** Companies have to be represented by counsel (instructed by solicitors). If litigants wish to be represented, they can only appear through counsel.

## The Court of Appeal

**1.79** This court hears appeals from the EAT and the High Court. Apart from litigants in person (but see paras. 19.41–43) everyone has to be represented by counsel instructed by solicitors.

## The House of Lords

**1.80** Appeals from the Court of Appeal go to the House of Lords, although there is a procedure where an appeal can go there direct from the High Court in very special circumstances. Apart from litigants in person (but see paras. 19.46–47) all parties have to be represented by counsel instructed by solicitors.

## The European Court of Justice

**1.81** This Court, which was set up under the Treaty of Rome, sits at Luxembourg. It has power to deal with all the employment law laid down in the Treaty, and Regulations and Directives made under it.

**1.82** It can either give a decision in favour of an individual petitioning it, or the Commission (set up under the Treaty). The Commission can take proceedings against any member nation, where that State defaults in passing legislation giving its citizens various rights, or imposing various duties on them.

**1.83**

*Dzodzi v. Belgium*
*The Times, Jan. 7,*
*1991, ECJ*

Our own courts are responsible for giving effect to decisions from the European court. The latter court tries to ensure that there is uniform interpretation of the Treaty and that there is no divergence between the case laws of the Community and national courts.

### Representation

**1.84** Parties who are litigating must be represented by a lawyer entitled to practice before a court in the member state. The lawyer must submit credentials from the Bar Council or the Law Society.

**1.85** Member States and institutions of the Community may be represented by an agent, who may be helped by an adviser or a duly accredited lawyer. The agent is not required to be legally qualified, so a minister could appear if he wished.

### The European Court of Human Rights

**1.86** This Court, which sits at Strasbourg, can only pronounce judgment against the United Kingdom on a complaint by another signatory country to the Treaty or on the petition of a person who alleges a country is in breach of the Convention (see paras. 1.42–44).

**1.87** There is no machinery by which its decisions are directly enforceable, although in practice there is usually compliance.

### Representation

**1.88** A litigant may present his case in person before the court although it is highly desirable that he is assisted or represented by a barrister, a solicitor, or any other lawyer. The person appearing must have been approved by the Court.

## POWER TO CONFER SOME 'COMMON LAW' POWERS ON TRIBUNALS

**1.89**

*EP(C) Act 1978*
*s. 131*

Under the Employment Protection (Consolidation) Act, 1978, there is power to confer some 'common law' jurisdiction (see Chapter 8) on Industrial Tribunals.

**1.90** These include damages for breach of contract of employment, or a sum due under such a contract, or a claim for recovery of a sum in pursuance of any enactment relating to the terms of performance of such a contract (see paras. 8.12–19). It must arise out of or is outstanding at the termination of the employment and is brought concurrently with proceedings for breach of statutory proceedings.

**1.91** By conferring these powers, duplication of actions would be avoided, thus saving costs. For instance, an employee might claim that he was unfairly dismissed and that he was owed four weeks for money in lieu of notice at the time. Even if he wins before the tribunal on his unfair dismissal claim, he still has to go before the County Court to recover his money in lieu.

**1.92** This power to confer jurisdiction has not been exercised because initially of objections from the T.U.C. (but see para. 1.48), but there are alleged drafting difficulties. However, by a side-wind it has been held that a tribunal can determine claims for non-payment of certain sums due to an employee under the Wages Act 1986 (see paras. 15.124–135).

## ACAS-CENTRAL ARBITRATION COMMITTEE

### Advisory, Conciliation and Arbitration Service ['ACAS']

**1.93**
*EP Act 1975 s.1(2)*

This statutory body, which was created in 1975, is charged with the duty of:

> "promoting the improvement of industrial relations, and in particular of encouraging the extension of collective bargaining and the development and where necessary, reform of collective bargaining machinery."

**1.94**
*EP Act 1975 s.2(1)*

Where there is a dispute, or one is apprehended, it may offer its services to try to effect a settlement, if approached by a party or by an interested person.

**1.95**
*EP Act 1975 s.133(6)*

One of its tasks is to seek to settle any dispute between an employee and his employer or former employer. Any advice given is confidential and cannot be disclosed in any subsequent proceedings (see para. 2.57).

**1.96** The Service has very considerable experience in assessing the likely outcome of proceedings. It will give the parties its views but it does not advise. In doing so, it is able to settle nearly two-thirds of cases brought before the tribunals. Not all result in a cash settlement – a number are withdrawn, either because of a technicality, e.g., the employee is out of time, or because the claim lacks merit.

**1.97**

*EP Act 1975 s.3(1)(b)*

The Service may also refer a matter in dispute to arbitration or to the Central Arbitration Committee, provided it has the consent of the parties, and they have exhausted all their agreed procedures, or there are some special reasons to justify arbitration.

**1.98**

*EP Act 1975 s.6*

It is also responsible for issuing Codes of Practice (see paras. 3.162–166), and can give guidance on matters relating to collective bargaining and time-off work to enable an employee to carry out certain duties (see para. 15.7).

**1.99**

*EP Act 1980 s.19(b) & sch.2*

It no longer has power to make a recommendation that a union be recognised by an employer for the purposes of collective bargaining (see para. 4.57).

## Central Arbitration Committee ['C.A.C']

**1.100**

*EP Act 1975 s.10*

This body was also created by the Employment Protection Act, 1975 and inherited the duties formerly exercised by other arbitration boards or bodies. It arbitrates in disputes referred to it by ACAS.

**1.101**

*EP Act 1975 ss. 17, 18 & 19*

It deals with complaints that an employer has failed to make disclosure to recognised unions (see paras.15.113–119) of certain information that is required for collective bargaining purposes.

**1.102**

*ACTSS v. Chloride Legg Ltd.
CAC Award 84/15
(unreported)*

But an employer cannot be forced to give information about groups of employees or issues for which the union is not recognised. Even where it is, the information is privileged where it relates to individuals who have not given their consent for disclosure.

# CERTIFICATION OFFICER

**1.103**

*EP Act 1975 s.7*

*TU Act 1913 s.3*

The Certification Officer, who is appointed by the Secretary of State, is responsible for:

(a) ensuring observance of statutory procedures governing the setting up and operation of political funds and dealing with member's complaints concerning breaches of fund rules;

*TU(A) Act 1984 ss.1 & 4*

(b) ensuring compliance with statutory procedures for mergers and transfers of engagements, and complaints about the conduct of merger ballots;

*TU & LR Act 1974 (as amended by EP Act 1975) s.8*

(c) maintaining a list of unions and employer's bodies ensuring that they keep proper accounts and that superannuation schemes conform to requirements for actuarial examination;

*E Act 1980 s.1*

(d) reimbursing unions for certain expenditures incurred in conducting secret postal ballots;

*TU Act 1984 ss.1 & 13*

(e) approving the ballot rules of any union wishing to continue spending money on political objects, and dealing with complaints that unions have not held secret ballots for elections to certain offices.

**1.104**

*Reg. v. Certification Officer, ex p. Electrical Power Engineer's Association [1990] ICR 682, HL*

A payment under para. 1.103 (c) above is made under the Trade Union Ballot Regulations, 1984. Some discretion has to be exercised. A union in applying their rule book reasonably disallowed a candidate who had won the highest votes, because an area was over represented. It was held they were not be debarred from receiving an indemnity. Only weighted voting, block voting or voting through an elected college would result in the payment being lawfully withheld.

**1.105**

*Reg. v. The Certification Officer, ex p. Royal College of Nursing of the United Kingdom [1991] IRLR 258, DC*

The Royal College of Nursing sought the views of their members in a ballot over whether their rule book should be altered to permit striking or taking industrial action. Only a Committee could decide ultimately whether there should be a change. It was ruled that attention shouldbe paid to the purpose behind the regulations. Too narrow a construction should not be applied. Even though the regulations restricted reimbursement to ballots that asked members whether there should be a strike or industrial action, and not whether the rule book should be altered, it was held that the College was entitled to the payment.

**1.106**

*EP Act 1975 s.8(1)*

A union whose name is on the list maintained by the Certification Officer, may apply to him for a certificate that it is independent. If, having made such inquiries as he thinks fit and taking into account relevant information, he finds that

(a) the union is not under the domination or control of the employer, and

(b) it is not liable to interference by the employer,

then he will issue a certificate.

**1.107**

*EP Act 1975 (as amended by EP(C) Act 1978 sch.16 para.23(2)(c)) s.8(9)*

If he refuses to issue one, then a union may appeal to the EAT (see paras. 19.1–35). If, on appeal, the Appeal Tribunal is satisfied that a certificate should have been issued, it will make a declaration that one should have been issued and give the appropriate directions.

# CHAPTER TWO

# Matters of mutual concern to Common and Statutory Law

## 'EMPLOYEE'/SELF-EMPLOYED

**2.1**    Many important consequences depend upon whether a person is an 'employee', or is an independent contractor. The employer is liable for all the wrongdoing of his worker that are committed in the course of his employment. He is responsible for tax deductions, for national insurance deductions and contributions, and for levies payable in respect of 'employees'. There are many duties and obligations to an 'employee'.

**2.2**    If the person working for him is an independent contractor, then he can escape a lot of these liabilities and responsibilities.

**2.3**    Some of the Acts and statutory instruments provide a definition of the word 'employee'. Except for those cases where the word is specifically stated to include a restricted class of independent contractor, as in the Race Relations Act 1976 (see para. 14.25), the ordinary common law tests apply.

**2.4**

*O'Kelly v. Trusthouse Forte plc [1983] ICR 708, CA*

In deciding whether a person is an 'employee', the Courts will look at a series of matters: the main ones being the following.

(a) Is there some measure of control indicative of an employer-employee relationship?

(b) Is the person carrying out the work for and on behalf of the employer or is he in business on his own account?

(c) Is he free to accept or refuse work at will?

(d) Is he supplied with a uniform and equipment?

(e) Is he subject to disciplinary or grievance

procedures?

(f) Does he have to take holidays as directed?

(g) Is he paid regularly either weekly or monthly, and is it paid gross or net of tax?

(h) What has been agreed with the Inland Revenue?

**2.5**

*Narich Pty. Ltd. v. Commission of Pay-Roll Tax [1984] ICR 286, PC*

No one test is decisive but the

"most important . . . criteria for determining the relationship . . . is the extent to which the person . . . is under the direction and control of the other party . . . with regard to the manner in which he does his work . . .".

**2.6**

*Massey v. Crown Insurance Co. Ltd. [1978] ITR 5, CA*

If the relationship between the parties

"is in doubt or . . . is ambiguous, so that it can be brought under the one relationship or the other, it is open to the parties by agreement to stipulate what the legal situation between them shall be" (per Lord Denning, M.R.).

**2.7**

*Wicken v. Champion Employment [1984] ICR 365 EAT*

It is not possible for the parties to change the true relationship between them by putting the wrong label on it. A girl had an agreement with an employment agency under which she was employed under a 'contract of service' but worked as a 'temp' for various client firms of the agency. It was held that she was not an 'employee'. There was a minimum of control over her, there were no mutual obligations to provide or accept work, there was no continuity and it did not resemble any contract of service.

**2.8**

*Ironmonger v. Movefield Ltd. t/a Deering Appointments [1988] IRLR 461, EAT Construction Industry Training Board v. Labour Force Ltd. [1970] 3 AER 220, DC*

Problems can sometimes arise over the true status of agency-supplied workers. Are they employed by the agency, the firm for whom they are working, or are they self employed? If they are unable to bring their status under one of these headings they will be classified as on a contract of 'sui generis' [a contract 'of their own kind'].

**2.9**

*Daley v. Allied Suppliers Ltd. [1983] ICR 90, EAT*

A Youth Opportunities Programme trainee was held to be not an 'employee' as there was no contract between her and the firm that was providing her with work experience. She was paid a training allowance and had to comply with instructions given to her as a trainee, but her attendance was optional.

**2.10**

*City of Glasgow DC v.
McNullity
Nov. 29, 1983, EAT
(unreported)
Dyson v. Pontefract & DC
CVS CP Scheme
Jan. 13, 1988, EAT
(unreported)*

On the other hand, where a person was engaged in carrying out such a scheme, he was an 'employee' because he fell within all the tests. So, too, was a person who participated in a Community Programme because he was paid a 'wage' and was otherwise treated as an 'employee'.

**2.11**

*McLaren v. Home Office
[1990] IRLR 338, CA*

There are several occupations where the relationship between the parties indicates the existence of a contract of employment, but where there is in law none, e.g., prison officers. But where there is power to enter into a contract of employment, and the parties do so then they will be bound by the terms agreed.

**2.12**

*Cowell v. Quilter Goodison
& Co. Ltd. & anr.
[1989] IRLR, CA
P. Act 1890, s.1
Santokh Singh v. Guru
Nanak Gurdwara
[1990] ICR 309, CA*

Further, sometimes the nature of the relationship precludes a person from being an employee. So equity partners, who under the statutory definition are 'carrying on business in common with a view to profit', do not have any employment relationship with each other. Nor, too, is there normally a contract of service between a minister of religion and a church, and this extends to priests in a Sikh temple.

**2.13**

*Massey v. Crown
Insurance Co. Ltd
[1978] ITR 5, CA*

An employee who has deliberately put a false label on his relationship to obtain fiscal advantages may find himself debarred from obtaining other statutory advantages:

> "He gets the benefits of it by avoiding tax deductions and getting his pension contributions returned. I do not see that he can come along afterwards and say it is something else . . . Having made his bed as being 'selfemployed', he must lie on it" (per Lord Denning, M.R.).

## BURDEN OF PROOF

**2.14**

Frequent references are made in the different Acts for one party or the other having to 'prove' some fact or to 'satisfy' the tribunal on some particular matter. Irrespective of the actual wording used, the standard of the burden of proof is always the same, namely, that of on a 'balance of probabilities'.

**2.15**

This means that the tribunal will decide a point based on which allegation is more probable in the circumstances. The members must take into account all the evidence they have heard, their assessment of the reliability of witnesses and use their experience in life and common sense.

**2.16**

*The Financial Times Ltd. v. Byrne & ors. Jan. 7, 1992, EAT (unreported)*

This has some practical importance because sometimes the burden is on one party at one point and then switches to the other for the next. A failure somewhere along the line might result in an otherwise sound case failing (see para. 5.21).

**2.17**

*London Borough of Barking and Dagenham v. Camara [1988] ICR 865, EAT Baker v. Cornwall County Council [1990] ICR 432, CA*

In (direct) discrimination cases, the burden does not pass to the employer to prove that he has not discriminated, except where the

"circumstances [are] consistent with the treatment being based on grounds of sex or race [when] the industrial tribunal should be prepared to draw the inference that the discrimination was on such grounds unless the alleged discriminator can satisfy the tribunal that there was some other innocent explanation" (per Neill, LJ).

**2.18**

*Quereshi v. London Borough of Newsham [1991] IRLR 264, CA King v. Great Britain China Centre [1991] IRLR 513, CA*

Where a party relies on inferences to be made from primary facts to prove discrimination, there must be some hint of prejudice on racial or sexual grounds before a tribunal can hold that a person has been treated unfavourably on either ground in comparison to others. If the explanation given for the treatment is unsatisfactory then a tribunal may infer discrimination.

**2.19**

*Bessenden Properties Ltd. v. Corness [1974] IRLR 338, CA*

Where an allegation of failure to mitigate damages is raised, the tribunal has to assess whether there has been adequate mitigation by an employee. The onus still remains on the employer to prove it (see para. 2.76).

## OBLIGATION TO PROVIDE WORK

**2.20**

*Langston v. Amalgamated Union of Engineering Workers [1974] IRLR 15, CA*

It is now settled law that it is implied in every contract of employment that an employee is not only given the right to be paid the agreed wage but also the right to have the opportunity of doing his work when it is available.

**2.21** Para. 9 of the Code of Practice (see para. 3.162) says:

> "management should recognise the employee's need to achieve a sense of satisfaction in his job and should provide for it so far as practical".

**2.22**

*RH&DT Edwards Ltd. v. Evans & Walters July 16, 1985, EAT (unreported) Miller v. Hamworthy Engineering Ltd. [1986] ICR 846, CA*

Unless a contract allows an employer to lay off an employee without pay, then an attempt to do so would amount to a fundamental breach of contract. That would entitle the employee to leave and to claim compensation on the grounds that he has been unfairly (constructively) dismissed (see para. 3.37(c)). Alternatively he could remain in employment but claim damages equivalent to the lost wages.

**2.23**

*A. Dakri & Co. Ltd. v. Tiffen [1981] ICR 256, EAT Kenneth MacRae & Co Ltd. v. Dawson [1984] IRLR 5, EAT*

Even if the contract does allow an employer to lay off without pay, then he can only do so for a reasonable time. If it goes beyond that period, the employee can leave and claim compensation. But where the contract does provide that the employee may be laid of *indefinitely*, then the length of the passage of time would be irrelevant.

**2.24**

*Devonald v. Rosser & Sons [1906] 2 KB 726, CA*

Where an employee's income is (mainly) dependent on the employer providing work, e.g., he is paid at an hourly rate without there being a minimum number of hours, or, on a nominal basic salary plus commission, there would be an implied term that the employer would supply him with a *reasonable* amount of work.

**2.25**

*McClelland Fergusson & Ptnrs. v. Fergusson Jan. 1, 1985 EAT (unreported)*

A sales director, who was employed on a commission basis, fell ill and sales dropped dramatically. It resulted in a big drop in his earnings. It was held that the employers breached their implied duty under contract by failing to take steps to maintain sales and so deprived the employee of most of his income. He was entitled to leave and claim 'constructive dismissal' (see para. 3.37(c)).

**2.26**

*Withers v. General Theatre Corporation [1933] 2 KB 536, CA*

In certain occupations, like acting where publicity is an important part of the contract, there is an implied right to work. A person has the right to enhance his reputation. An actor who was entitled to be advertised as playing a leading part was wrongly prevented from appearing. It was held that he was entitled to recover damages flowing from that breach. It did not extend to any injury to his existing reputation or feelings.

## ILLEGAL CONTRACTS

**2.27**

*Napier v. National Business Agency Ltd [1951] 2 AER 264, CA Tomlinson v. Dick Evans U Drive Ltd [1978] IRLR 77, EAT*

If both parties enter into a contract that is wholly or partly illegal, the employee generally is not entitled to invoke the benefits of the Acts. This applies even if there is, for instance, a manifest case of unfair dismissal, and it matters not whether the point has been raised by a party. Once the tribunal or court (including appeal courts) learns about it or suspect that it has occurred, it has a duty to investigate.

**2.28**

*Broaders v. Kallare Property Maintenance Ltd. [1990] IRLR 421, EAT*

The illegal contracts generally fall into two groups. Those that are illegal from the start and those that are legal on the face of them but become illegal because of the mode of carrying them out. The latter generally involve defrauding a third party, often the Revenue, but it does not extend to dishonest conduct by an employee against his employer.

**2.29**

*Miller v. Karlinski [1945] 62 TLR 85, CA*

Those which are illegal at inception can never be enforced, whether an employee is aware or not of the illegal nature of the contract. Furthermore they are not restricted to criminal acts. Browne-Wilkinson, J (as he then was) said that contracts would not be enforced where they are:

*Coral Leisure Group v. Barnett [1981] ICR 503, EAT*

"entered into for the purposes which are . . . (although not forbidden by the general law) immoral . . . The word 'immoral' connotes only sexual immorality . . . 'Illegal contracts' . . . include not only contracts to do criminal acts but also contracts to achieve an immoral purpose."

**2.30**

The fact that a person has during his employment committed an unlawful or immoral act will not necessarily, by itself, prevent him from enforcing his rights, unless the contract was entered into for one of those purposes. So the lorry driver who knowingly uses an over-weight vehicle on frequent occasions or the door-man of a hotel who procures prostitutes for guests can pursue a claim. Whether it will succeed on merits may be a different matter.

**2.31**

*Corby v. Morrison t/a the Card Shop [1980] ICR 564, EAT Newland v. Simon & Willer (Hairdressers) Ltd. [1981] ICR 521, EAT*

If there is an agreement that part of the worker's pay should not go through the books and so avoid tax, this would be illegal. The employee will not be able to enforce his common law or statutory rights. But where the employee was unaware that the employer was acting illegally, e.g., tax was being deducted from his wages or he thought it was, but no returns were sent to the Inland Revenue, then he will not be debarred from making a claim. The test to be applied is not, *ought* he to know, but *did* he know of the illegality?

**2.32**

*Hyland v. J H Barker (North West) Ltd. [1985] ICR 861, EAT*

After an illegality ceases, an employee can pursue his statutory rights if he has the necessary qualifying period of employment (see para. 3.22) that will only *start to run* from when the illegal practice stopped.

**2.33**

*Hewcastle Catering Ltd. v. Ahmed & Elkamark [1991] IRLR 473, CA*

Where an employee helps an employer to defraud a third party from which he derives no benefit, public policy may not preclude him from bringing a claim. This is especially so where the contract of employment was not illegal at inception and where the employee had co-operated in the prosecution of the employer for the fraud.

## FRUSTRATION OF CONTRACT

**2.34**

*Davis Contractors Ltd. v. Fareham UDC [1956] AC 696, HL*

Frustration occurs where the main provision of a contract cannot be performed due to circumstances outside the control of either party and that were not foreseen or provided for in the contract. Thus where there is an agreement to rent a chalet but it is burnt down beforehand, then that event effectively brings the contract to an end without any action by either party.

**2.35**

The doctrine, which is usually to be found in commercial contracts, does not depend on an opinion, or intention, or even knowledge of any of the parties, but on the occurrence of the event that renders the performance of the contract radically different from that which was agreed. In the absence of any terms to the contrary, all the liabilities of each party under the contract cease.

**2.36**

*National Carriers Ltd. v. Penelpina (Northern) Ltd. [1981] I AER 161, QB*

It has now been settled in the House of Lords that all contracts are subject to this doctrine. In the employment field, it usually applies in sickness and imprisonment cases. Not all the reported ones can be reconciled.

**2.37**

The significance in employment cases is that there will *not* have been a 'dismissal' and hence the employee loses many of his statutory rights (see paras. 4.1 & 5.20), and some of his 'common law' ones as well.

**2.38**  The general rule is that self-induced frustration does not bring the doctrine into operation. So if a singer, for instance, was to lose her voice intentionally by walking in the rain in winter without a coat, then she would not be able to resist a claim for damages for breach of a contract to sing at a concert by claiming that there had been frustration through laryngitis.

**2.39**

*Chakki v. The United Yeast Co. Ltd. [1982] ICR 140, EAT*

Again, there is not unanimity of opinion on the point, but in imprisonment cases, the weight of judicial pronouncements is that it is because the employee is not available for work, and not that he has been sent to prison, that brings about the frustrating event. He could obviously avoid doing the act that would be likely to result in his losing his liberty.

**2.40**  Consequently, if he is sent to prison for a short period, e.g., for three weeks for non-payment of his wife's maintenance, then that would not be long enough to constitute a frustrating event. There would be times when he would be away in the normal course of events for that length, e.g., on leave, or perhaps sickness and so on, and his job would continue during these absences.

**2.41**

*Harrington v. Kent C.C. [1980] IRLR 353, EAT*

On the other hand a sentence of 12 months imprisonment would be a frustrating event. A minimum absence of some months (assuming the earliest release) would make the carrying out of the contract radically different from that contemplated when it was made.

**2.42**

*F.C. Shepherd & Co. Ltd. v. Jerrom [1986] ICR 802, CA*

Even where there was a special procedure for dismissing apprentices for absences (for any reason) it has been held that the concept of frustration still applies. Where a youth had been sent to borstal training, there had been no dismissal by the employer, because the contract had been frustrated.

**2.43**

*Egg Stores (Stamford Hill) Ltd. v. Leibovici [1977] ICR 260, EAT*

Sickness or serious injury can also be a frustrating event. If a tyre fitter gets knocked down and is confined to a wheel chair for the rest of his life, then the contract would be frustrated. Similarly, the contract of a violin player who loses a hand would be frustrated. For less serious matters, it can be difficult to determine the point when there is frustration. The general considerations applied are:

*Williams v. Watsons Luxury Coaches Ltd. [1990] ICR 536, EAT*

(i) the length of the previous employment and (if relevant) how long it would have been expected to continue;

(ii) the type of job involved, and the need for the employer to get the work done and/or find a replacement;

(iii) the nature of the illness or disabling event, and the prospect of recovery;

(iv) whether a reasonable employer could be expected to wait any longer;

(v) any terms regarding sick pay.

**2.44**

*Notcutt v. Universal Equipment Co. (London) Ltd. [1986] ICR 414, CA*

Where the circumstances are appropriate, the doctrine applies to contracts that can be ended at short notice. An employee with 26 years' service suffered a coronary that prevented him from working again. It was held that the illness had automatically frustrated the contract; the employer did not have to take any action.

**2.45**

*Lawton v. Bowden International Ltd. Dec. 13, 1990, EAT (unreported)*

The margin between whether there has been frustration or not is necessarily blurred. An employer should be wary of assuming that a contract of employment has ended. If he takes any action inconsistent with the continuance of a contract, then he may run the risk of it being held that he had dismissed the employee. It may turn out to be unfair on procedural grounds (see paras. 5.62–71). In a dubious case, it may perhaps be better to deal with the problem as a sickness dismissal(see paras. 5.86–102).

**2.46**

*Glenboig Union Fireclay Co. Ltd. v. Stewart [1971] ITR 14, CS EP(C) Act 1978 sch.13 para.9*

If a person is kept on by his company, perhaps on nominal pay, during an extended sickness absence, then if the employer takes him off the books, that will be deemed to be a 'dismissal'. On the other hand, if there is no contract of employment for more than 26 weeks then that would break the 'continuity of employment' (see paras. 3.25–35). The employee would lose most of his statutory rights.

## REPUDIATORY OR FUNDAMENTAL BREACH

**2.47**

*Western Excavating (EEC) Ltd. v. Sharp [1978] ITR 132, CA*

Where a party does some act that puts it out of his power to continue to carry on with a contract, or has indicated that he no longer intends to do so, then that act or statement amounts to a repudiatory act, which may be accepted by the other side (see para. 3.58).

**2.48**

*London Transport Executive v. Clarke [1980] ICR 532, CA*

Thus the conduct of an employee in going on an extended holiday to the West Indies in defiance of a refusal by his employers to give him permission was held to be repudiatory. He had made himself unavailable for work. When this was accepted by the employers, that ended the contract (see para. 3.58).

**2.49**

*Northgate Laundries Ltd v. Jenner Feb. 5, 1982, EAT (unreported)*

It is not necessary for the act to amount to any form of industrial misconduct. The test is an objective one. Thus where an employee was absent from work through illness and during that time the employers closed down the premises where he worked, it was held that:

> ". . . the closing of the works does constitute a dismissal by way of repudiation even though the employee at that particular time is not fit to work. . . . that repudiation was accepted by [the employee] asking for redundancy payments" (per Browne-Wilkinson, J.).

**2.50**

*Lewis v. Motorworld Garages Ltd. [1986] ICR 157, CA*

Fundamental breach generally occurs where one party commits a breach that goes to the root of the contract. Thus if an employer unilaterally halves the salary of a member of his staff, that would amount to a fundamental breach. Or it could arise from several acts, which if added up, go to the root of a contract (but see para. 3.40).

**2.51**

*Western Excavating (EEC) Ltd. v. Sharp [1978] ITR 132, CA Rigby v. Ferodo Ltd. [1988] ICR 29, HL*

If there has been a fundamental breach, then either party can withdraw from the contract. An employee could leave the employment and seek redress on the basis that he had been 'constructively dismissed' (see para. 3.37(c)). But he must act swiftly otherwise he will be deemed to have waived his rights by 'affirming' the contract. Furthermore there must be some overt acceptance of the repudiation; the contract does not automatically end by a wish of a party that it should do so.

**2.52**

*Norwest Holst Group Administration Ltd. v. Harrison [1985] ICR 668, CA*

If the employer informs an employee that he is going to take some unlawful action in the future [an 'anticipatory breach'] then the employee need not wait for it to occur. But if before he acts the employer retracts and notifies the employee, the right of the employee to take action on it is lost.

**2.53**

*Lewis v. Motorworld Garages Ltd., [1986] ICR 688, CA*

An employer's behaviour can be taken into account, along with other breaches, to determine whether cumulatively they amount to repudiatory conduct (but see para. 3.40).

**2.54**

Many constructive dismissal cases occur where it is alleged that there has been a breach of the implied term of mutual trust and confidence (see paras. 5.55–59).

## 'WITHOUT PREJUDICE'

**2.55**

*EP(C) Act 1978 s.133*

Many parties to proceedings would wish to try to settle their claims without going to the expense of an action. In tribunal cases, ACAS has a statutory duty to attempt to resolve disputes between employers and their staff (see paras. 1.95–96).

**2.56**

Frequently a party feels that there is justice in his claim or defence, and no amount of persuasion will make him change his mind, even if it comes from an independent and objective source.

**2.57**

*EP(C) Act 1978 s. 133(6)*

Any negotiations that take place through ACAS are privileged. Nothing can be revealed as to what has been said or as to the outcome or that would indicate a view taken by ACAS.

**2.58**

If a party wishes to negotiate in writing direct with the other side without risking the contents of any offers being subsequently disclosed, then it can be done by means of 'without prejudice' correspondence. It can be done orally as well, but if there is a dispute over whether it was 'without prejudice' then the conversation, or some of it, may have to be revealed and the damage done. If the letters are marked 'without prejudice' then the question brooks of no argument.

**2.59**

*Re. Daintrey, ex p. Holt [1893] 2 QB 116, QBD*

But it is necessary for there to be a dispute or for somenegotiations to be taking place when a 'without prejudice' letter is written, otherwise there will be no privilege.

**2.60**

The trouble with making an offer is that it tends to suggest an acknowledgement of some liability, leaving only the question of the amount to be decided. An employer (or other respondent – see paras 3.178–179) may only be trying to rid himself of a troublesome case or save expense.

**2.61** Hence, it is usually felt that it is better that the adjudicating body should not know what has gone on before the case is heard. Indeed in the High Court, and County Court, the judge is not allowed to know about it or about any 'payment into court' (see paras. 18.116 & 18.124) until after he has made his findings on liability.

**2.62**

*Walker v. Wiltshire*
*[1889] 23 QBD 355, QB*

Once correspondence is marked 'without prejudice', it is said to be 'privileged'. It can only be produced in proceedings if both sides agree.

**2.63**

*Norwest Holst Group*
*Administration Ltd. v.*
*Harrison*
*[1985] ICR 668, CA*

A consequence of this is that a party cannot rely on a 'without prejudice' letter purporting to 'accept' repudiatory conduct (see paras. 2.47–49), and so bring the contract to an end, because the letter is ineffective and in any event it cannot be shown to the court (except by agreement).

**2.64**

*Cutts v. Head & Anr.*
*[1984] 1 AER 597, CA*

Where there is a claim for something other than a monetary one, for instance, for a declaration about some matter, and one party put forward proposals 'without prejudice' to settle the action, that letter can be produced after liability has been determined. The court can then decide what order for costs is appropriate. Notice of an intention to take this course should be given to the other side.

**2.65**

*IT (R of P) Reg 1980*
*rule 11(1)*

A similar procedure can be adopted in the tribunals where there is no procedure for making a 'payment into court' (see paras. 18.100 & 18.111). An employer might offer a former employee the sum of £500 'without prejudice' in settlement of his claim. If the applicant fails to obtain an award above that figure, then the tribunal can be shown the letter and asked to make an order for costs against him. It will be on the basis that the proceedings have been carried on unreasonably (see paras. 18.76–81).

## 'IN HONOUR ONLY'

**2.66**

*TULR Act 1974 s.18*

Usually a union which has come to a collective agreement with another organisation, does not wish to be exposed to a claim for damages in the event of a breach of contract. They are protected under the 1974 Act which provides that parties to a collective agreement are required to state in writing that it is to be legally enforceable before it can be subject to the scrutiny of the Courts.

**2.67**

*Marley v. Forward Trust Group [1986] ICR 891, CA*
*Robertson v. British Gas Corporation [1983] ICR 351, CA*

But where some of the terms of a collective agreement between an employer and a union were incorporated into a contract of employment, and included the words,

'This agreement is binding in honour only . . .'

it was held that this clause did not prevent an employee from relying on the terms that formed part of his own contract. The exclusion clause was not incorporated into the contract of employment.

**2.68**

*National Coal Board v. NUM & ors [1986] ICR 736. ChD*

Only those terms that were apt to be enforced were included, e.g., those fixing terms of pay, hours of work, disciplinary proceedings etc. Those relating to procedures designed to resolve disputes between employers and employees' representatives were excluded.

**2.69**

*Alexander & ors v. Standard Telephones & Cables plc. [1991] IRLR 286, QB*

Where there is a redundancy clause contained in a Collective Agreement, an employee seeking can rely on it in two ways. Either he can show that it has been expressly incorporated into his contract of employment. If not able to do so he may be able to establish an implied incorporation by showing an intent that is apparent within the contract. The wording must be sufficiently clear to show that it was intended to be contractually binding.

## 'EX-GRATIA' PAYMENTS

**2.70**

The essence of an award of damages or compensation is that the injured party should be placed in the same position that he would have been but for the breach of contract or statutory duty, or any other wrong-doing. He should be compensated, so far as is possible, for the loss and damage he has suffered.

**2.71**

Sometimes, an employer makes an 'ex-gratia' payment to a former employee for a variety of reasons. He may want to 'buy off' a prospective action, or he may be doubtful about whether he has any liability, or he may merely want to be generous.

**2.72**

*Chelsea Football Club v. Heath [1981] ICR 323, EAT*

Whatever the reasons for a payment, if the employee subsequently brings proceedings, then provided the payment to him was expressly or by implication in settlement of any claim he might have, then the amount paid 'ex-gratia' can be set off against the liability. The loss will have been mitigated to the extent of that payment.

**2.73**    Difficulties sometimes arise where an employer is found by the tribunal to be partly responsible for bringing about his dismissal (see paras. 5.109–114) and an 'ex-gratia' payment has been made.

**2.74**

*Parker & Farr v. Shelvey [1979] ICR 896, EAT Clement-Clarke International Ltd. v. Manley [1979] ICR 74, EAT*

For instance, if the total award is £2,000 but the employee is 25% to blame (and thus entitled to £1,500), and an 'ex-gratia' payment of £1,000 has been made, should the 25% be taken off the £1,500 or off £1,000 (£2,000 – £1,000)? There is a difference of judicial views, but it would seem that on general principles the latter view is correct (see para. 5.124–126).

**2.75**

*McCarthy v. British Insulated Cables plc [1985] IRLR 94, EAT UD(I of CL) Order 1991*

The ex-gratia payment will have to be taken off the gross amount of the loss and not from the statutory limit placed on an award. Thus an employee who has suffered an actual loss of £20,000, and who has received £6,000 ex-gratia, will still be entitled to £10,000, i.e., the maximum compensation (see para. 5.126).

## 'MITIGATION' OF LOSS'

**2.76**

*EP(C) Act 1978 s.74(4) Gallear v. J F Watson & Son Ltd. [1979] IRLR 306, EAT A G Bracey Ltd. v. Iles [1973] IRLR 210, NIRC Archbold Freightage Ltd. v. Wilson [1974] IRLR 10, NIRC*

It is a cardinal principle of law, and a statutory requirement in unfair dismissal claims, that a person who suffers damage as a result of the wrongful act of another must attempt to 'mitigate' his loss by making all reasonable efforts to reduce the extent of the damage. That duty will usually be discharged where it can be said that he has acted

    'as a reasonable person would do if he had no hope of seeking compensation from his previous employer.'

**2.77**

*Bessenden Properties Ltd. v. Corness [1974] IRLR 338, CA Johnson Hobart Manufacturing Co. Ltd July 20, 1990, EAT (unreported)*

The onus of proving failure to mitigate, both under the common law and statutory law, lies on the employer. The test applied is whether the employee has acted reasonably. All the surrounding circumstances including any relating to his personal situation have to be considered. This does not mean that any whim or fancy will justify a refusal to take a suitable job.

**2.78**

*Daley v. Dorsett (Alma Dolls) Ltd [1981] IRLR 385, EAT Gardiner-Hill v. Roland Berger Technics Ltd. [1982] IRLR 498, EAT*

The economic climate locally will be important. In difficult times an employee will generally be expected to accept lower-paid or level employment, or travel further afield; and he must take energetic steps to secure another job. Becoming self-employed or seeking retraining may amount to mitigation in appropriate circumstances.

**2.79**

*Gunton v. Richmond-upon-Thames B.C. [1980] ICR 755, CA*

Under the '*common law*', when a dismissal is wrongful (see para. 8.33) a contract of employment can subsist in special circumstances. As an employee is only entitled to be paid for work that he performs, he is bound to seek alternate employment and thus 'mitigate' his loss.

**2.80**

*Robt. Cort & Sons Ltd. v. Charman [1981] ICR 816, EAT*

Under the statutory law, a repudiatory act by the employer brings the employment to an end immediately, and consequently the employee should seek alternate work, unless it is his intention to seek reinstatement or re-engagement (see para. 5.147–156). Then he must apply to the tribunal as soon as possible.

**2.81**

*EP (C) Act 1978 s.71(5) Fyfe v. Scientific Furnishings Ltd. [1989] ICR 648, EAT*

Where an offer of reinstatement or re-engagement is made by the employer but unreasonably refused, then that will be treated as a failure to mitigate. If the employee had been treated in a humiliating manner whilst in employment or if the terms of re-engagement will result in a big drop of earnings or loss of benefits, then he will usually be entitled to decline returning.

**2.82**

*TBA Industrial Products Ltd. v. Locke [1984] ICR 228, EAT Addison v. Babcock Fata Ltd. [1987] ICR 805, CA Isleworth Studios Ltd. v. Richard [1988] ICR 432, EAT*

The rules relating to mitigation do not apply to a redundancy payment (see Chapter 4) or the 'basic award' in an unfair dismissal claim (except as set out in para. 5.159(a)(i)): these sums are payment for past service. Nor do they *usually* apply to the notice period (see paras. 3.10–25) and any earnings during that time normally have to be disregarded to compute the loss (see para. 3.159(b)(i)).

**2.83**

*Hoover v. Forde [1980] ICR 239, EAT W. Muir Ltd v. Lamb [1985] IRLR 95, EAT Williams v. Loyds Retailers Ltd. [1973] IRLR 262,IT*

There is conflicting authority over whether a failure to use an internal appeal procedure can amount to a breach of duty to mitigate. The better view is that it might do so in appropriate circumstances. However, where an employee does pursue an appeal, then a failure to seek alternate employment before the hearing does not amount to a failure to mitigate his loss.

**2.84**

*City & Hackney Health Authority v. Crisp [1990] ICR 95, EAT*

They do not apply also to the sum payable to the employee for the period between dismissal and an order of reinstatement or re-engagement (see para. 5.154) even though the employee delayed instituting proceedings. But if an employer fails to comply with such anorder, then the tribunal will bear in mind any failure by the employee to mitigate in deciding at what point within the relevant period (see para. 5.159(c)) to assess an Additional Award.

## AGENTS AND REPRESENTATIVES

**2.85** Under the ordinary law of contract, the act of a person (an 'agent') who is employed on behalf of another will bind that other (the 'principal') if he acts within his actual or ostensible authority. Thus a manager who unfairly sacks a worker will make the employers liable for the consequences.

**2.86** The extent of this principle is questionable when applied to a member of a union, where the union has been consulted by the employers over proposed redundancies. One division of EAT thought that no reasonable employer was entitled to infer that individual employees were privy to the employer's discussions with the union. Another division doubted the correctness of that decision.

*Huddersfield Parcels Ltd. v. Sykes [1981] IRLR 115, EAT McClafferty v. Tesco Stores Ltd., Feb. 20, 1985, EAT (unreported)*

**2.87** A distinction is drawn between the powers of a union representative to act for an employee in general matters from in a *specific context*. Thus a union may negotiate wage rates for its members but it cannot, in the absence of express authorization, accept a notice of dismissal on behalf of a member.

*Ramalheira & ors. v. Bloomsbury Health Authority Dec. 15, 1988, EAT (unreported)*

**2.88** A union formally agreed with an employer that being at work under the influence of alcohol was a serious misdemeanour that could warrant summary dismissal. It was held that the employers were

*Gray Dunn & Co Ltd. v. Edwards [1980] IRLR 23, EAT*

> "entitled to assume that all employees who are members of the union know of and are bound by its provisions. There could be no stability in industrial relations if this were not so" (per Lord McDonald).

## ACTS OF SOLICITORS AND OTHER SKILLED ADVISERS

**2.89** A solicitor or other person or body holding himself (or

*Allen v. Hammett*
*[1982] ICR 227, EAT*

themselves) out as a skilled adviser is an agent for the party for whom he (or they) act. Consequently, if a litigant leaves the conduct of his case in the hands of a solicitor, a legal advice centre, or the Citizen's Advice Bureau, and through an error, no Originating Application (see para. 18.10) was lodged in time, then that failure is deemed to be the mistake of the litigant. The litigant may then be unable to prosecute his claim, but he will have a right of action for negligence or breach of contract against his adviser.

**2.90**

*Jones v. Jones*
*[1980] 2 QB 577, CA*

Where a solicitor or other skilled adviser fails to take action in time because of an erroneous view of the law, and the court or tribunal has discretion to allow the omission to be put right, then the principle that is applied is whether 'there was good cause or sufficient reason' for the error. Salmon, L.J., put it this way:

> "That was in my judgment a wrong view of the rules. Was it, however, a view which any trained lawyer could reasonably take? I think undoubtedly it was. For one thing, a very experienced practice master who, when asked the question, rather late, obviously took the same view. It would be difficult for this court to say that the solicitor could not reasonably take the view which had been adopted by the practice master: and it must be remembered that until this case there had been no authority at all upon the construction of [the rule]."

**2.91**

Where there is some question mark over which of two dates is correct, a prudent lawyer or adviser should generally play safe. He should assume that the action should be taken at the earlier date.

**2.92**

*Riley v. Tesco Stores*
*[1980], ICR 323, CA*

The same principles regarding the exercise of discretion by a court or tribunal apply where a person consults a solicitor or other skilled adviser and is given advice that turns out to be incorrect. Was there 'good cause of sufficient reason' for it? (see paras. 3.85–86).

**2.93**

Skilled advisers means anyone who holds themselves out as experts in a particular field, either expressly or by implication. Rather like motor car drivers there is no differentiation made over the standard of skill: they are all expected to be of a minimum standard, whatever their experience.

**2.94**

Both under the statutory and the common law, where a

solicitor or other representative negligently fails to take action in time resulting in a claim being lost, then that person will be exposed to an action for damages in the ordinary civil courts.

**2.95**

*Siraj-Eldin v. Campbell Middleton Burness & Dickson [1989] IRLR 208, CS*

But if it is shown that the proposed claim in the tribunal would have failed because, for instance, the evidence called in the civil court established that it would have been within the reasonable response of a reasonable employer to dismiss (see paras. 5.42–43) and the particular employer would have sacked him, then he will recover nothing from the solicitor or representative. He would have suffered no loss.

**2.96**

*Freeman v. Sovereign Chicken Ltd. [1991] ICR 853, EAT*

A solicitor or other skilled adviser instructed to act for a litigant has 'ostensible authority' to settle a case through ACAS. It is binding on the parties and it matters not that the litigant had given instructions that the case was not to be compromised, unless the other side knew of the restriction on the authority. Further, the settlement can include other potential claims arising out of the employment relationship.

**2.97**

*Harber v. North London Polytechnic [1990] IRLR 198, CA*

Although the general rule in litigation is that a person is bound by the acts of his representative, there are circumstances where a court or tribunal can go behind an agreement or concession. Such discretion is subject to well established principles. For instance, if a mistake is induced by a failure of one side to send all the relevant documents to the other, or there has been a mis-statement of the law by a Judge or Chairman, then the interests of justice may require that litigation be reopened. It may perhaps subject to the payment of costs.

**2.98**

Under the *common law* the ostensible authority is limited to those issues that are raised in the pleadings. Counsel or solicitors could not bind a litigant on other matters unless expressly instructed to do so.

# CHAPTER THREE

# Statutory Law in general

## ACTS OF PARLIAMENT HAVE TO APPLY

**3.1** Parliament, having regulated the rights and duties of employers and employees, did not intend that they could be by-passed. In particular, it did not want a strong employer to be able to force an employee to sign his rights away.

**3.2**

*EP(C) Act, 1978 (as amended by E Act 1980 sch.1 para.20 & sch.2) s.140*

Consequently, even if an employee was to sign an agreement that precluded him from exercising his right to go to a tribunal, that would not be enforceable except in the circumstances set out below (and see para. 3.45).

**3.3**

*EP(C) Act 1978 ss.140(1) & 134*
*Dupont Furniture Products Ltd v. Moore [1982] ICR 84, HL*

A settlement made in respect of a dismissal claim may be effected through the conciliation service ACAS (see para. 1.95), in which case, it is binding provided they have 'taken action' by 'endeavour[ing] to promote a settlement . . . without it being determined by the industrial tribunal'.

**3.4**

*Gilbert v. Kembridge Pictures Ltd. [1984] ICR 188, EAT*
*Slack v. Greenham (Plant Hire) Ltd. [1983] IRLR 271, EAT*

The Act requires the conciliation officer to attempt to promote *reinstatement* or *re-engagement* on equitable terms. Where the employee does not wish it, or it is not practical, his duty is restricted to some minimum involvement in recording the cash settlement or other agreed terms. He does not have to inform them of their legal rights but he will usually explain the binding nature of the agreement. The terms do not have to be in writing: once genuinely agreed they are binding.

**3.5**

*Courage Take Home Trade Ltd. v. Keys [1986] ICR 874, EAT*

Even if a tribunal has found that a dismissal was unfair and sent the parties away to settle the compensation, and they have agreed a figure, an employee can still contest the amount. Only if the agreement is effected through ACAS, or it is incorporated into the tribunals' decision (see paras. 18.83–87) is a party prevented from proceeding further.

**3.6**

*Hennessy v. Craigmyle & Co. Ltd.*
*[1986] ICR 461, CA*
*Oatley v. EMI (UK) Ltd*
*Mar 7, 1983, EAT*
*(unreported)*

Economic duress, lack of capacity, or even mistake are capable of rendering an agreement void, but they are only likely to succeed in the most unusual circumstances.

**3.7**

*Trafford Carpets Ltd. v. Barker (Case A)*
*Nov. 13, 1990, EAT*
*(unreported)*

An agreement recorded in a COT 3 form was a sham to enable an employee to gain a benefit under a Government Enterprise Scheme. It was held that the terms set out in the agreement were not binding.

**3.8**

*EP(C) Act 1978 ss.133(2) & (3) & 140(g)*

For non-dismissal cases other than those in para. 3.9 below, the agreement not to proceed in the tribunal will be valid so long as a conciliation officer has attempted to promote a settlement. This does not extend to the consideration of possible remedies.

**3.9**

*SD Act 1975 s.77(4)*
*RR Act 1976 s.72(4) W Act 1986 s.6(3)*

For discrimination, equal pay and Wages Act claims, the test is whether there has been a contract that settled the case, made with the assistance of a conciliation officer.

## NOTICE PERIODS

**3.10**

*EP(C) Act 1978 (as amended by E Act 1982 sch. 2 para.3(1)) s.49(1)*

Under the Employment Protection (Consolidation) Act 1978, the undermentioned periods are the minimum required for notice of dismissal:

(a) at least one week's notice, if the employee has been employed for one month or more;

(b) at least two weeks' notice, if employed for two years;

*West v. Kneels Ltd.*
*[1987] ICR 146, EAT*
*Misset v. Council of the European Communities*
*The Times, March 23, 1987, ECJ*

(c) one additional week's notice for each further year of service up to a maximum of 12 weeks' notice, but, in computing the period, the day on which notice is given has to be disregarded.

**3.11**

*EP(C) Act 1978 s.55(5)*

If the employer fails to give such notice, then for the purposes of establishing whether an employee has a 'qualifying period of service', (i) for various statutory rights and (ii) for calculating redundancy pay (see paras. 4.44–49) and (iii) the 'basic award' in unfair dismissal claims (see para. 5.159(a)), the employment shall be *deemed* to continue up to the end of the period laid down.

**3.12**

For instance, if a man has been employed for six years, then he must be given six weeks' notice. If dismissed with only two weeks' notice, then the employment will be deemed to have continued for a further four weeks.

**3.13**

EP(C) Act 1978 s.43(3)
Secy. of State for
Employment v.
Staffordshire C.C.
[1989] IRLR 360, CA

Even where there is an agreement to accept money in lieu of notice or to a reduction of the notice period, the deeming provisions (in para. 3.11 above) still apply.

**3.14**

EP(C) Act 1978 s.55(4)

For other purposes, the employment ceases on the day specified by the employer. So the time limits for commencing proceedings for unfair dismissal or redundancy starts from that day.

**3.15**

At 'common law' (see Chapter 8) the notice period is either that specified in the contract of employment, or if nothing is said, then it is that which is implied by law. The length of an implied period is that which is reasonable in the circumstances. This will depend on the nature of the employment, the seniority of the employee, the general customs in that sort of occupation, and perhaps also on the period in which pay is calculated.

**3.16**

Hill v. C A Parsons & Co.
Ltd.
[1971] 3 AER 1345, CA
Brindle v. H W Smith
(Cabinets) Ltd.
[1973] ITR 69, CA
Adams v. Union Cinemas
Ltd
[1939] 3 AER 136, QB

It can vary very considerably, with a senior manager being entitled to over six months in appropriate circumstances. A director and secretary of a small company was held to be entitled to three months; whereas the period for a controller of several cinemas was six months.

**3.17**

EP (C) Act 1978 (as
amended by E Act 1982
sch.2 para.3(1)) s.49(1)
EP(C) Act 1978 s.1(3)(e)

An employee can now rely on the minimum statutory periods. The contractual terms (see paras. 9.15–45) have to be served on him within thirteen weeks of the commencement of the employment (see paras. 9.1–2). As they must include the notice periods (see paras. 9.35–37), the problems over implied minimum terms are likely to be rare.

### Summary Dismissals

**3.18**

EP(C) Act 1978 s.49(5)

If the employee engages in conduct that entitles an employer under the *common law* to dismiss him summarily, then no notice need be given. The test that has to be applied is whether there has been a wilful disregard of some essential aspect of the contract that amounts to a repudiation.

**3.19**

*Sanderson v. Mirror Group
of Newspapers Ltd.
May 22, 1986, EAT
(unreported)*

A chief sports writer of a paper was annoyed at restrictions placed on his activities. He gave vent to his feelings at a press conference that he held at a rival newspaper. His dismissal on the grounds that his damaging public attack had undermined the trust and confidence that must exist between a journalist and his paper was held to be fair. What had to be considered was whether his conduct was

*Wilson v. Racher
[1974] ICR 428, CA*

"insulting and insubordinate to such a degree as to be incompatible with the continuance of the relation of master and servant" (per Edmund Davies, LJ.).

**3.20**

*Laws v. London Chronicle
(Indicator Newspapers) Ltd
[1959] 1 WLR 698, CA*

Disobedience to lawful orders will often come within this category. It has to be established that there was an intentional repudiation. An employee was given two contradictory instructions by senior line managers, and was uncertain which to follow. She chose to comply with that given by her immediate superior and was then sacked by the more senior manager. It was held that the summary dismissal was unlawful.

**3.21**

*Denco Ltd. v. Joinson
[1991] ICR 172, EAT*

On the other hand where an employee, who was a shop steward, deliberately used an unauthorised password to enter into his employer's computer that contained sensitive information, it was held that the conduct prima facie warranted summary dismissal. The only way he could escape was to show that there were exceptional circumstances.

## 'CONTINUITY OF EMPLOYMENT'

**3.22**

*CE Act 1963 sch.1 now
EP(C) Act 1978 (as
amended by E Acts 1980 &
1982) sch.13*

Parliament created the concept of 'continuous employment' in 1963 and many rights and duties depend on those words. For instance, the requirement of having worked for a qualifying period for different rights, the length of notice for dismissal that has to be given (see para. 3.10), the amount of redundancy pay (see paras. 4.44–45) and the 'basic award' (see para. 5.159(a)) and so on all depend on the length of 'continuity of employment'.

**3.23**

*EP(C) Act 1978 (as
amended by E Act 1982
s.20 & Sch.2) sch. 13 paras.
1 & 17
Secretary of State for*

When ascertaining an employee's period of employment there is a presumption that, unless the contrary is shown, it shall have been continuous. But where there has been a change of employer, the onus lies on the employee to prove continuity. This can be shown by

*Employment v. Cohen & anr.*
*[1987] ICR 570, EAT*

establishing that there was no real change in the employment apart from the name of the employer.

**3.24**

*General of Salvation Army v. Dewsbury*
*[1984] ICR 498, EAT*

The employment commences on the day the employee starts work under his contract of employment, and not when he commences his duties. It ends on the day he is dismissed (or leaves), although the date can be extended under the deeming provisions (see paras. 3.10–13 & 3.64–71).

**3.25**

*EP(C) Act 1978 (as amended by E Act 1982) sch.13 para.1(1)*
*Jennings v. Salford Community Service Agency*
*[1989] ICR 399, EAT*

The general rule is that a break of a week, running from the beginning of Sunday to the following Saturday midnight, or longer, breaks the 'continuity of employment'. The employee loses all his acquired rights. But if he worked for *any* time during a week, continuity would be preserved.

**3.26**

*Thornberry v. Cement Gun Co Ltd*
*May 24, 1979, EAT (unreported)*

Furthermore, it matters not if he leaves and takes another job but returns before there is a clear week's absence. The Act still preserves continuity.

**3.27**

*EP(C) Act 1978 sch.13 paras.3 & 4*
*Secretary of State for Employment v. Dearey*
*[1984] ICR 413, EAT*
*Rennie v. Scottish Amicable Life Assurance*
*EAT No 242 of 1982*

In order for a week to count during this period of 'continuous employment', there must be at least 16 hours of work each week. If there is a contract to work those hours or more, it does not matter whether fewer hours are worked. Nor does it matter if less than 16 hours are stipulated in the contract, if in practice 16 or more hours are worked. In both cases continuity is preserved. If an employee has been employed for 5 years or more, then the figure is reduced to 8 hours.

**3.28**

Further if, prior to the five years, the contract is to work 16 or more hours per week, but is temporarily varied (by consent) to work less than 16 hours but more than 8 hours per week for not more than 26 weeks, then continuity is preserved.

**3.29**

*Surrey County Council v. Lewis*
*[1987] ICR 982, HL*

Where there are concurrent contracts, but separate and independent from each other, with the same employer, the hours spent on each cannot be aggregated to raise the total hours above the 16 (or 8) hours to retain continuity.

**3.30**

*EP(C) Act 1978 sch. 13 para.9(1)(a) & 2*

Where there has been a break of a week or more (but see para. 3.25) continuity of employment is also preserved in the circumstances hereunder.

(a) He is absent through sickness or injury, but not beyond a period of 26 weeks unless it was agreed that he should remain an employee during this period.

(b) He is absent because of temporary cessation of work. Where a teacher was employed over an eight year period under a series of fixed term contracts, it was held that it was necessary to find out the reason for the non-renewal of her contracts on each occasion. As each time there was a 'temporary cessation of work' that was of a 'transient' nature, her continuity was preserved. The Court applied a mathematical approach, because the pattern was regular, e.g., time at work compared to being away?

*Ford v. Warwickshire CC*
*[1983] ICR 273, HL*
*Sillars v. Charrington Fuels*
*Ltd.*
*[1989] ICR 475, CA*

Where the pattern of work is irregular, the broad approach should be followed, looking back at the *entire* previous period of employment. It is necessary to consider, *not* whether a temporary absence of work was caused by a cessation *of* work, but whether the absence from work was caused by a temporary cessation *from* work.

*Fitzgerald v. Hall, Russell &*
*Co Ltd.,*
*[1970] AC 984, HL*
*Flack & ors. v. Kodak Ltd.*
*[1986] ICR 775, CA*

Continuity is lost where there is a break, caused not by an general diminution of work, but because the employer spreads the work amongst others in the same pool of casual labour as the employee.

*Byrne v. Birmingham D.C.*
*[1987] ICR 519, CA*

A break was caused by lack of funds, during which an employee was not paid. It was held that it did not break the continuity.

*University of Aston in*
*Birmingham v. Malik*
*[1984] ICR 492, EAT*

(c) He is absent in circumstances in which, by arrangement or custom, he is regarded as continuously employed. A skipper had worked on the employers' trawlers for over 35 years signing off at the end of each voyage. He was told when work got short that they had not finished with his services and was promised consideration for their last remaining vessel. When nothing occurred he brought proceedings. It was held that custom and practice in their relations over the years resulted in continuity of employment being preserved even though the final break lasted 9 months.

*Boyd Line Ltd. v. Pitts. Nov.*
*11, 1985, EAT*
*(unreported)*
*Murphy v. A. Birrell & Son*
*Ltd.*
*[1978] IRLR 458, EAT*

On the other hand, continuity was not preserved when an employee had been told, before he left to start up his own business, that he could return to his old job if he was not successful. The venture failed and he came back after five months. An

*Secretary of State for*
*Employment v. Davis*
*July 19, 1985, EAT*
*(unreported)*

agreement was made that continuity would be preserved during this period of absence. It was held that because the agreement was retrospective, it was unenforceable under the statute (against the Secretary of State).

*EP(C) Act 1978 ss.82 & 84*

(d) Where the employee is given notice of dismissal on the grounds of redundancy, but before his employment ceases

(i)   The is offered a fresh contract on either the same terms, or

(ii)  on different terms and/or at a different place

by the same employer or by an 'associated employer' (see paras. 3.153–161) to commence not later than four weeks after the end of the current employment, or if it is on a Friday, Saturday or Sunday, then the time is on the fifth Monday thereafter, and he takes up the offer.

*EP(C) Act 1978 sch. 13 para. 9(1)(a)*

(e) She is absent:

(i)   wholly or partly because of pregnancy or confinement up to a maximum of 26 weeks: or

*EP(C) Act 1978 (as amended by E Act 1980 sch 2) s.33(3)(b)*

(ii)  she exercises a statutory right to return to work after complying with notice requirements and commences work within 29 weeks of the birth of her child, or, in special circumstances, within 33 weeks (see para. 13.7); or

*EP(C) Act 1978 s.48(1)*

(iii) she exercises any enhanced common law rights to return to work on a later agreed date, again having complied with the notice requirements (see para. 13.25); or

(iv)  where the contract of employment remains in existence, through the employee not resigning, or the employer failing to dismiss her;

*Secretary State for Employment v. Doulton Sanitware Ltd. [1981] ICR 477, EAT*

but if she gives notice of her intention to return under the statute, she cannot generally, (under (i) & (ii) above), add the period of maternity leave to her length of service for the purpose of computing 'continuous employment' if she fails to recommence employment.

*EP(C) Act 1978 sch. 13, para. 15 Express & Star Ltd. v. Bundy & ors. [1987] ICR 379, CA*

(f) He is absent as a result of a lock-out by the employer. The test to be applied is whether the employers were closing the place of employment to compel employees to comply with the old or accept new terms of employment, which may or may not involve a breach of contract.

EP(C) Act 1978 sch. 13 para. 14
Weston v. Vega Space System Engineering Ltd [1989] IRLR 429, EAT

(g) He is working temporarily abroad, but not beyond 26 weeks: but for claims for redundancy, time abroad does not count for computing the length of continuous service.

LR (C of E) Reg 1976 reg.4.
Ingram v. Foxon [1984] ICR 685, EAT

(h) Where there is reinstatement or re-engagement in consequence of a complaint of unfair dismissal, with the same or an 'associated employer' (see paras. 3.153–161), or where there issuch a potential complaint and ACAS successfully intervenes. It is not necessary for an Originating Application (see para. 18.10) to have been presented.

EP(C) Act 1978 sch. 13 para. 15

(i) He is out on strike, whether official or unofficial, but returns to work at the end of it. The period out does not count towards the total length of the employment.

Bloomfield & ors. v. Springfield Honey Finishing Co. Ltd [1972] ICR 91, NIRC

It matters not whether a worker is sacked during the dispute provided the employer does not replace him permanently or the employee does not take another permanent job.

EP(C) Act 1978 sch.13, para.7

(j) If the contract of employment is temporarily varied to provide for between eight and 16 hours work each week, up to a maximum of 26 weeks; but this does not apply to employees with five or more years of service (see paras. 3.27–28).

But where an employee has qualified for a right through continuous employment, then that accrued right will be preserved unless both the contractual hours are reduced below eight hours *and* he works less than 16 hours per week.

Lloyds Bank Ltd. v. Secretary of State for Employment [1979] ICR 258, EAT
Corton House Ltd. v. Skipper [1981] ICR 307, EAT

Thus if an employee works alternate weeks of 15 hours and 35 hours to fit in with her employer's work pattern, she will not acquire 'continuity' because there would be a break every time she works only 15 hours. Yet, if she contracts to work, or does work, 16 hours only on each alternate week but does not work in between, she would retain 'continuity'.

Turner v. Sarah Lou Ltd. May 20, 1985, EAT (unreported)
Suffolk C.C. v. Secretary of

In computing the hours, only the hours on duty count, so if an employee has to remain on the premises during tea breaks, or at the beginning or

*State for Environment & anr.*
*[1985] IRLR 24, HL*

end of the working day, to sign in and out, then that time can be added. This does not apply to the time that a 'retained' fireman is on call.

**3.31**

*Ladbroke Hotels Ltd. v.*
*Otto*
*Feb. 10, 1985, EAT*
*(unreported)*

If a contract is rendered illegal at any stage – by for instance an agreement that part of an employee's income should not be declared to the Inland Revenue – then that will result in a break in the continuity. The qualifying time only starts to run again when the unlawful practice ceases.

**3.32**

*Nokes v. Doncaster*
*Amalgamated Collieries*
*Ltd.*
*[1940] AC 1014, HL*

Under the common law, the transfer of a business automatically brings all contracts of employment to an end, but in the following circumstances continuity is preserved. To meet our obligations under the Treaty of Rome (see paras. 1.29–32) the provision (d) below was enacted but it overlaps to some extent with those set out in (a) to (c).

*EP (C) Act, 1978 sch. 13*
*para.17(2)*
*Melon v. Hector Power Ltd.*
*[1981] ICR 43, HL*

(a) Where the worker is employed in a 'trade, or a business or an undertaking' or in an identifiable part of it that is sold. It must be purchased as a 'going concern' and this will usually include the goodwill, know-how, benefits of existing contracts etc.

*Macer v. Abafast Ltd.*
*[1990] ICR 234, EAT*

A break in the employment of more than one clear week (see para. 3.25) is not necessarily fatal, where it is used as a device to avoid responsibilities under the Act.

*EP(C) Act 1978 sch.13*
*para.18*

(b) Where the employee transfers from one firm to another, where that other is an 'associated employer' (see paras. 3.153–161).

*EP(C) Act 1978 sch.13*
*para.17(5)*
*Wynne v. Hair Control*
*[1978] ITR 401, EAT*
*Jeetle v. Elster*
*[1985] ICR 389, EAT*
*Allen & Son v. Coventry*
*[1980] ICR 870, EAT*

(c) Where there is a change of partners. There is some doubt whether this applies where there is a transfer from one person (a 'sole partner') to several partners, or from several partners to a single person. Usually the employee's position is protected by para. 17(2) of sch. 13 to the Employment Protection (C) Act 1978 (see (a) above).

*TU (P of E) Regs. 1981 reg.*
*2(1) reg. 3(1)*

(d) Where there is a 'transfer' of 'any trade or business but . . . not includ[ing] any undertaking or part . . . which is not of the nature of a commercial venture', and the worker was employed in it 'immediately before' the transfer.

*Berg v. Besselsen*
*[1990] ICR 396, ECJ*

The transfer does not require the consent of

employees – it takes place automatically, and even against their wishes where they oppose it. It is open to them to resign: and in appropriate circumstances to claim constructive dismissal (see paras. 2.50–54).

Landorganisationen i
Danmark v. Ny Molle Kro
[1989] ICR 330, ECJ

There has to be a 'transfer from one person to another'. Under our domestic law an acquisition of control by a share buy out is precluded; but the European Court of Justice has held that the Acquired Rights Directive (on which the Transfer of Undertakings Regulations was based) provides protection where there is a change in the natural or legal person responsible for the running of anundertaking.

Kenmir Ltd. v. Frizzell
[1968] ITR 159, DC

A 'part' of a business does not mean that it was previously carried on as a separate or self contained entity; suffice that it is capable of being run as a business by the new owner, whether he chooses to do so or not.

JMA Spijkers v.
Gebroeders Benedik
Abbatoir CV & anr.
[1986] 2 CMLR 296 ECJ
McLellan v. Cody & Cody
Oct. 7, 1986, EAT
(unreported)
Safebid Ltd. v. Ramiro &
ors.
May 3, 1990, EAT
(unreported)

There has to be a transfer of a 'going concern', so that the purchaser can carry on without interruption. This will usually include the goodwill. Where there was a change of tenants at a public-house that was owned by a brewery it was held that continuity was preserved for an employee who worked there. The new tenant had been put into possession of a going concern and was running the same business as that run by his predecessor. The fact that the brewery owned the goodwill was not fatal.

Caterleisure Ltd. v. T G W U
& ors.
Oct. 14, 1991, EAT
(unreported)

But where a firm holding a concession stopped operating a catering business prematurely, and it was then carried on temporarily with a different sort of catering facility by the company that granted to concession, it was held that this was not a 'relevant transfer'.

Foreningen af
Arbejdsledere i Danmark v.
Daddy's Dance Hall A/S
[1988] IRLR 41, EAT
LMS Drains Ltd. & Metro-
Rod Services Ltd. v. Waugh
June 6, 1991, EAT
(unreported)

Furthermore it matters not how many transfers take place and between whom, provided that there is an economic entity in existence that the final employer carries on in some capacity, e.g., as purchaser of the business, franchisee, licensee.

Woodhouse v. Peter
Brotherhood Ltd.
[1972] ICR 186, CA
Crook & ors. v. H. Faiman
Ltd.
October 10, 1989, EAT
(unreported)

It is wrong to look at the transactions from how they appear to the employee. The correct test is whether the purchaser had become the owner of the business in succession to the vendor. If it is a *different* business after the transfer, then continuity is broken.

Woodcock & anr. v.
Committee of Friends
School & anr.
[1987] IRLR 98, CA
Expro Services Ltd. v.
Smith
[1991] ICR 577, EAT

Whether it is a 'commercial venture' is very much a matter of first impression. The phrase is not defined further and there is likely to be a large 'grey area'. A situation can arise where the vendor does not come within that definition whereas the purchaser does; thus depriving an employee of the necessary continuity of employment to obtain relief.

P Bork International A/S v.
Foreningen af
Arbejdsledere i Danmark
[1989] IRLR 41, ECJ
Litster v. Forth Estuary
Engineering Ltd.
[1989] ICR 341, HL
Wendleboe v. L J Music
Aps
[1985] I ECR 457, ECJ

The phrase 'immediately before' is given a wide interpretation. It covers any person in the employ of the vendor who is dismissed in consequence of the proposed sale, whether there was a binding agreement or not (see para. 5.14). It could apply where a liquidator trims his workforce before seeking purchasers to make a business more attractive, but not where he has run out of work and there is a true redundancy situation.

**3.33**

Ford v. Warwickshire C.C.
[1983] ICR 273, HL

In ascertaining whether there has been 'continuity of employment', it is necessary to look backwards from the date of dismissal to see what has happened in practice: but for computing the total length of reckonable service, only those weeks that count may be considered (see para. 3.30(i)).

**3.34**

Secretary of State for
Employment v. Globe
Elastic Thread Co.
[1979] ICR 706 HL

The parties can agree amongst themselves how they regulate their relationship, but they cannot alter in any way the status or rights of employees arising under the Acts.

**3.35**

MSA (Britain) Ltd. v.
Docherty
Aug. 18, 1982 EAT
(unreported)

For instance, an agreement to count a period of previous employment with the same or with another employer to which he is not entitled under the Act to give extended 'continuity', is incapable of conferring any *statutory* rights. An employer who breaks such an agreement can be sued for breach of an agreement under the common law but not under the Act.

**3.36**

E Act 1982 s.21
Liveridge v. London
Residuary Body
[1989] ICR 228, EAT

Sometimes a statute will confer continuity, not by amending s.153(4) but by expressly providing for it. This was done to protect teachers moving from one local authority to another, providing they were engaged in relevant local government service. They would otherwise have lost continuity.

## DISMISSAL

**3.37**

EP(C) Act 1978
ss.55(2) & 82(2)

Before an employee can claim a redundancy payment or compensation for unfair dismissal, he must have been 'dismissed'. The Act provides that this can occur in three ways:

(a) the employer can terminate the employment either orally or in writing;

(b) the contract may be for a fixed term and end without being renewed;

Western Excavating (EEC)
Ltd v. Sharp
[1978] ITR 132, CA

(c) the employer may be in breach of a fundamental term of the contract thereby entitling theemployee (under his ordinary common law rights: see paras. 8.13–18) to leave, with or without notice. This is known as constructive dismissal'.

**3.38**

Wadham Stringer
Commercials (London) Ltd.
& anr v. Brown
[1983] IRLR 46, EAT

In determining whether there has been a breach of a fundamental term, it is necessary to see whether the default goes to the root of the relationship. There must be a *contractual* breach, not merely a failure to act reasonably.

**3.39**

Rank Xerox Ltd. v.
Churchill & ors
[1988] IRLR 280, EAT

A mobility clause in a contract of employment operated harshly against a particular employee, who in consequence resigned. It was held it was irrelevant that the employer behaved unreasonably in enforcing it. The test was whether there was a fundamental breach of contract.

**3.40**

Watson v. Bedford Bakery
Ltd.
January 20, 1988, EAT
(unreported)

Further, where there are several breaches, and the employee resigns in respect of one of them, having waived his rights under the others, then he will normally lose his entitlement to claim constructive dismissal if that one does not amount to a fundamental breach (but see paras. 2.50 & 2.53).

**3.41**

Briggs v. Oates
[1990] ICR 473, ChD.

There does not have to be any nefarious conduct by the employer. Breach can occur quite innocuously. For instance, this happened when a partnership of 2 solicitors was dissolved and that resulted in an employee losing his job. As he was on a fixed term contract with a period outstanding, this was in law repudiatory conduct by the employer. When the employee accepted it, the contract was brought to an end. It also relieved the employee of his obligations under the contract (which related to restrictive covenants: see para. 10.8) because the employer was in default.

**3.42**

*Halstead v. Marshall of Wisbech Ltd. Oct. 5, 1989, EAT (unreported)*

A contract permitted an employer to demote a member of staff who did not attain a satisfactory level of performance. Following a series of warnings relating to administrative errors and a failure to keep up with paper work, a manager was demoted. He left and claimed constructive dismissal. It was held that the employers had acted within the terms of contract (but see para. 5.51).

**3.43**

*WE Cox Toner (International) Ltd v. Crook [1981] ICR 823, EAT*

If an employee wishes to leave following a breach by the employer, then he must act reasonably promptly. Otherwise he will be deemed to have 'affirmed' the contract and lose his rights to resign (see paras. 2.50–54).

**3.44**

*Tanner v. D T Kean [1978] IRLR 110, EAT*

Once an unconditional notice of dismissal has been given, or a resignation notified, then it cannot be unilaterally withdrawn. There must be consent to the cancellation, either express or implied, from the other side.

**3.45**

*EP(C) Act 1978 s.142(1) & (2) E Act 1980 s.8(2)*

An employer can avoid liability under para. 3.37 (b) above if the employee has agreed in writing, after December 6, 1965, to fore-go his right to claim either redundancy pay, or, after February 28, 1971, to make an allegation of unfair dismissal. The contract must be for a fixed period of two years or more and cannot be ended earlier.

**3.46**

*Allders International Ltd. v. Parkins [1981] IRLR 68, EAT*

If an employer tells an employee that if he does not resign he will be dismissed, then even though the employee resigns this will be deemed to be a 'dismissal' by the employer. This is because there would be a breach of an implied term in the contract of employment of 'mutual trust and confidence' that exists between the parties.

**3.47**

*Caledonian Mining Co. Ltd. v. Bassett & Steel [1987] ICR 425, EAT*

Further, where an employee resigns in consequence of a trick or false information being given to him by his employer, this will still amount to a 'dismissal' by the employer.

**3.48**

*Sheffield v. Oxford Controls Co Ltd. [1979] ICR 396, EAT Birch & Humber v University of Liverpool [1985] ICR 470, CA*

On the other hand, if the employer tells the employee that he wants him to leave, and thereafter they agree severance terms, or if an employee who is facing disciplinary proceedings is given the option of resigning and there is no certainty that he would ultimately be

*Martin v. MBS Fastening
[1983] IRLR 198 CA*

sacked, then, in both cases, if the employee chooses to quit, there would be no 'dismissal'.

**3.49**

*Tanner v. D T Kean
[1978] IRLR 110, EAT
Norrie v. Munro's
Transport (Aberdeen) Ltd.
Dec. 7, 1988, EAT
(unreported)*

Sometimes an employee, in a moment of anger, tells the employer that he "wants his cards". If each side knows that the employee is not intending to leave but is merely giving vent to his anger, then this would not be a resignation. Similarly, if after telling an employee twice that he was not being dismissed for failure to carry out his duties, the employer added "you might as well put your jacket on", it was held that the latter statement was not clear. The surrounding circumstances should be taken into account and they indicated that he was not being dismissed.

**3.50**

*Sothern v. Franks Charlesly
& Co.
[1981] IRLR 278, CA
Walmsley v. C & R
Ferguson Ltd.
[1989] IRLR 112, CS
Goodwill Inc. (Glasgow)
Ltd. v. Ferrier
Aug. 8, 1989, EAT
(unreported)*

But if the employee states in unambiguous terms and perfectly normally that she is resigning then she will be bound by it. It does not matter that she did not intend that the employer should not act on her statement. The criterium is, what is the legal effect of what she said. The position may be different where the employer should reasonably be in doubt about the employee's intention, and consequently seeks confirmation of the position by writing to him.

**3.51**

*Senews Ltd. v. Baker
Feb. 11, 1988, EAT
(unreported)*

A woman at a heated meeting with her manager tendered her resignation that was accepted, but she later sought to retract it. The response of the employer was to give her one month's notice. It was held to be an employer's dismissal. Although the resignation could not be unilaterally withdrawn, it was implicit in the employer's action that he accepted that withdrawal. He then chose to give her a month's notice of dismissal (see para 3.44).

**3.52**

*Sovereign House Security
v. Savage
[1989] IRLR 115, CA
Peebles Publishing Group
Ltd. v. Black
Aug 8, 1991, EAT
(unreported)*

Where an employee is of very limited intellect, or he has been 'jostled' by some action of the employer, or is under severe stress, it is necessary to determine exactly what it is that he is seeking to do. Is he really intending to resign, or is he trying to say something different?

**3.53**

*Igbo v. johnson Matthey
Chemicals Ltd.
[1986] ICR 505, CA*

Even if an employee agrees that his contract of employment will be automatically ended if he fails to report for work on a specific date (usually following an extended holiday abroad) then a delayed return to work would not bring about a cessation of the employment. Such a provision would 'purport to exclude or limit' the operation of the Act and so be unenforceable (see para.3.1–2).

**3.54**

Haseltine Lake & Co v.
Dowler [1981] ICR 222, EAT
Ready Case Ltd. v. Jackson
[1981] IRLR 312 EAT

A notification that there will be a dismissal at some indefinite time in the future, perhaps on the closure of a factory, does not entitle an employee to leave and claim that he has been (constructively) dismissed. If the date is fixed, but the employer leaves earlier, having given notice of it to his employer, then this will (generally) be deemed to be a 'dismissal' by the employer.

**3.55**

North East Coast
Ship-Repairers v. Secretary
of State for Employment
[1978] IRLR 149, EAT

Apprentices, who are usually on a fixed contract for three years or more, may find that the normal rules do not apply to them. This is due to the special nature of their contracts, e.g., because they are for 'once and for all'. Although there is technically a 'dismissal', they do not fit within the definition of redundancy (see para. 4.15) and it is usually not unfair to fail to renew their contracts.

**3.56**

Notcutt v. Universal
Equipment Co (London)
Ltd.
[(986] ICR 414, CA

Contracts of employment can end in many ways without there being any 'dismissal'. For instance, if the employer dies, or the employee is sent to prison for five years or is permanently disabled, there would be frustration (see paras. 2.34–46).

**3.57**

Birch & Humber v.
University of Liverpool
[1985] ICR 470, CA
Morley v. C T Morley Ltd.
[1985] ICR 499, EAT

Both sides can also mutually agree that a contract should be ended. This does not become a 'dismissal'. But mere acquiescence by two directors in their redundancies forced on them by their companies' financial circumstances did not prevent them from being 'dismissed'. It did not matter that they had voted for their own dismissals. At that time, theu were 'wearing their directors' hats'.

**3.58**

London Transport
Executive v. Clarke
[1980] ICR 532, CA
Hindle Gears Ltd v.
McGinty
[1985] ICR 111, EAT

A 'dismissal' can also occur if an employee is guilty of repudiatory conduct (see paras 2.47–49) and the employer 'accepts it'. He thereby dismisses the person. There is conflicting authority as to the date when the dismissal becomes effective, but the better view is that it occurs when the employee is notified, either expressly or impiedly.

**3.59**

Vose v. South Sefton
Health Authority
Oct. 15 1985, EAT
(unreported)
Bliss v. SE Thames
Regional Health Authority

The acceptance of the repudiatory action must be clear and unambiguous before it becomes effective. The receipt of pay after an employer commits repudiatory breaches may be construed as an 'affirmation' of the contract. If it is accompanied by protests or perhaps

*[1987] ICR 700, CA*

accepted on a 'without prejudice' basis (see paras. 2.55–65) then the employee's rights may be protected.

**3.60**

*Wiltshire C.C. v. Natfhe [1980] ICR 455, CA Scottish Council for Civil Liberties v. Godwin July 14, 1988, EAT (unreported)*

There can also be a discharge by performance, e.g., where a person is taken on for a specific task that has been completed. There is no 'dismissal' by the employer.

**3.61**

But there is a 'dismissal' when a compulsory winding up order of a company is made. The contracts of all staff are automatically ended, except those kept on by the liquidator.

**3.62**

It would seem that there will be no dismissal where, during his employment, an employee has different terms imposed on him against his will, unless he leaves and claims constructive dismissal.

*Wood v. York City Council [1978] ICR 849, CA*

"Even though a man may change his job from, say manual work to clerical work, even though he may change the site of his work from one place to another, even though he may change the terms of his contract of employment and enters into a new contract of employment, as long as he is with the same employer all the way through, then it is continuous employment" (per Lord Denning),

*Hogg v. Dover College Nov. 29, 1988, EAT (unreported) Tipper v. Roofdec Ltd. [1989] IRLR 419, EAT*

although the Employment Appeal Tribunal (see paras. 19.1–35) in another case said that an employer, in imposing fundamentally different terms on an employee, had effectively dismissed him. Another division of the Appeal Tribunal pointed out that unless there was a break of a week or more, the contract of employment would be continuous.

**3.63**

There are special statutory provisions relating to a 'deemed' dismissal in respect of a refusal by an employer to take back an employee following a period of maternity leave (see paras. 13.14–15).

## 'EFFECTIVE DATE OF TERMINATION'

**3.64**

*EP(C) Act 1978 s.55(4) & (5)*

There may be two 'effective date[s] of termination of employment'. Dates are important because various statutory rights depend on an employee having a qualifying period of service and taking action within various time limits. A failure to present a claim in the tribunal within the specified time is generally fatal (see paras. 3.74–92).

**3.65**

*EP(C) Act 1978 (as amended by E Act 1982 sch.3 para.1) s.55(5) Chapman v. Letherby & Christopher Ltd. [1981] IRLR 440, EAT*

When the employer or the employee gives notice of termination of employment, the 'effective date' is the date on which that notice expires. If the employer sends an ambiguous letter to the employee from which it would be possible to deduce two dates, the later one will be construed as the 'effective date'. Where the dismissal is partly oral as well as in writing the following question should be posed:

*Leech v. Preston B.C. [1985] ICR 192, EAT*

> "how would any reasonable employee in the employee's position have interpreted the terms of his dismissal when those terms are regarded as a whole, looking to the spoken words . . . and the confirmatory language of the letter . . .?" (per Waite J.).

**3.66**

Sometimes it is not clear whether a worker, who is not required to work out his notice, remains an 'employee' up to the end of the notice period, or whether the employment ends on his last day at work.

**3.67**

*Stapp v. Shaftesbury Society [1982] IRLR 326, CA Christie & Ors. v. Mirror Group Newspapers Ltd. Dec. 11, 1984, EAT (unreported)*

Generally, he will cease to be an 'employee' on the date he stops work, unless there are indications to the contrary, e.g., tax has been deducted from the money given to him in lieu of notice, or he is told that he will remain on the books until the end of the period.

**3.68**

*Batchelor v. British Railway Board [1987] IRLR 136, CA J. Sainsbury Ltd. v. Savage [1981] ICR 1, CA EP(C) Act 1978 s.55(4)*

Where no notice is given, then the general rule is thatthe dismissal takes effect immediately. This applies even though the dismissal is in breach of contract. It may also apply where the employee appeals against the dismissal and is suspended pending the hearing, provided the decision to dismiss is upheld on appeal. If the appeal was successful, the notice of dismissal would be cancelled with retrospective effect.

## Time of Dismissal

**3.69**

*Octavius Atkinson & Sons Ltd. v. Morris [1989] IRLR 158, CA*

A summary dismissal without notice generally brings the employment to an end forthwith. It matters not that the employee has been paid until the completion of the working day or has been paid for travelling time.

**3.70**   Where the employee is on a fixed term and it is not renewed then the 'effective date' is the date on which that term expires.

**3.71**   Where an employer is required to give notice to an employee (see para. 3.10) then for the purpose only of ascertaining

*EP(C) Act 1978 s.49(5)*
*EP(C) Act 1978 (as amended by E Act 1982, sch.2 para.3(1)) s.55(5)*

(a) the qualifying period of service necessary for:

    (i) requiring written reasons for dismissal (see paras. 15.66–72), or

    (ii) for making unfair dismissal claims (see Chapter 5), and

(b) in calculating the amount of redundancy pay (see paras. 4.44–47) and the basic award (see para. 5.159(a)),

*Secretary of State for Employment v. Staffordshire County Council & anr. [1988] IRLR 111, CA*
*EP(C) Act 1978 s.49(3)*

the 'effective date' is deemed to be the date on which, had the statutory notice been given (see para. 3.10), it would have expired and this applies even where the employee has waived his right to notice by, for instance, accepting money in lieu, but not where the employer has the right to dismiss summarily for misconduct (see paras. 3.18–21).

**3.72**   Where an employer sends a notice of dismissal by post, it is only effective from the date when it is received, or is deemed to have been received, and not when it is posted.

*Brown v. Southall & Knight [1980] ICR 617, EAT*

**3.73**   But where an employee wishes to 'accept' his employer's repudiatory conduct and terminate the employment (see paras. 2.47–54), the contract only ends when he has adequately communicated his intention to hisemployer. This may be done indirectly. For instance, if the employer has been informed by the Department of Employment that the employee had applied for unemployment pay, then this would be effective notice. The Department is obliged to obtain confirmation from the employer that the person is no longer in their employ.

*Norwest Holst Group Administration Ltd v. Harrison [1985] ICR 668, EAT*
*Wight v. Blackstone Franks Smith & Co April 2, 1988, EAT (unreported)*

## TIME LIMITS

**3.74**   The law requires that certain acts and applications must be done within certain fixed periods. Failure to comply may result in a good case being lost, or, more rarely, a party being debarred from defending an unmeritorious claim against him. There has to be some finality to litigation.

**3.75**

Hetton Victory Club Ltd. v.
Swainston
[1983] ICR 341, CA

An Act generally requires that a claim has to be made within a fixed period. Unless the written application – and it does not matter whether it is on the proper form, provided the appropriate information is given – is 'presented' at the tribunals before midnight on the last day, then it will be out of time. There is an outside letter box at most of the regional tribunal offices.

**3.76**

Ford v. Stakis Hotels &
Inns Ltd.
[1987] ICR 943, EAT

When the last day for presenting the document is a bank holiday, then that day does not count, as it is technically a 'dies non' (a non day), and time is extended to the following day.

**3.77**

EP(C) Act 1978 s.101(1) &
(2)

Sometimes a tribunal does not have discretion to extend the time. For instance, unless an employer has been notified in writing about it, no claim for redundancy can be entertained if it is first made after one year following the dismissal (see para. 4.50).

**3.78**

EP(C) Act 1978 ss.67(2) &
101(2)

In other cases, the tribunal may extend time where it is shown that it was 'not reasonably practical' to have presented it in time, or where it is 'just and equitable'. The Acts lay down which test has to be applied; they are dealt with in this book under each type of claim.

**3.79**

Palmer & Saunders v.
Southend-on-Sea B.C.
[1984] IRLR 119 CA

'*Not reasonably practical*' means that there must be some physical or cogent reason why a claim was not made in time. For instance, if an employee is ill, and is unable to attend to his affairs, or was abroad at the time, or the documents were sent off in good time to arrive within the time limits but were inexplicably held up in the post, then those sort of reasons would come within the definition.

**3.80**

St Basil's Centre Ltd. v.
McCrosson
[1991] IRLR 455, EAT

Where documents are sent by first class post, then following the *Practice Direction (QBD:Postal Service) [1985] 1 WLR 489]* they will be expected to arrive, in the ordinary course of events, on the second working day after posting. For second class post the time lapse is the fourth working day after posting.

**3.81**

Beanstalk Shelving Ltd. v.
Horn
[1980] ICR 273, EAT

If there is a postal strike on or other reason to believe that the documents will not be delivered in the usual time, then allowance for that should be made. If necessary other means of delivery should be arranged.

**3.82**

*Porter v. Banbridge Ltd.*
*[1978] IRLR 271, EAT*
*United Co-operatives Ltd.*
*v. Mansfield*
*July 27, 1988, EAT*
*(unreported)*

The excuse of ignorance of the law is now generally not good enough, in view of the wide publicity given to employees of their rights, *and*, of the time limits. Nor is deferring a decision pending the outcome of criminal proceedings or domestic appeals acceptable.

**3.83**

*Machine Tool Industry*
*Research Association v.*
*Simpson*
*[1988] ICR 558, CA*
*Grampian Health Board v.*
*Taylor*
*June 27, 1991, EAT*
*(unreported)*

But where the ignorance relates to the factual basis of a claim that was fundamental to bringing it, e.g., an employee made redundant is unaware that another employee has been recruited to the post immediately afterwards, then discretion will generally be exercised. The employee *must* act promptly after learning of the true position.

**3.84**

*James W Cook & Co.*
*(Wivenhoe) Ltd. v. Tipper*
*& ors.*
*[1990] ICR 716, CA*

The onus lies on the employee to show that it was not 'reasonably practical' (see para. 2.14–19) and that can turn out to be difficult. In one instance, the burden was discharged by dismissed employees proving that their former employers had misled them into believing that they would be reemployed after a short break. They delayed submitting their claims until the firm went into liquidation.

**3.85**

*Riley v. Tesco Stores Ltd.*
*[1980] ICR 323, CA*

If a person is given advice by a solicitor, or by any other skilled adviser such as the Citizen's Advice Bureau or a union, and there is a failure to take action in time, or wrong guidance is given, then a claim may be lost (see paras. 2.89–98). It has been succinctly put this way:

*Trusthouse Forte (UK) Ltd.*
*v. Halstead*
*June 10, 1986, EAT*
*(unreported)*

". . . the sins of the negligent or incorrect adviser do have to be visited on the applicant for the purposes of considering . . . what was reasonably practical" (per Garland J.).

**3.86**

*Rybak v. Jean Sorelle Ltd.*
*[1991] ICR 127, EAT*

But where an employee received erroneous directions from a member of the staff at an office of the Industrial Tribunals, and put her claim in late, it was held that she was entitled to rely on the advice. Consequently she proved that it was 'not reasonably practical' to have presented her claim in time.

**3.87**

*Hutchinson v. Westward*
*Television Ltd.*
*[1977] ITR 125, EAT*

'Just and equitable' is a less stringent test. A tribunal is entitled to:

". . .take into account anything which it judges to be relevant . . . to say how far it thinks it necessary to look at the circumstances of the matter complained of. No doubt it will want to know what it is all about; it may want to form some fairly rough idea as to whether it is a strong complaint or weak complaint, and so on" (per Phillips J.).

**3.88**

*Clarke v. Hampshire Electro- Plating Co. Ltd. [1991] IRLR 490, EAT*

Where a person suspects that there has been an act of discrimination against him but only acquires proof of it after the time limit has expired, then provided the period of time is not excessive and he acts promptly normally leave to proceed will be granted.

## Amending to include other claims

**3.89**

*British Newspapers Printing Corporation (North) Ltd. v. Kelly & ors. [1989] IRLR 222, CA Ketteman & ors v. Hansel Properties Ltd. [1987] 2 WLR 312, HL*

Where an amendment is sought to add or substitute a new claim out of time to an Originating Application, the test to be applied is different. A tribunal would have to consider the relative hardship and injustice that both parties would suffer if the amendment was permitted. If reference in the facts was impliedly made to such a claim, it would normally be allowed. But the ordinary tests would apply where there was a change in the identity of the respondent.

## Change in the Law

**3.90**

*Foster v. South Glamorgan Health Authority [1988] ICR 526, EAT*

Where on an appeal there has been a declaration that the lower courts have previously misinterpreted the law, litigants with similar cases who seek to bring claims out of time will have to obtain leave. A tribunal would have to consider in each case:

(i)   the period involved, and
(ii)  the reason for the late claim
      and in respect of cases where the 'reasonably practical' test applies
(iii) whether the claim has been lodged within a reasonable time of the change in the law.

**3.91**

In some instances a Chairman alone – or a tribunal (see para. 18.25 & 18.41) – is empowered to extend the time limits, merely using his discretion. For instance, he may validate a Notice of Appearance that has been filed outof time.

**3.92**

*7 Snooker Club v. Shirley Apr. 28, 1988, EAT (unreported) Aspris & Sons Ltd. v.*

Although discretion is normally exercised because of the importance of trying to get at the truth in a case, nevertheless time limits should not be taken too lightly. An adverse decision made by a Chairman may be

*Demetriou
[1989] ICR 246, EAT* difficult to over-turn on appeal. However, before an order refusing an application can be made, the employer must be sent a written notice giving him the opportunity to show cause why an extension should be made before a decision is made on the application.

## WHO 'ORDINARILY WORKS' IN GREAT BRITAIN

**3.93**

*EP(C) Act 1978 s.141(1–)
s.141(4)*

Employees who ordinarily work outside Great Britain under their contracts are normally excluded from the benefits of the Acts. So far as an entitlement to redundancy pay is concerned, such an employee will not be excluded if on the date he is dismissed he is in Great Britain in accordance with his employer's instructions.

**3.94**

*EP(C) Act 1978 s.141(5)
Wood v. Cunard Line Ltd.
[1991] ICR 13, CA
Smith v. Stages & anr.
[1989] ICR 272, HL*

A person employed on a ship registered in Great Britain or on an aircraft or a hovercraft registered in the United Kingdom and operated from Great Britain is also protected unless he is not ordinarily resident in Great Britain or his work is wholly outside territorial waters. Travelling to and from the U.K. to take leave, when the ship is operating wholly abroad, does not alter the position.

**3.95**

In deciding where a person "ordinarily works", the tribunal does not just consider what has actually happened but what was contemplated at the time the contract was made. If it was later mutually varied, then the position at that time would have to be considered.

**3.96**

Where the precise terms, whether written or oral, are in the contract of employment, e.g., "You will work in Bahrain for 11 months of each year," the position will be clear. But where the matter is left to the discretion of the employer, the tribunal will have to consider what is the reality.

**3.97**

*Wilson v. Maynard Ship-
building Consultants A.B.
[1978] ITR 23 CA*

An employee, who was a consultant on engineering matters, had a contract with a Swedish Company, which contained no reference to where he was to work. He worked more weeks abroad than in Great Britain before being dismissed. It was held that the test to be applied is not where he was at the end of his employment, but to consider where his:

> "base [was] to be. It is, in the absence of special factors . . . likely to be the place where he is to be treated as ordinarily working. Terms . . . which

indicate where the travels involved in his employment begin and end: where his private residence – his home – is, or is expected to be: where, and perhaps in what currency, he is to be paid; whether he is to be subject to pay national insurance contributions in Great Britain. These are merely examples of factors which . . . may be relevant . . . looking to the whole normal, anticipated, duration of employment" (per Megaw, L.J.).

**3.98**

*Janata Bank v. Ahmed*
*[1981] ICR 791, CA*

On the other hand, staff working in branches in the United Kingdom of foreign companies, but who may be transferred to another branch overseas, normally have no protection under the Acts.

**3.99**

*Sonali Bank v. Rahman &*
*Choudhury*
*[1989] ICR 314, EAT*

But, where an employment contract with a foreign company contains an international mobility clause but is otherwise inconclusive in its terms, it is necessary to look beyond the clause. 'A degree of common sense and realism' has to be applied, in speculating into the future in the light of what has happened in the past.

**3.100**

Those working on oil rigs in British territorial water and in designated areas of the Continental Shelf and the Frigg Gas Field are covered by most of the legislation.

## WHAT IS A 'WEEK'S PAY'?

**3.101**

In assessing the amount of compensation to be paid to employees under the various statutes, the tribunal has to work out the 'week's pay'. This presents little difficulty where the hours are fixed and there is an agreed rate.

**3.102**

*Cooner v. P S Doal & Son*
*[1988] ICR 495, EAT*
*W Act 1986 s.16(1)*

Normally speaking, the 'week's pay' consists of gross pay (but see paras. 3.104–105 below) that the employee receives under his contract. If this does not include the amounts to which he is statutorily entitled under a Wages Order, then the latter figure will be used for calculation purposes.

**3.103**

*EP(C) Act 1978 sch.14*
*para.4*

If the employee is paid by piece rates or on commission, the general rule is that the average pay for the previous 12 weeks is taken. This must not include any non-compulsory overtime element or travel allowance.

**3.104**

If a bonus or merit payment or other amount is regu-

*Palmanor Ltd. v. Cedron [1978] IRLR 303, EAT*

larly made, then this forms part of the 'week's pay', and the correct proportion has to be computed. Tips are not included unless they emanate from an obligatory service charge paid to the employer who then distributes it in fixed proportions to staff.

**3.105**

*Tarmac Roadstone Holding Ltd. v. Peacock [1973] ICR 273, CA British Coal Corpn. v. Cheesborough & anr. [1990] ICR 317, HL*

Where an employee is bound, under his contract of employment, to work overtime or at hours at which a higher rate of pay applies, then the week's pay must include those additional amounts. But if he works overtime voluntarily and/or at the employers' discretion, then this may not be included even though it has the effect of diluting the average hourly rate.

**3.106**

*EP(C) Act 1978 (as amended by EP(V of L) Order 1992) sch.14 para.8(1) UD(I of CL) Order 1991*

When assessing the amount of redundancy (see paras. 4.44–47) or 'basic award' in an unfair dismissal claim (see para. 5.159(a)), the 'week's pay' is based on the gross wage, subject to a maximum of £198 in respect of dismissals (see para. 3.60) up to April 1, 1992 and thereafter £205. For the compensatory element in an unfair dismissal claim (see para. 5.159(b)), the net figure is used, subject to an limit of £10,000.

## NORMAL RETIRING AGE

**3.107**

*EP(C) Act 1978 (as amended) s.64(1) & 82(1)*

Generally an employee is debarred from claiming a redundancy payment or from bringing a claim for unfair dismissal where he has reached 65 years. But where there is another 'normal retiring age' for an employee holding the position that he [or she] holds, then that age applies except for redundancy where there is no entitlement to redundancy pay above the age of 65 (but see para. 4.49).

**3.108**

*EP(C) Act 1978 s.153(1)*

In determining his position, it is necessary to take into account his:

> 'status as employee, the nature of his work and his terms and conditions of employment . . .'

**3.109**

*Barber v. Thames Television plc [1991] ICR 253, EAT Hughes v. Department of Health & Social Security [1985] ICR 419, HL*

It is necessary to identify the relevant group in which an employee fits. Any term which only deals with retirement and is not linked to another facet of the employment is not relevant. Nor is it appropriate to consider the history of persons within the group. If persons in a group are basicly doing the same job and some are retired at one age and the rest at another, then there is no 'normal retiring age'.

**3.110**

*Waite v. Government Communications Head-quarters [1983] ICR 653, HL*

There is a presumption that the 'normal retiring age' is that specified in the contract. This can be rebutted byevidence that in practice employees in the same position tend to and reasonably expect to retire at a specific age, in which case that other age applies. If they retire at *different* ages then the fall-back position applies, namely 65 years.

**3.111**

*Swaine v. Health and Safety Executive [1986] ICR 498, EAT*

If the employers, as a matter of administrative policy, change the age at which they require a group of their staff to retire, then that new age will apply (normally). But where the facts showed that the reduction was from 65 years to a band between 62 and 63, it was held that the age was too imprecise to constitute a new age and so the fall-back position applied.

**3.112**

*Whittle v. Manpower Services Commission [1987] IRLR 441, EAT Brook & ors. v. British Telecommunications plc [1991] ICR 286, CA*

Where it is shown that there were abnormal or particular circumstances of a temporary nature which necessitated retirement beyond the contractual retiring age, e.g., a shortage of staff through long term sickness, then the 'normal retiring age' would remain that provided in the contract. Further it is not permissible only to look as the reasonable expectations for those approaching retirement age: the expectations for *all* those in the group have to be taken into account

## DOMESTIC HEARINGS

**3.113**

Usually employers have laid-down procedures for adjudicating when it is decided to take disciplinary proceedings against a member of their staff, that may result in a dismissal. If there is not one the ACAS Code of Practice provides guidelines on the procedure that should be followed (para. 3.159).

**3.114**

*Ward v. Bradfield Corporation [1971] LGR 27, CA*

The approach of tribunals and courts to these hearings was succinctly put by Lord Denning thus:

"We must not force these disciplinary bodies to become entrammeled in the nets of legal procedure. So long as they act fairly and justly, their decisions should be supported."

**3.115**

Disciplinary proceedings should not be conducted like a court of law. All that is required is that certain basic rules should be followed, which may have to be adapted to deal with a particular problem. It is possible to identify certain areas where employers have been held to be in default.

**3.116** In some instances, a decision of the employer can only be reviewed by the Tribunal; in others by the ordinary courts. As Tribunals have to apply the statutory provisions with some common law super-imposed, the result may be different from that obtained in the ordinary courts where the common law only is applied.

**3.117** The over-riding requirement is that a tribunal (or a person) must comply with the rules of natural justice. What constitutes it cannot be defined. It is a provision which casts its net widely and is generally readily recognisable.

**3.118** The *first* requirement is that there must be openness. The employee must know what is alleged against him. Further he must be given the opportunity to state his own case and of repudiating that of his accusors.

*Khanum v. Mid Glamorgan Health Authority [1979] ICR 40, EAT*

**3.119** So where allegations were made against an employee that he had started a fight, natural justice required that not only must he have a chance to put his side, but he must also know in sufficient detail what was being said against him.

*Bentley Engineering Co. Ltd. v. Mistry [1979] ICR 47, EAT McGann v. TSB Trustcard Ltd. (Case A) Dec. 14, 1988, EAT (unreported)*

**3.120** This can be done by either allowing him to hear what a witness is alleging against him, or showing him a written statement of the person. Otherwise he may not know in sufficient detail the case against him and any dismissal is likely to be adjudged to be unfair. In appropriate circumstances, he should be allowed to cross-examine witnesses who make allegations against him.

*Louies v. Coventry Hood & Seating Co Ltd [1990] ICR 54, EAT Shakespeare & anr. v. British Coal Corpn. Mar. 30, 1988, CA (unreported)*

**3.121** A chief constable had received a report from a delegated officer that contained assessments on a probationary police officer. It recommended his dismissal. The probationer was not shown it. The court held to be a breach of natural justice to dismiss him, relying on a document which was not shown to him.

*Reg. v. Chief Constable of Thames Valley Police, ex p. Stevenson, The Times, April 22, 1987, QBD*

**3.122** The *second* matter that should be borne in mind is that an employee should be given the opportunity to be represented or at least accompanied by his union or work colleague.

**3.123** The employee's mind might freeze when confronted

by senior management. He might fail to put over his case effectively so that the employer might dismiss on erroneous information. That could turn out to be unfair, or even wrongful. This is more likely to be so if the employee is very young, or a bit 'simple', or likely to be over-awed.

**3.124**

*Sharma v. British Gas Corporation July 27, 1983, EAT (unreported)*

There is no requirement, in the absence of an express agreement, that an employee should be allowed to insiston being legally represented as

> "the ordinary realities of every-day industrial relations do not permit of quasi-legal trials on every disciplinary occasion" (per Browne-Wilkinson, J.).

**3.125**

*British Railways Board v. Kugler May 16, 1989, EAT (unreported) Ulsterbus Ltd. v. Henderson [1989] IRLR 251, CA (Northern Ireland)*

*Thirdly*, it may be advisable to allow an employee to meet her accusors face to face, or at least permit her representative to interview them or call them at a hearing. This is especially so where acts of violence are concerned, or where the issues are complex and it may be difficult to find out the truth.

**3.126**

*Khanum v. Mid-Glamorgan Health Authority [1979] ICR 40, EAT*

The same principle applies when dealing with complaints made by others against an employee. But where written complaints from several patients about a nurse were produced at the disciplinary hearing, and objection was limited to the panel reading them but there was no request for the patients to be called, it was held that the dismissal was fair.

**3.127**

Problems sometimes arise where an employee gives information about a fellow employee and fears for his own safety should his identity become known. Further, the writer of an anonymous letter informing on others engaged in industrial misconduct might be identified if a copy of it is disclosed. What should an employer do?

**3.128**

*Barr & ors. v. Kay Metzeler Ltd. Mar. 5, 1991, EAT (unreported)*

Every case must depend on its own facts. Providing there is a full investigation that is reasonable in the circumstances, and there is sufficient independent evidence to support the allegations, then a disciplinary hearing (and any appeal) may act on the evidence without disclosing the source of the information. An employer would have to be satisfied, though, that there would be a real risk of danger should the identity of the informants be disclosed or ascertainable.

**3.129**

*Calvin v. Carr [1980] AC 573, PC*

*Fourthly*, there must be good faith and fairness by the adjudicators in the conduct of the proceedings. They must get at the truth, so far as is possible.

**3.130**

*Reg. v. Hertfordshire C.C. ex p. NUPE & Ors. [1985] IRLR 258, CA*

A disciplinary body at a hearing is required to exercise discretion on what matters it may or may not consider. The decision must be one that a reasonable employer could reach, i.e., one that is not

*Associated Provincial Picture Ltd. v. Wednesday Corporation [1948] 1 KB 223, CA*

"so absurd that no sensible person could have dreamt that it lay within the powers of the authority. [For] example . . . the red haired teacher dismissed because she had red hair. It isso unreasonable that it might also be described as being done in bad faith" (per Lord Greene, MR).

**3.131**

*Reg. v. General Medical Council, ex p. Gee The Times, May 2, 1988, HL*

It must ensure that there is no 'duplicity' in the charges, in the sense that each allegation should be made separately. A decision must be given on each. The accused can know how to proceed and, in particular what mitigation to put forward, or whether to appeal.

**3.132**

*Read v. Phoenix Preservation Ltd. [1985] ICR 164, EAT*

Where police officers were called to a disciplinary inquiry and questioned an employee, a dismissal based on the answers given was held to be unfair. The employee had been 'cautioned' that he need not say anything, and was inhibited from telling his full side of the story.

**3.133**

*Dhaliwal v. British Airways Board [1985] ICR 513, EAT*

On the other hand, where an employee was interviewed by police quite separately and made a written confession, which lead to criminal proceedings, it was held that although the judge at the trial ruled the confession 'inadmissible', it did not preclude an employer from acting on its contents provided he reasonably believed it was true.

**3.134**

If there are a lot of documents, an employee should be given them in good time, so that he can examine them. An important point could turn on something recorded in them. If he has difficulty in reading, or is not very intelligent, it is very important to ensure that there is someone there to help him.

**3.135**

*Peter Simper & Co. Ltd. v. Cooke [1986] IRLR 19, EAT Wiseman v. Borneman [1971] AC 279, HL*

*Fifthly*, not only must justice be done in a particular case, it 'must be manifestly seen to be done'. This principle is subject to a degree of flexibility according to the circumstances. It is not possible to define precisely where the borderline between where a breach does or does not occur but it can usually be recognised.

**3.136**

*Slater v. Leicestershire*

Generally, it is advisable to place the investigative and disciplinary functions in different hands to avoid the

Health Authority.
Mar. 17, 1988, CA
(unreported)

accusation of bias. A failure to do so may be a breach of procedure (for which there may be a remedy in the civil courts: see paras. 8.25–30), but it may not make a dismissal unfair. It would be a factor to take into account when considering the reasonableness of a dismissal (see para. 5.44).

**3.137**

Reg. v. Chief Constable of
South Wales, ex.p.
Thornhill
[1987] IRLR 313, CA

A Chief Constable adjourned a disciplinary hearing against a police sergeant to confer with a senior officer concerning other urgent matters. That officer had preferred the complaint against the sergeant. It washeld that in the special circumstances the sergeant could have no valid grievance. There was no breach of the rules of natural justice.

**3.138**

Campion v. Hamworthy
Engineering Ltd.
[1987] ICR 966, CA

On the other hand, it would be a serious breach of natural justice for a person hearing an internal appeal to have a private discussion on the case with the person who took the original decision to dismiss or who presents the employer's case on the appeal.

**3.139**

Haddow & Ors. v. I.L.E.A.
[1979] ICR 202, EAT
Woodroffe v. British Gas
Corporation
Dec. 2, 1985, CA
(unreported)

*Sixthly*, no man should be a judge in his own cause. However, in the end the only thing that really matters is that the disciplinary body should act fairly and justly.

**3.140**

Reg. v. Oxford Regional
Mental Health Review
Tribunal ex. p. Mackman
The Times, June 2 1986,
DC

But where a person who has presided at a tribunal that heard and rejected an application by an aggrieved, then he will not normally be debarred from adjudicating at a later hearing by the same individual concerning other applications.

**3.141**

Rowe v. Radio Rentals Ltd.
[1982] IRLR 177, EAT

If there are several tiers of appeal, then those who make decisions at a lower level should not sit in judgment at a higher stage. A person cannot be expected to be impartial if he is considering an appeal from his own decision. It does not mean that there cannot be any contact between people at different levels, but they must all act fairly and justly.

**3.142**

*Lastly*, where criminal proceedings have been taken against an employee, and he is acquitted of the charges, an employer may nevertheless institute disciplinary proceedings relying on the same facts.

**3.143**

Saeed v. Greater London
Council (ILEA)
[1986] IRLR 23, QBD

Not only is the burden of proof lower, but an employer may have lost confidence in the employee to perform a particular function. The dismissal has to be judged in the light of those and other industrial matters.

## Consequence of a Breach

**3.144**   A breach of the rules of natural justice will not automatically make a dismissal unfair. It depends largely on whether a decision is being reviewed by the ordinary courts or by the tribunals.

**3.145**

*Polkey v. A E Dayton Services Ltd. [1988] ICR 142, HL*

If a *tribunal* finds that there has been a breach of fair play by the employer, but nevertheless on the facts known to the employer at the time there was an overwhelming case, and the result would have been the same had there been no breach, then the dismissal willnot normally be unfair.

**3.146**   In the *courts*, if it is found that the employer has breached contractual or statutory procedures, then any illegal action taken will (probably) be set aside by the courts, usually under the 'judicial review' procedure (see para. 1.60–65).

**3.147**   Before an application for review will be accepted by the Courts, it must be shown that the duties being performed, in respect of which complaint is made, were in the public domain. The fact that they arose from statutory powers or royal prerogative is not conclusive.

**3.148**

*Reg. v. Disciplinary Cte. of the Jockey Club, ex. p. Massingberd-Munday The Times, Jan. 3, 1990, DC*

A royal Charter was granted to the Jockey Club. The club purported to discipline one of its members. It was held that as that power arose out of a contract between the club and its member and not under the Charter, it was not susceptible of judicial review by the Courts.

**3.149**

*Reg. v. Chief Constable of Thames Valley Police, ex. p Cotton [1990] IRLR 344, CA*

If the allegation is that there has been a breach of natural justice because of a failure to give an employee an opportunity to state his own case, the courts apply the following test, namely would there be any

"real, . . . sensible, . . . substantial chance of any further observations on the applicant's part in any way [which would] alter . . . the final decision."

## Internal Appeals

**3.150**

*Shearlaw v. British Aerospace plc Dec. 17, 1987, EAT (unreported)*

If there has been an internal appeal consisting of a complete rehearing as opposed to a review of the findings of fact made at the disciplinary hearing, then any defect in the earlier proceedings may be cured provided

*Calvin v. Carr [1980] AC 573, PC*

". . . at the end of the day, there has been a fair result reached by fair methods . . .".

## INDEPENDENT PUBLIC LAW BODIES

**3.151**

*Reg.v. Civil Services
Appeal Board, ex p.
Cunningham
[1991] IRLR 297, CA*

If an Industrial Tribunal has no power to hear a claim which is normally within its jurisdiction, and an employee's only redress is to take his complaint to an independent law body, then there is a duty imposed on that body to give outline reasons for its decision. It becomes a fully judicial body and must conduct its proceedings in the appropriate manner.

**3.152**

*Reg. v. Army Board of
Defence Council ex p.
Anderson
[1991] ICR 537, DC*

A non-tribunal body was required to hear a complaint relating to an alleged breach of the Race Relations Act 1976, which would otherwise be adjudicated upon in the Industrial Tribunals. It was held that that body must ensure fairness in its procedures. There must be a proper hearing at which the relevant evidence is considered by all the panel members before a decision is reached. The complainant is entitled to see all the relevant material. The proceedings need not be as formal as in a tribunal, but the relevant provisions of the Act must be applied correctly.

## 'ASSOCIATED EMPLOYER'

**3.153**

*EP(C) Act 1978*

This phrase, which crops up frequently in the statutes, is defined in s.153 as under:

'Any two employers are to be treated as "associated" if one is a company of which the other (directly or indirectly) has control, or if both are companies of which a third person (directly or indirectly) has control'.

**3.154**

*Co Act 1985 s.735 Merton
London Borough Council v.
Gardiner
[1981] ICR 186, CA
Hancill v. Marcon
Engineering Ltd.
[1990] ICR 103, EAT*

A 'company' means a company limited under the Companies Act 1985, or if it is a foreign firm then it must, in its essentials, be similar to a British limited company. A US 'Inc' was held to be similar to 'Ltd'.

**3.155**

*Wynne v. Hair Control
[1978] ITR 401, EAT
Zarb & Samuels v. British
& Brazilian Produce Co.*

'Control' is restricted to cases where a person is a major shareholder in a company with voting rights attached. That a person operates with 'de facto' control is not enough, nor if it consists of an ability, by holding 50

**3.156**

Strudwick v. Iszatt Brothers
Ltd.
[1988] ICR 796, EAT
South West Laundrettes v.
Laidlow
[1986] ICR 455, CA
Cardiff Galvanizers (1969)
Ltd. v. Parsons
Oct. 20, 1989 EAT
(unreported)

**3.157**

Payne v. Secretary of State
for Employment
[1989] IRLR 352, CA

**3.158**

**3.159**

Wynne v. Hair Control
[1978] ITR 401, EAT

**3.160**

Gardiner v. London
Borough of Merton
[1981] ICR 186, CA

**3.161**

Cox v. E.L.G. Metals Ltd.
[1985] ICR 310 CA

[1978] IRLR 78, EAT
Hair Consultants Ltd. v.
Mena
[1984] IRLR 386, EAT

percent of the shares with voting rights, to block any resolution.

It is now established that the 'third person' has to have voting control in each of the two relevant companies that together form the associated employers. Generally, the 'third person' may not consist of two persons who normally act in concert, but where it does, then it must be the same combination of persons in each company. Where a husband solely controls company 'A', and he and his wife control company 'B', those two companies are not associated.

Where justice demands it, the rules become stretched on occasion. A person employed by a builder was transferred to a limited company temporarily for a particular job. That firm was owned by the builder and his wife equally, the wife's position being nominal to comply with requirements under the Companies Acts. It was held that the builder and the firm were the same employer.

This provision is applied in several situations. As most statutory rights depend on continuity of employment being preserved (see paras. 3.22–36) it has to be strictly construed. This has led to some curious results.

A girl worked in a hairdressing business for a sole proprietor, and then moved to another salon that was jointly owned by the same proprietor and a partner. It was held that they did not come within the definition of an 'associated employers'. Neither were limited companies. But continuity of employment may be preserved under another provision of the Act (see para. 3.32).

Similarly where an employee worked for four Local Authorities for over 12 years doing similar work in each, it was held that they were not 'associated employers'. Neither was a limited company and no third person had control over them, nor did one control the other.

Where reference is made to the number of employees with an 'associated employer' who have to be added to those employed by the employer of the worker, then those who work for employers abroad may be counted.

## CODES OF PRACTICE

**3.162**  The 'Code of Practice' on industrial relations was initially produced by the Department of Employment and issued with the authority of Parliament. It came into force on February 28, 1972. Subsequently it was adopted by ACAS (see para. 1.93) when that body was set up on a statutory basis. Various amendments and additions to it have been made since then.

**3.163**   Its purpose was to provide guidance to help improve industrial relations, and in particular to help both sides to formulate procedures for settling disputes. In effect, it is a 'Highway Code' for use in industrial situations.

**3.164**   The Code is comprehensive, covering every aspect of relations, from the responsibility of managements, of unions, the planning and use of manpower, communication and consultation, employee representation, to grievance and disputes procedures. Most of the provisions are common sense and have been in force in many companies for many years before its introduction.

**3.165**   The Disciplinary Procedures set out in Code have been superseded by a new 'Code of Practice 1', which is more all-embracing. It deals with promoting fairness, setting standards and so forth. Further Codes of Practice have been issued by ACAS up-dating the duties of both sides of industry.

**3.166**   ACAS has issued a revised edition of '*Times off for Trade Union Duties and Activities*' that has taken account of changes made by the Employment Act 1989.

**3.167**   A failure to observe any provision does not in itself give rise to a claim, but if there are any proceedings, then a breach of the Code could be taken into account when the decision is made. Tribunals tend, first, to see whether there has been a failure to follow procedural requirements contained in the contract of employment. Only if there are no terms do they turn to the rules in the code.

**3.168**

*Polkey v. A E Dayton Services Ltd. [1988] ICR 142, HL*

An employer can still avoid liability for an unfair dismissal when in breach of the rules where on the facts known to the employer *at the time* the failure was purely technical, and where compliance with the requirements would have been useless and could not have effected the result (see paras. 5.53–68).

**3.169**   Codes of Practice have been drawn up by other bodies dealing with race relations (see paras. 14.47–49), with sexual equality (see para. 11.123), with health and safety at work (see para. 16.6), and with picketing (see para. 7.4).

**3.170**  A Code covering the employment of disabled persons, has been published by the Manpower Services Commission (see paras. 15.99–100). It is for use purely on a voluntary basis.

## MEANING TO BE GIVEN TO STATUTES

**3.171**  The ordinary rules of construction of a statute require that where the meaning is clear, then effect much be given to it (but see para. 1.40). But where it is possible to interpret the words in a statute in two ways, the one that gives effect to the apparent intention of Parliament should be adopted. In determining that intention, the courts are entitled to take into account the background leading to the passing of the legislation.

*Secretary of State for Employment v. Cox [1984] IRLR 437, EAT British Coal Corporation v. Cheesborough & anr. [1990] ICR 317, HL*

**3.172**  The words in the Race Relations Act 1976 'on racial grounds' were capable of a narrow interpretation or a broad meaning. E.A.T. said:

*Showboat Entertainment Centre Ltd. v. Owens [1984] ICR 65, EAT*

> "It seems to us that Parliament must have intended such an employee to be protected so far as possible from the consequence of doing his lawful duty by refusing to obey such an instruction [to discriminate],"

and held that broad meaning would be applied.

**3.173**  On the other hand, because a section had not "been aptly drafted to cover the rather exceptional circumstances of [a] case", a claim failed. It mattered not that it fell "within the mischief aimed at" by the legislature. Lord Dilhorne put it this way:

*Stock v. Frank Jones (Tipton) Ltd. [1978] ITR 289, HL*

> "If it . . . appear[s] that an Act might have been better drafted, or that amendment to it might be less productive of anomalies, it is not open to the courts to remedy the defect. That must be left to the legislature. The existence of anomalies, if they exist, cannot limit the meaning to be attached to clear language in a statute".

**3.174**  The House of Lords has proceeded in a contrary direction in interpreting Orders based on an EEC Directive. It added the words, 'as between the woman and the

*Pickstone & ors. v. Freemans plc [1988] ICR 697, HL*

*Litster & ors. v. Forth
Estuary Engineering Ltd.
[1989] ICR 341, HL*

man with whom she claims equality' in an equal pay claim to enable a statute to be interpreted in a manner they thought necessary to give effect to a Directive.

**3.175** Normally speaking, to seek out the meaning of an Act, or a Regulation or Order, it is not permissible to look at extraneous sources. What is contained in a White Paper, or what was said in Parliament may not be considered.

**3.176** The construction of an Act or a statutory instrument is a matter of judgment by our own courts and tribunals. It is determined in the light of the circumstances prevailing at the date of enactment.

*Duke v. GEC Reliance Ltd.
[1988] ICR 339, HL[em]*

### European Law

**3.177** The European Court has jurisdiction to give preliminary ruling on the interpretation of any provision of the European law. It is anxious to avoid divergences developing in the courts of the Member states.

*Dzodzi v. Belgium
The Times, Jan. 7, 1991,
ECJ*

## WHO CAN BE THE PARTIES TO A DISPUTE

**3.178** Generally, it is an employer who is the 'respondent' (e.g., the person on the other side to the 'applicant' employee) and who is responsible for paying any compensation ordered by the tribunal.

**3.179** Where a dismissal arises out of union pressure because an employee is not a member of a union (see para. 5.7(c)), or, where 'action short of dismissal' (see Chapter 6) is taken against him for the same reason, then the employer *or* the employee can 'join' the union and/or person(s) bringing pressure (see also paras. 15.93–100).

*EP(C) Act 1978 (as
amended by E Act 1982,
s.7 & sch.4) s.76
EP(C) Act 1978 (as
amended by E Act 1982
s.11) s.26*

**3.180** The procedure is that an application is made to the tribunal (by letter) at any time before the hearing for an order to 'join' the union and/or person(s) exercising pressure, and it must be made.

**3.181** If proceedings are taking place, the tribunal has discretion to make or refuse an order. There will have to be a good reason for the failure to have applied before the hearing started. Perhaps the employee was unaware of the material facts until some evidence was given.

*EP(C) Act 1978 (as
amended by E Act 1982
ss.7 & 11) ss.26A(1) & 76(1)*

**3.182**
*ss.26A(2) & 76(2)*

There is no power to make such an order after the Decision (see para. 18.83–87) has been given.

**3.183**
*ss.26A(3) & 76(3)*

When the tribunal awards compensation to an employee, it may order the union and/or person(s) exercising pressure, who have been 'joined' in the case, to make a payment direct to the employee, where it would be right and fair. It may also order both (or all) parties to make a contribution towards the award in any proportions.

# CHAPTER FOUR

# Redundancies

## GENERAL INFORMATION

**4.1**  In 1965 Parliament introduced a new concept into employer/employee relations by providing for the payment of compensation to staff dismissed because of redundancy. The amount was computed by multiplying the number of years' service by one week's pay, subject to variations and limitations.

**4.2**  The idea was not to punish the employer or for it to be a recipe for under-employment. The intention was to make the employer conscious of the need to keep his staff intact wherever possible by trying to find alternate employment. The consequence has been that employers are more cautious about taking on staff, and are more selective when they do. For the worker, the system does provide some security. It also builds up a nest-egg with each year of service.

**4.3**

*EP (V of L) Order 1992*
*Marshall v. Southampton*
*& S.W. Hampshire Area*
*Health Authority*
*(Teaching) (No.2)*
*[1990] ICR 136, CA*

The payment of redundancy, which has a maximum of £5,940 for dismissals (see paras. 3.61–70) up to April 1, 1992 and thereafter £6,150 does not attract tax, nor effect entitlement to unemployment benefit. The amount is not reduced even if the worker gets another job the next day. It has been held that if proceedings are brought under a Directive made under the Treaty of Rome, the statutory limit imposed under our own law still applies.

**4.4**

*UD(I of CL) Order*
*1991*

It is generally more advantageous to bring proceedings against an employer on the grounds of unfair dismissal rather than redundancy (but *not* unless the evidence warrants it). In the former case, the Tribunal orders the payment to the employee of not only a 'basic award' (which is the same as a redundancy payment except that the period under 18 years also counts) but also a compensatory element. Under this latter provision there is a maximum of £10,000. The amount can be increased in special circumstances (see para. 5.159(b) (c) & (d)).

**4.5**  The consequence of this is that there are now very many cases where the employer alleges that the worker was sacked for redundancy whereas the employee contends that no redundancy situation existed and that he was in truth unfairly dismissed, or, where it did exist, that he was unfairly selected for redundancy. This hasmade the interpretation of the various Acts extremely difficult because the draftsmen of the legislation do not appear to have foreseen this position arising.

**4.6**

*E Act 1989 s.17*

From an employer's point of view it is usually better to make a redundancy payment than give compensation for unfair dismissal.

## WHO IS NOT ENTITLED TO REDUNDANCY PAY?

**4.7** Generally, every 'employee' (see paras. 2.1–13) is entitled to redundancy pay (but see para. 3.45), but the following, amongst others, are specifically excluded by statute:

*EP(C) Act 1978 s.144(2)*
*s.144(2)*

(a) share fishermen;

(b) certain merchant seamen;

*s.99*

(c) Crown servants, or employees in a public office or in the National Health Service;

*EP(C) Act 1978 (as amended by the E Act 1982 sch.4) s.100(2)*

(d) a domestic servant who is a close relative (other than a spouse).

**4.8**

*EP(C) Act 1978 (as amended by E Act 1982 sch.2 para.6 & 7, & sch. 4) ss.81(4) & 151(4)*

An employee may be rendered ineligible in the following cases, amongst others, where he/she:

(a) has not completed at least two years of reckonable continuous service (see paras. 3.23–36) since the age of 18 years;

*EP(C) Act 1978 (as amended by E Act 1989, s.16(1)) s.82 EP (C) Act 1978 sch.13 para.5*

(b) is 65 years of age or over, unless there was an earlier 'normal retiring age' in which case that specified age applies (see paras. 3.106–115);

(c) is a part-time worker, who normally works less than 16 hours per week (but with exceptions; in particular see paras. 3.27–30);

*EP(C) Act 1978 (as amended by E Act 1980), s.142(1) & (2)*

(d) is on certain fixed terms contracts (see para. 3.45);

*EP(C) Act 1978 s.141(3) & (4) EP(C) Act 1978 ss.82(3) & 84(1) Benton v. Sanderson Kayser Ltd. [1989] ICR 136, CA*

(e) normally works outside Great Britain in accordance with his/her contract (but see paras. 3.93–100), except where he/she is in Great Britain in accordance with instructions at the time of dismissal;

(f) is offered suitable fresh employment on the same terms by the same employer or by an 'associated employer' (see paras. 3.153–161) and unreasonably refuses the offer; or on different terms or in a different place and, during a trial period of up to 4 weeks, also unreasonably refused to continue.

**4.9**

*National Carrier Control Services v. Urey Sept. 14, 1990, EAT (unreported)*

In determining whether the new job offered is suitable and whether the employee was reasonable in rejecting it, the tribunal must consider the personal circumstances of the employee. In appropriate cases, his or her standards and aspirations, should be taken into account provided they are reasonable 'in the round'.

**4.10**

*Gloucester C.C. v. Spencer & Anr. [1985] ICR 401, CA*

School cleaners declined to accept a new contract providing for reduced hours of work to carry out their previous duties, and left. Even though the employers were prepared to agree to lower standards, the cleaners were held to be not acting unreasonably. They were entitled to redundancy pay.

**4.11**

*McKindley v. William Hill (Scotland) Ltd. [1985] IRLR 492, EAT*

The offer of a new job should specify the material facts, e.g., remuneration, status, job description and so forth. There must be sufficient detail to show any deviation from the old contract, but it need not contain all those items that are required to be in writing under the Act (see paras. 9.15–44).

**4.12**

*Burton, Allton & Johnson Ltd. v. Peek [1975] IRLR 87, EAT Birch & Humber v. University of Liverpool [1985] ICR 470, CA*

A volunteer for redundancy is usually entitled to a redundancy payment. However, where a scheme for early retirement was put forward and two employees decided to apply for it, it was held that the agreement to retire early did not amount to a 'dismissal'. The employees were debarred from recovering any redundancy pay. The critical question is, what brought the employment to an end?

**4.13**

*Lee v. Nottingham C.C. [1980] IRLR 284, CA*

It does not matter if, when the employee is taken on, it is anticipated that his work will fall away and result in a dismissal.

## WHEN DOES REDUNDANCY ARISE?

**4.14**

It is only possible to deal with this complex subject in very broad terms. If a particular case is complicated, then expert advice should be sought. The Acts are difficult to understand, and there are many exceptions to be found on different aspects: they have given the courts much trouble.

**4.15**

EP(C) Act 1978 (as amended by E Act 1982) s.81(2)

The position is that any dismissal (see para. 3.37) ispresumed to be because of redundancy, that is to say, that it is attributable *wholly* or *mainly* to the fact:

(a) that the employer has ceased, or intends to cease:

   (i) to carry on the business upon which the worker was employed, or

   (ii) to carry on that business at the place where the worker was employed, or,

(b) the requirements of the business for the employee to carry out work of a particular kind at his workplace or elsewhere have ceased or diminished or it is expected that they will do so.

**4.16**

This presumption can be countered by the employers bringing evidence that a dismissal was wholly or mainly due to another cause, e.g., the worker was sacked for incompetence or dishonesty, or there has been no loss or contraction of the business.

**4.17**

*Halfords v. Roche Jan. 30, 1989, EAT (unreported)*

The fact that the amount of *work* within a firm remains the same but increased efficiency or reorganisation or mechanisation result in an employee being dismissed will generally not debar that person from claiming redundancy pay. The Act preserves his rights where there has been a diminution in the requirements of the business for the *employee* to do the work in the place where he was engaged.

**4.18**

*Gorictree v. Jenkinson [1985] ICR 51, EAT*

Further, an employee is not precluded from recovering redundancy:

(a) where a business is sold and he is dismissed for an 'economic, technical or organisational reason' (see paras. 5.13–14) before or after the sale; or

*Sutton v. Revlon Over-seas Corporation Ltd. [1973] IRLR 173, NIRC Murphy v. Epsom College [1985] ICR 80, CA*

(b) where there is a reallocation of duties following a reorganisation or mechanisation in the business and the employee is dismissed as a result of there being a cessation or diminution of work previously carried out by him and it matters not that there has been no general reduction in the employers' business.

**4.19**

*Fay v. North Yorkshire C.C. [1986] ICR 133, CA*

To be eligible for redundancy pay, an employee must bring his case strictly within the statutory definition. A part time teacher was displaced by a full time master, who had been transferred from another school that was overstaffed. As there was no diminution of work, and the part-timer was not entitled to redundancy pay upon her dismissal.

**4.20**

*Cowen v. Haden Ltd.*
*[1983] ICR 1, CA*

The contractual position of the parties is important to determine whether there is an entitlement to redundancy. So if the employee can be required, under the terms of his contract, to transfer to other work and he unreasonably refuses to do so, he will lose his entitlement to it.

**4.21**

*Tipper v. Roofdec Ltd (No. 2) Mar. 11, 1991, EAT (unreported)*

A HGV driver who was disqualified from driving was given temporary alternate work at another depot whilst a permanent job was sought for him. That other site closed and no other position could be found, so he was dismissed. It was held that the termination was *mainly* attributable to the loss of his license and so he was not entitled to a redundancy payment.

**4.22**

*Macfisheries v. Findlay*
*[1985] ICR 160, EAT*
*Johnson v. Nottingham*
*Combined Police Authority*
*[1974] ICR 170, CA*

The phrase 'work of a particular kind' may include, in appropriate circumstances, a change from night to day duty. So where employees were not contractually bound to change, but were dismissed for refusing to do so, they could still claim redundancy pay.

**4.23**

*Marriott v. Oxford & District Co-Operative Society Ltd.*
*[1969] ITR 377, CA*

Difficulties sometimes arise where an employer, who is running out of work for a particular employee, tells him that he must either accept other work, on less favourable terms, or leave and the worker reluctantly accepts for a short time, and then leaves.

**4.24**

*Western Excavating (E.E.C.) Ltd. v. Sharp*
*[1978] ITR 132, CA*
*(as explained in W.E. Cox Toner (International) Ltd. v. Crook*
*[1981] ICR 823, EAT)*

If there was not a true agreement by the employee to the variation in the contract, the effect in law will be that this amounts to a dismissal by the employer (see paras. 3.37 & 8.13–14). The employee will be entitled to recover his redundancy pay; but if he delays too long he "will be regarded as having elected to affirm the contract".

**4.25**

*Spinpress v. Turner*
*[1986] ICR 433, EAT*

The right to redundancy pay will only arise where there is a '*reduction*' in work provided to the employee, being work of a kind that he is employed to do. Accordingly, if the employee refuses to do the work or the reduction of his pay is self-induced, he will not be eligible.

## INSTANCES OF SUCCESSFUL REDUNDANCY CASES

**4.26**
*Exec. of Everest v. Cox*
*[1980] ICR 415, EAT*

A canteen manageress of a firm with a concession at a police station was offered suitable employment elsewhere when the concession ended. She refused because the company taking over the work led her to believe she would be employed by them, but in the event she was not.

*Held*: she was entitled to redundancy as her conduct was not unreasonable at the time she took the decision.

**4.27**
*Bromley & Hoare v. Evans*
*[1972] ITR 76, NIRC*

Employer's business as builders and decorators had been increasing but they found it more economical to use self-employed staff rather than their own men. Two employees were dismissed and the work was taken over by outside labour.

*Held*: that the need for employees had diminished and so the two were entitled to redundancy pay.

**4.28**
*Hebden v. Forsey & Son*
*[1973] ITR 8, NIRC*

Employee ceased work to have an eye operation. His return to work was delayed by a further operation to the other eye. During the whole period he kept in touch with his boss who agreed he could remain off sick. When he returned after a total of 10 months, his employers refused to take him back on the grounds of frustration of contract.

*Held*: if the employer considered period too long, he could have given him notice to terminate, which had not been done. So he was entitled to redundancy pay.

**4.29**
*Lee v. Nottingham County*
*Council*
*[1980] IRLR 284, CA*

Lecturer took job knowing that work-load would slacken because of reduction in number of student teachers over a period and that his job would go.

*Held*: knowledge was not the test: only whether a dismissal, as occurred here, was wholly or mainly attributable to a fall in work, creating a redundancy.

## INSTANCES OF CASES THAT FAILED

**4.30**
*Lesney Products & Co. Ltd.*
*v. Nolan & Others*
*[1977] ITR 6, CA*

Employers reorganised the work in their factory to increase efficiency resulting in a cutting of overtime, but the amount of work remained the same. Nine employees refused to accept the position and left.

*Held*: that as the amount of work had not ceased or diminished, the claim for redundancy failed.

**4.31**

*J. Stott & Son Ltd. v.*
*Stokes*
*[1971] ITR 50, QBD*

Employee, an alleged trouble-maker, was sacked for absenting himself from a site when he should have been working. He claimed it was a cover-up for redundancy.

*Held*: as it was proved the dismissal was due to conduct entitling the employer summarily to sack, then even though a redundancy situation existed, the employee was not entitled to redundancy pay.

**4.32**

*Jones v. Wagon Repairs*
*Ltd.*
*[1968] ITR 361, QBD*

An employee, with 17 years service, became ill with a chronic disability in May, 1966 but returned in November, 1966. He became ill again in December, 1966, and nine months later, in September, 1967, formal notice of ending of his job was sent to him. He was invited to apply for old post when fit. In October, 1967, the works closed down. In March, 1968, the employee was well enough to return to work and claimed that he was entitled to redundancy up to September, 1967.

*Held*: a long time before September, 1967, the contract had been frustrated, and a redundancy situation only arose in October, 1967.

**4.33**

*O'Hare v. Rotaprint Ltd.*
*[1980] ICR 94, EAT*

Employers anticipated increased sales and took on additional workforce. The work failed to materialise, and they reduced staff back to the original level.

*Held*: there was no cessation or diminution of work, and a redundancy payment ought not to have been made.

## LAY-OFF AND SHORT TIME WORKING

**4.34**

*EP(C) Act 1978 s.87*

*s.88*

If an employee, who is available for work, gets no pay of any kind ('Lay-Off') or less than half his normal week's pay that does not include any overtime element ('Short-Time Working') for four consecutive weeks, or for a broken series of at least six weeks in a 13-week period, or a mixture of both, then he is entitled to leave and apply for a redundancy payment.

**4.35**

He must serve a written notice on his employer stating his intention to claim on one or both grounds, and this notice must be served within four weeks of the end of the 4th or 13th week period. His entitlement to the redundancy payment is not affected by his giving notice of termination of employment.

**4.36**

*EP(C) Act 1978 s.89*
*Fabar Construction Ltd. v.*
*Rose & Sutherland*
*[1979] IRLR 232, EAT*

An employer can contest liability by serving a counter notice within seven days in which he *must* dispute the employee's entitlement to redundancy pay. Further, *at the time* of the service of the employee's notice, there must be a reasonable prospect of normal full-time employment. This must commence not later than four week's of the notice, for a period of not less than 13 weeks.

**4.37** If the employee disputes that there is a reasonable prospect of work and he still wants his redundancy pay, then the matter will have to be adjudicated upon by the tribunal.

**4.38** If no counter notice is served, the employee must give notice to leave his job within four weeks. If one is served but subsequently withdrawn, then he must do so within three weeks of the withdrawal. If a Decision is made by the tribunal, it has to done within three weeks of the notification to the employee of the tribunal's Decision (see paras. 18.83–94).

**4.39** In any event, the employee is not entitled to any pay-ment while still employed. He *must* give a *minimum* notice of seven days or such other (longer) period as is stipulated in his contract of employment for the ter-mination of his employment.

**4.40**

*A. Dakri & Co. Ltd. v. Tiffen*
*[1981] ICR 256, EAT*

This provision is strictly construed and if the employee cannot bring his case within the time limits, then he will lose his right to a redundancy payment.

## STRIKES

**4.41** If a worker goes on strike, his employer is generally entitled to dismiss him without being liable to pay him redundancy pay. It matters not that a redundancy situation exists, e.g., the employer was going to dismiss him because of shortage of work.

**4.42**

*EP(C) Act 1978 s.92*

If the worker goes on strike after being given notice, he may still obtain some part or all his redundancy pay by applying to the tribunal, which has the power to make an award where it is 'just and equitable', the amount being determined by the tribunal.

**4.43**

*EP(C) Act 1978 sch.13*

If the worker resumes his job at the end of the strike, the employment is deemed to be 'continuous'. Time *para.15* spent off work is not counted as reckonable when computing his total period of service (see paras. 3.30(i) & 3.33).

## CALCULATION OF REDUNDANCY PAY

**4.44**

*EP(C) Act 1978 (as amended by E Act 1982 sch.2 para.7(1)) s.151 & sch.4*

There must be a complete year of continuous service, all the weeks of which must be reckonable. Those when an employee is out on strike do not count (see para. 4.43). The relevant time is calculated back from the date when the notice expires (but see paras. 3.10–12).

**4.45**

*EP(C) Act 1978 (as amended by E Act 1982 sch.2 para.6(5)(a) & (b) & sch.4) sch.4 para.7(1) & (2)*

The following scale is applied for each complete year of service, up to a maximum of 20 years. The computation is based on each year of service up to the age stated:

(a)  18 but under 22 = $\frac{1}{2}$ week's pay
(b)  22 but under 41 = 1 week's pay
(c)  41–65          = $1\frac{1}{2}$ weeks' pay

**4.46**

*EP (V of L) Order 1992*

The redundancy payment is calculated by ascertaining the age of the worker at the time of the effective date of dismissal (see paras. 3.64–73), working out the number of weeks applicable and multiplying that number by the week's pay (see paras. 3.101–105). The latter figure is subject to a maximum of £198 for dismissals up to April 1, 1992, and thereafter £205.

**4.47** For convenience, the chart in Appendix A (on page 292) may be used to calculate the amount.

**4.48** Thus, the redundancy pay for a man of 50 who has been continuously employed for 15 years and was earning £145 per week gross at the time of his dismissal, would be as under:

35 to 40 years = 5 years @ 1 week per year = 5 weeks
41 to 50 years = 10 yrs @ 1 wks per year  = <u>15 weeks</u>

20 weeks

Therefore 20 (weeks) £145 = £2,900

**4.49**

*EP(C) Act 1978 (as amended by E Act 1989 s.16) sch.4 para.4*

Certain adjustments to these figures are necessary where:

(a) the worker is approaching his/her 65th birthday, when the award is reduced by one-twelfth for each complete month commencing with the 12th month before attaining the 65th year. Thus a person aged 64 years and 3 months on the effective date of dismissal (see paras. 3.64–73) would have three-twelfths of the award deducted;

RPP Reg. 1965
Royal Ordinance plc v.
Pilkington
[1989] ICR 437, CA

(b) an employee is entitled to a pension upon a dismissal. The amount to be off-set depends on the total length of continuous employment (see paras. 3.22–36) and this includes periods with previous employers except where the pension (or a lump sum) was being (or had been) paid before the dismissal.

An employer is permitted to exclude or limit theright to a redundancy payment provided he gives notice of his intention to do so within a reasonable time of learning of the employee's intention to claim a redundancy payment.

## TIME LIMITS

**4.50**

EP(C) Act 1978 ss.91(1) &
101(1)(b)&(c)
Price v. Smithfield &
Wanenburg Group Ltd.
[1978] IRLR 80, EAT

A written claim to the employer must be made within six months of the end of the employment. It does not have to be in any particular form, but merely indicate an intention to seek redundancy. Alternately a claim may be made to the tribunal (see para. 18.10) during that period.

**4.51**

EP(C) Act 1978
s.101(2)

The tribunal has power to extend the time for a further 6 months, e.g., 12 months in all (*but no more*) in both cases. The test to be applied is 'just and equitable' having regard to the 'reason shown by the employee and . . . to all other relevant circumstances' (see para. 3.87).

## FAILURE OF EMPLOYER TO PAY

**4.52**

EP(C) Act 1978 s.106

An employee, who has made reasonable efforts to get his redundancy pay, but without success, may apply to the Secretary of State. The latter is obliged to make the payment and he may recover the amount from the employer. It is not necessary for the employee to have commenced legal proceedings.

## REDUNDANCY NOTICES

**4.53**   Where redundancy is contemplated, it is the duty of an employer, who is selecting one or more employees of any description who belong to an independent trade union which is recognised by the employer, to consult *at the earliest opportunity* with the union representatives.

**4.54**

*EP Act 1975 (as amended by EP (H of R) Var. Order 1979) s.99(3)*

No time scale for consultation is laid down where up to and including 9 employees are to be dismissed for redundancy. But where, at one establishment, the undermentioned numbers are to be dismissed then the following notice periods must be given:

   10 or more persons: 30 days notice.
   100 or more persons: 90 days notice.

**4.55**

*Barratt Developments Ltd. v. UCATT [1978] ICR 319, EAT*

'One establishment' has been held to cover several building sites where each had a temporary hut that was connected to their headquarters by telephone.

**4.56**

*TGWU v. R A Lister & Co. May 21, 1986, EAT (unreported)*

The period for consultation is calculated from the time of the notification of redundancies until the date when it is proposed that they should take place. It is not when they actually occur. So if employees leave earlier as a result of negotiation or other reasons, then there is not breach of the Act.

**4.57**

*N.U.G.S.A.T. v. Albury Brothers Ltd. [1979] ICR 86, CA EP Act 1975 s.99(2)*

'Recognised' means the recognition of the union, to any extent, for the purpose of collective bargaining. That is to say, it must be concerned with one or more of the matters set out in para. 7.24(a)-(g) (see paras. 15.113–118).

**4.58**   The employer must disclose to the representative of the trade union in writing:

(a) the reasons for the dismissals;
(b) the number and description involved;
(c) the proposed method of selection;
(d) the method of carrying it out;
(e) total work-force at establishment.

**4.59**

*EP Act 1975 s.99(7)*

The information should be disclosed before the negotiations begin; and the talks must not be a sham. The employer must consider any representations made to him by the union and reply in writing, giving his reasons if he rejects any of the union's contentions. Only then can the notices be sent out.

**4.60**   If he negotiates with more than one union concerning employees who come within the description of those to be dismissed, then he must consult with each union.

**4.61** Employees need not belong to a particular union that is recognised by the employers for these purposes. They may nevertheless benefit from the provisions, if they come within the description of employees who are being considered for redundancy (see para. 4.53).

**4.62** If there are:

*EP Act 1975 s.99(8)*

(i) special circumstances that render it not reasonably practical for the employer to comply with any of the requirements, then

(ii) he must take all such steps towards compliance as are reasonably practical in the circumstances (see paras 3.79–86).

**4.63** 'Special circumstances' arise where:

*Clarks of Hove Ltd. v. The Baker's Union [1978] IRLR 366, DC*

"for example, sudden disaster strikes a company, making it necessary to close the concern, then plainly that would be a matter which was capable of being a special circumstance: and that is so whether the disaster is physical or financial. If the insolvency, however, were merely due to a gradual rundown of the company, then those are facts on which the industrial tribunal can come to the conclusion that the circumstances were not special. In other words, to be special the event must be something out of the ordinary, something uncommon . . ." (per Lane, L.J.).

**4.64** If the 'special circumstances' render it not reasonably to comply, it is still necessary for the employer to do his best to comply with the obligation to consult with the union at the earliest opportunity.

**4.65** If more than ten employees are to be dismissed, he must notify the Secretary of State, and this duty arises whether or not there is a union to consult.

*EP Act 1975 s.100*

**4.66** These provisions do not confer any personal rights on the employee other than the benefit to a 'protective award' (see para. 4.67). Certain classes of employees are excluded, like those in Crown employment, registered dockers engaged in dock work, those who work outside Great Britain, and certain merchant seamen, amongst a few others.

*EP Act 1975 ss.99(9) & s.119*

## 'PROTECTIVE AWARD' UPON FAILURE TO CONSULT

**4.67**

*EP(C) Act 1978 s.101(1)*
*French v. USDAW*
*[1980] ICR 31, EAT*

Where there has been a breach of these requirements to consult a union (see paras. 4.57–58 & 15.113–118) then it may present a complaint to the tribunal. If the tribunal finds the case proved, it *must* make a declaration to that effect and *may* also make a 'protective award', the amount being dependent on the 'seriousness of the default'.

**4.68**

*Sovereign Distribution Services Ltd. v. Transport & General Workers Union*
*[1990] ICR 31, EAT*

The purpose of the section is not to punish defaulting employers but to ensure compliance. Consequently if there was a genuine attempt at consultation but the employer still breached the Act, then the tribunal would make a declaration in favour of the union. There might not be an award to the employees.

**4.69**

*EP Act 1975 s.101(2)*

At these proceedings, it is a defence for the employer to prove that:

(a) there were special circumstances that rendered it not reasonably practical to comply with the requirement to give notice; and

(b) he took all such steps as were reasonably practical in the circumstances.

**4.70**

*EP Act 1975 (as amended by EP (H of R) Var. Order 1979) s.101(4) & (5)*

An order made by the tribunal covers all employees of the description specified, whatever their length of service or whether a member of the union or not. It requires the employer to pay remuneration for such part of the 'protected' period as the tribunal deems fair and equitable in all the circumstances.

**4.71**

*TGWU v. Ledbury Preserves (1928) Ltd. [1986] ICR 855, EAT*

The effect of an award is to preserve the employment for such period as is stipulated by the tribunal. It may commence with the proposed date of the first dismissals if they have been specified (and not when they first took effect), or with the date of the award, whichever is earlier, for a maximum of:

*EP Act 1975 s.101(5)*

28 days for up to 10 employees;
30 days for up to 99 employees;
90 days for 100 employees or more,

**4.72**

*Angus Jowett & Co. v. NUTGW [1985] ICR 646, EAT*

An employer who sold his business gave notice of dismissal to all his staff, without consulting their union. It was held that liability for a protective award remained with him and was not transferred across to the purchaser.

**4.73**
*EP Act 1975 s.101(6)*
A complaint must be made to the tribunal by the union before the proposed dismissal takes effect or before the end of three months beginning with the date when the dismissal takes effect. When it is not reasonably practical to present it within the 3 months then it must be done within such further period as is reasonable (see paras. 3.80–86).

# CHAPTER FIVE

# Unfair dismissal and the closed shop

## GENERAL INFORMATION

**5.1**

*IR Act 1971 s.22 now EP(C) Act 1978 s.54*

In 1971, Parliament provided that employees should have the right not to be unfairly dismissed, to be dealt with exclusively in the Industrial Tribunals. That is a different remedy to a claim for damages for wrongful dismissal (see paras. 8.28–35).

**5.2** The adjective 'unfair' is frequently misunderstood. Circumstances can and do arise where the most scrupulously fair employer finds himself being classified as 'unfair' and having to pay out compensation to an employee for various technical reasons. Similarly, a genuine meritorious employee might be denied compensation because of some hitch. He may not have made his claim in time (see paras. 3.74–92).

**5.3**

*Cook v. Thomas Linnel & Sons Ltd. [1977] ITR 330, EAT*

It should be borne in mind that the legislation is not intended to impede efficient management of a business; it is only to prevent a dismissal for an unfair reason.

**5.4**
It is easy to legislate for the general principles to be applied; it is in carrying them out that the difficulties arise. Consequently, this part of the law has now become highly complex and technical. If a case is *approached* in the right way, it is generally possible to arrive at the correct answer.

## WHO IS PROTECTED?

**5.5**

*EP(C) Act 1978 s.142(2)*

The aggrieved person must be an 'employee' (see paras. 2.1–11). However, some employees are not eligible to bring proceedings, e.g.,

*EPI(C) Act 1978 s.142(2)*

(a) a share fisherman,

*ss.133(3) & 146(2)*

(b) member of the armed forces and police,

*s.65*

(c] those exempted by Order of the Secretary of State for Employment,

(d) certain others (e.g., some staff at the Palace of Westminster).

**5.6**

*Smith v. Hayle Town Council [1978] ICR 996, CA*
*EP(C) Act 1978 (as amended by UD (V of QP) Orders 1979 & 1985) s.64*
*EP(C) Act 1978 (as amended by E Act 1982 sch.3. para.19) ss.58 & 64(3)*

Even when a worker is an 'employee', he will be debarred from bringing a claim in the following instances. The onus will be on him to prove that there is jurisdiction for the tribunal to adjudicate.

(a) Where he has not completed *two* years of continuous reckonable service (see paras. 3.30–36), except where the dismissal is automatically unfair (see para. 5.7). Where the dismissal is as a result of a medical suspension (see paras. 15.1–6) the qualifying period of employment is 1 month.

*EP(C) Act 1978 sch.13 paras.3–6*

(b) Where he is a part-time worker, who normally works less than 16 hours per week. But in certain restricted circumstances and where he has less than five years' service, he is not debarred provided he works not less than eight hours. Where he has more than five years' service, eight or more hours per week is sufficient (see paras. 3.27–29). For computing the number of hours, see para. 3.30(j).

EP(C) Act 1978 (as amended by E Act 1982 sch.3 para.19) ss.58 & 64(3)

These restrictions do not apply where the dismissal is automatically unfair (see para. 5.7).

EP(C) Act 1978 (as amended by E Act 1982 sch.2 para.19 & SD Act 1986 s.3(2)) s.64(1)(b) & (3)

(c) Where the worker is 65 years of age or over on the effective date of dismissal (see paras. 3.61–70) unless there is another 'normal retiring age' (see paras. 3.107–112).

EP(C) Act 1978 (as amended by E Act 1982 sch.3 para.19) ss.58 & 64(3)

These restrictions do not apply where the dismissal is automatically unfair (see para. 5.7).

EP(C) Act 1978 (as amended by E Act 1980) ss.8(2) & 142(1)

(d) When he is on a fixed contract of two years or more made before October 1, 1980 and has agreed in writing during that time to forego his right to compensation at its expiry (but see para. 3.45): thereafter the period of the fixed term is reduced to one year.

EP (C) Act 1978 (as amended by E Act 1982 s.9(2) & (4) & E Act 1990) ss.62 & 62A Highland Fabricators v. McLaughlin [1985] ICR 183, EAT

(e) Where, at the *time* of dismissal, the employee complaining of unfair dismissal was taking part in an *official* strike or in *official* other industrial action, *unless* one (or more) of the other workers (the 'relevant employees') at the place where the (complaining) employee works, who was on strike was:

(i)   not dismissed, or

(ii)  if he was dismissed, then he was offered employment at any time within 3 months of his dismissal *and* the (complaining) employee brings proceedings within 6 months of his own dismissal.

Glenrose (Fish Merchants) Ltd v. Chapman & ors. Dec. 11, 1990, EAT (unreported)

For the words 'other industrial action' to apply, there does not need to be a breach of contract. It is generally sufficient that the action is concerned with pressure being applied by two or more employees to obtain an advantage, in relation to a 'trade dispute' (see para. 7.24). Anything said before and at the time of dismissal will be relevant.

Power Packing Casemakers Ltd. v. Faust [1983] ICR 292, CA

Thus a refusal to work essential overtime by several employees, which was not obligatory under their contracts of employment, was held to be 'industrial action'. Their motives in applying pressure on the employer over pay had to be considered.

*Manifold Industries Ltd. v.*
*Sims & ors.*
*[1991] ICR 504, EAT*

*Jenkins v. P & O European*
*Ferries (Dover) Ltd.*
*[1991] ICR 652, EAT*

It seems that a failure to comply with (i) and (ii) above strictly will be fatal to the employer. He will then have to contest the case on its merits. An objective test has to be applied as to whether the employee is away for reasons unconnected with the strike, e.g., was it for sickness? However if an employee resigns or retires at that time, then he is no longer an 'employee' and consequently his existence may be disregarded.

*Marsden & ors. v. Fairey*
*Stainless Ltd.*
*[1979] IRLR 103, EAT*

Time can be crucial. A dismissal notice sent by post will only take effect when received (see para. 3.72). If the striking workers have returned to their jobs before receiving the letters then they are not debarred from bringing proceedings.

*P & O European Ferries*
*(Dover) Ltd. v. Byrne [1989]*
*IRLR 254, CA*

The time for determining whether there exists any employee who has not been dismissed, when a strike is continuing, is at the conclusion of the tribunal proceedings. It matters not whether it is at a preliminary hearing to consider the point or at the full hearing (see paras. 18.49–53 & 18.66–89).

An employer will have sufficient time to dismiss the employee, having learnt his name during the proceedings, to defeat the employee's claim. In any event the identity of the employee can be obtained by way of Further Particulars before the hearing (see para. 18.21).

*Bigham & Keoch v. GKN*
*Kwikform Ltd.*
*[1991] IRLR 4, EAT*

Where an employee obtains reinstatement by using subterfuge, e.g., he gives a false name and address then an employer can escape liability. But if the employee's identity *ought* to have known, then the tribunal has jurisdiction to adjudicate.

*H. Campey & Sons Ltd. v.*
*Bellwood*
*[1987] ICR 311, EAT*

The same provisions apply where the employer was conducting a lock-out, save that the 'relevant employees' are those who were directly affected or interested in the dispute *at the date* of the institution of the lock-out (and see para. 3.30(f)).

*Williams & ors. v. National*
*Theatre Board Ltd.*
*[1982] ICR 715, CA*

*E Act 1990, s.9*

It is not necessary for the old job to be offered back but only one that is reasonably suitable. The employer is entitled to impose terms, e.g., that the employee will be treated as on a final warning.

(f) From January 1, 1991 employees will lose all their rights if at the time of dismissal they are taking part in an *unofficial* strike or *unofficial* other industrial action, unless none of them are members of a union.

*EP(C) Act 1978 s.141(1)*

(g) where, under the contract of employment, the employee is ordinarily required to work outside Great Britain (see paras. 3.93–100).

## DISMISSALS WHICH ARE AUTOMATICALLY UNFAIR

**5.7**

*EP(C) Act 1978 (as amended by E Act 1982 s.3) s.58*

If the (principle) reason for the dismissal is as under, then the dismissal will be treated as automatically unfair. The employee will be entitled to higher compensation (see para. 5.159(a)(ii), (b) & (d)).

(a) The employee was, or proposed to become a member of an independent trade union (see para. 1.106); or

(b) because he had taken part, or proposed to take part, in the activities of an independent trade union at an 'appropriate time', e.g., outside his working hours, or within them in accordance with an agreement with the employer; or

(c) because he was not a member of a trade union, nor of a particular one, nor had he refused or had proposed to refuse to join or remain a member.

**5.8**

*Fitzpatrick v. British Railways Board [1991] IRLR 376, CA*

The provisions set out in para. 5.7 (a) above have to be strictly construed. However protection is given to an employee where the dismissal is for his trade union activities with a *previous* employer and where it is *anticipated* that he will cause trouble in the future with his new one.

**5.9**

*Kooltech Ltd. v. Barr Feb. 21, 1990, EAT (unreported)*

A tribunal is entitled to hold on the all of the evidence that a dismissal, alleged to be because of conduct, was in truth for trade union activities. This may occur where a dismissal on the grounds of conduct are weak and the evidence discloses an underlying anti-union bias.

**5.10**

*Discount Tobacco & Confectionery Ltd. v. Armitage [1990] IRLR 14, EAT*

An employee sought the assistance of her union to resolve a dispute over terms and conditions of employment. Shortly afterwards she was dismissed. It was held that a tribunal was justified in finding that the underlying reason was membership of a union. Consequently the dismissal was automatically unfair.

**5.11**

If an employee is dismissed because of redundancy

EP(C) Act 1978 (as amended by E. Act 1980 sch.3 para.17) s.59

and

(a) the same circumstances apply equally to one or more employees doing similar work at the same undertaking, and

(b) the (principle) reason for the selection is any of those set out in para. 5.7 (A), (B) or (C), above, or

(c) the selection for dismissal was in contravention of a customary arrangement or an agreed procedure, unless there were special reasons justifying departure from them,

then the dismissal will be automatically unfair. In respect of (b) above (only), the employee will be entitled to a Special Award (see para. 5.159(d)).

**5.12**

Wellworthy Ltd. v. Singh & ors. April 21, 1989, EAT (unreported)

It is very difficult to obtain a finding that a dismissal is unfair where it follows an 'agreed procedure'. This is so even though it is based on an element of subjectivity and involves the application of guidance in the selection process.

**5.13**

Cook v. Kingston-upon-Hull CC, April 16, 1984 EAT (unreported) TU (P of E) Regs. 1981 reg. 8(1)

Where an undertaking or part of an undertaking, which must be of a commercial nature – and this would cover a private club that has a bar – is transferred from one person to another and an employee is dismissed as a result, then the dismissal will be treated as automatically unfair unless the employer (whether the vendor or purchaser) proves that:

Berriman v. Delabole Slate Ltd. [1985] ICR 546, CA TU (P of E) Reg. 1981 reg. 8(2)

(a) that the dismissal was for 'economic, technical or organisational reasons entailing changes in the work-force', or any one of those reasons, *and*

(b) it was fair and reasonable in the circumstances (see para. 5.44–45), but the employee will only be entitled to ordinary compensation (see para. 5.159(a)–(c) for a breach).

**5.14**

Litster & ors. v. Forth Estuary Engineering Ltd. [1989] ICR 341, HL

Without any instructions, the liquidator of an insolvent company dismissed the employees one hour before he sold the business to another firm. It was held that the dismissals were unfair as they were for a reason connected with the transfer. The liability of the liquidator to pay the compensation (which he was unable to do) was automatically passed to the purchaser.

**5.15**

Secretary of State for Employment v. Gilbraith & ors.

On the other hand the liability of the liquidator for redundancy payments was not passed on to the purchaser of the business. The employees had been dis-

July 10, 1987 EAT
(unreported)

missed by the time of the *completion* of the sale (see para. 3.29).

**5.16**

Crawford v. Swinton
Insurance Brokers Ltd.
[1990] ICR 85, EAT

Where an employee resigns in consequence of changes imposed on him by the transferee and establishes a constructive dismissal (see para. 2.50–54), the Tribunal has to decide what was the *reason* or *principle reason* that motivated the employer in their decision. Does it comes within the definition of 'economic, technical or organisational reasons'? If not the new employer is automatically liable.

**5.17**

Anderson v. Dalkeith
Engineering Ltd.
[1985] ICR 66, EAT

There is a difference of judicial views how far the requirements in para. 5.13(b) above have to be applied. One division of the EAT held that the receiver of a company that dismissed all the workforce at the insistence of the acquiring company could rely on the 'economic' ground. It added that no further evidence was required.

**5.18**

Wheeler v. Patel & anr.
[1987] ICR 631, EAT
Gateway Hotels Ltd. v.
Stewart & anr.
[1988] IRLR 287, EAT

Two other divisions of the EAT, in cases where the facts were not dis-similar, held that a Tribunal must still decide whether it was fair and equitable to dismiss. The basis of their decisions was that another course could have been followed by the employer.

**5.19**

Unlike the other automatically unfair dismissals (see paras. 5.7 & 5.11), the employees in these cases are not entitled to the extra compensation set out in para.

## A DISMISSAL – FAIR OR UNFAIR

**5.20**

EP(C) Act 1978 s.57(1) & (2)

Irrespective of the merits of a claim, before one can be brought, the employee must prove that he has been 'dismissed' (see paras. 3.37–63), and that he is eligible to take proceedings (see para. 5.5). Once he is over these hurdles, then it is up to the employer to prove that the dismissal was for a permissible reason, that is to say, for one of the following:

(a) it related to the *capability* of the employee,

(b) it was because of his *conduct*,

(c) it was due to *redundancy*,

(d) that it was the result of some *statutory restriction* placed on either the employer or the employee,

(e) it was due to '*some other substantial reason*'.

**5.21**

*P(C) Act 1978 s.57(2)(a)*

*Capability* may be relied upon where the 'skill, aptitude health or any other physical or mental quality' falls below that which is required for the job. The duties on which the worker is engaged must relate to 'work of a kind which he was employed . . . to do'.

**5.22**

*Sutton & Gates (Luton) Ltd v. Boxall [1979] ICR 67, EAT*

This will usually include incompetence where it relates to an inherent fault and not just to laziness or negligence.

**5.23**

*Conduct* would occur where an employee was putting in false claims for expenses, or where he was rude to his employer's clients. The matters would have to be serious to warrant a dismissal.

**5.24**

An employee might have an answer to the allegations. He might assert that there was a misunderstanding over what expenses he might claim, or he might deny that he was rude. The customer might have misheard the words used, or they may not have been offensive.

**5.25**

There is sometimes a thin dividing line between capability and conduct. For instance, an employee may keep on making mistakes despite being warned of the serious consequences. If he is dismissed, it may be difficult to determine whether he is wilfully in default or is just incapable of doing his work properly.

**5.26**

In such circumstances, if faced with a claim that the dismissal was unfair, it is perfectly proper for an employer to rely on the two defences jointly or in the alternative. It will be left to a Tribunal to put the correct label on it if it comes to a hearing.

**5.27**

*EP(C) Act 1978 (as amended by E Act 1982, sch.3 para.17) s.59*

Although a true *redundancy* is a defence, nevertheless the selection of an employee for dismissal will be deemed to be automatically unfair if it is proved that any of the circumstances set out in para. 5.7 (a), (b) or (c) exist (see paras. 5.11–13).

**5.28**

If the employee does show that there is a breach of the special provisions, then he will be entitled to claim the additional compensation: (see para. 5.159(a)(ii) & (d)).

**5.29**

*EP(C) Act 1978 s.59(b)*

For a dismissal in contravention of a customary arrangement or agreed procedure (see para. 5.11(c)) the tribunal does not have to consider whether it was fair and equitable (see paras. 5.44–45). The employee will only be entitled to ordinary compensation (see para. 5.159(a)–(c)).

**5.30**　Before the provisions in para. 5.29 above come into play, it must be shown that the redundancy situation equally applies to other employees in the *same undertaking* who hold *similar positions* to the dismissed employee.

**5.31**

*Henry v. Ellerman City*
*Liners Ltd.*
*[1985] ICR 57, CA*
*Rogers & ors. v. Vosper &*
*Thornycroft (U.K.) Ltd.*
*[1989] ICR 384, CA*

Such a procedure, as in para. 5.29 above, may be agreed expressly or by implication, and where made it may be mutually altered, again either expressly or by implication. Further, the agreement must relate to the criteria and process by which the comparison will be made. This does not include any preliminary steps such as the seeking of volunteers.

**5.32**

*Robinson & ors. v. Ulster*
*Carpet Mills Ltd.*
*[1991] IRLR 348, CA*
*Northern Ireland*

Where it is found that there is a departure from an agreed procedure that is justified then the ordinary 'fairness' test has to be applied. A dismissal will not be unfair unless it was outside the bands of reasonable responses (see para. 5.119).

**5.33**

*EP(C) Act 1978 s.60*

Pregnant women are given special statutory protection (see para. 13.15) but a breach only entitles them to ordinary compensation (see para. 5.159(a)–(c)).

**5.34**

*Stockton-on-Tees BC v.*
*Brown*
*[1988] ICR 410, HL*

A pregnant woman was given notice of the termination of her existing job to take effect when she would have been on maternity leave. At that time, she could have been re-engaged in an alternate post. It was held that the special provisions did apply, because the dismissal was *for a reason connected with* pregnancy, and therefore unfair. The only escape was to prove one of the special reasons (see para. 13.3)

**5.35**

*Clayton v. Vigers*
*[1989] ICR 713, EAT*

Furthermore it is no defence that special circumstances oblige an employer to dismiss an employee on maternity leave. So a dentist was held to have fallen foul of the law where he dismissed his dental nurse within a few days of the birth of her child. It was no defence to prove that he could only find a *permanent* replacement for her. At the time the nurse had not served a notice of her intention to return to work on a date within the 29 weeks (see para. 13.7).

**5.36**　*Statutory restriction* would arise, for instance, where a long distance lorry driver is banned from driving for a year. Alternatively there might be some statutory restriction placed on the employer's business forcing him to close down.

**5.37**

*Robinson v. British Island Airways [1978] ITR 111, EAT*
*Elliott Turbomachinery Ltd. v. Bates [1981] ICR 218, EAT*

*Some other substantial reason'* is a very wide provision. It gives the employer protection where, for instance, he carries out a genuine reorganisation to increase his efficiency, and in doing so he has to dismiss several of his staff. They would usually be entitled to redundancy pay.

**5.38**

*Hollister v. National Farmers Union [1979] ICR 542, CA*

The test to be applied in a dismissal arising from a reorganisation is whether there was

> "some sound, good business reason for the reorganisation . . . whether [it] was such that the only sensible thing to do was to terminate the employee's contract unless he would agree to a new agreement" (per Lord Denning),

*Polkey v. A E Dayton Services Ltd. [1988] ICR 142, HL*

but the terms offered must be 'reasonable . . . ones' in the circumstances. There must be real negotiations with the employee, or his representative, or an attempt made to do so where he is being difficult.

**5.39**

*Fay v. North Yorkshire CC [1986] ICR 133, CA*

Where a person is taken on for a fixed short term contract to stand in for staff away on secondment or to cover for those away sick, then the termination of his contract upon that other's return will not normally be unfair. The dismissal will be for 'some other substantial reason'; and he will not qualify for redundancy pay either (see paras. 4.14–25).

**5.40**

*EP(C) Act 1978 s.63*
*James Ferries & Co Ltd. v. Johnstone October 30, 1984, EAT (unreported)*

If pressure is brought on an employer by other workers or by their union to sack a man, this would not amount to 'some other substantial reason'. An employer's fear of industrial action would provide no defence to a claim that the dismissal was unfair.

**5.41**

*Yusuf v. Aberplace Ltd. [1984] ICR 851, EAT*

The fact that a man could not get on with fellow workers would be relevant in considering whether it was fair and equitable to dismiss. But that would have to be ignored if the threat of industrial action over the person's presence was the *real* reason for dismissal.

**5.42**

Normally speaking, an employer must prove that it was the matters that he had in mind *at the time* of dismissal or appeal that caused him to sack the employee to escape liability. The fact that he puts the wrong label in law on it is irrelevant, so long as the facts on which he relies comes within the definition of a permissible reason (see para. 18.17).

**5.43**

*Ely v. YKK Fasteners (UK) Ltd. Jan. 30, 1991, EAT (unreported)*

An exception to the rule lies in constructive dismissal cases. If an employer erroneously thought that an employee had resigned, but would have sacked him in any event, the employer may rely on those facts known to him at the time on which he would have decided to dismiss.

## Merits of Case

**5.44**

*EP(C) Act 1978 (as amended by E Act 1980 s.6) s.57(3)*

Once the employer proves that the dismissal was for a permissible reason (see para. 5.20), the tribunal will then have to consider whether in the circumstances and having regard to the size and administrative resources of the employer, he acted reasonably and in accordance with the equity and substantial merits of the case. The onus of proving that does not lie on either party (see paras 2.14–19).

**5.45**

*Abbotts & Standley v. Wessex-Glyndwood Steels Ltd. [1982] IRLR 51, EAT*

Bristow J summarised the principle as follows:

"[it] is concerned only with the reasonableness of what you do, not how you do it . . . Very often . . . the way in which you do something affects or may affect the question: was it reasonable for you to do it at all? If . . . you dismiss a senior employee or long standing at a moment's notice with no consultation whatever, you are not simply treating him with discourtesy . . . you are depriving yourself of the opportunity to explore with him the possibility of finding another slot in which to place him and on this basis it would be open . . . to find your action in dismissing him in the circumstances to be unreasonable."

**5.46**

*Rentokil Ltd. v. Mackin & anr. [1989] IRLR 286, EAT*

It is concerning this aspect that a great welter of law has arisen. It is important to remember that each case is decided on its own special facts (see para. 19.20), and this will sometimes result in different results, even in near similar cases.

**5.47**

*Cullion v. Scottish Midland Co-Operative Society Ltd. Sept. 27, 1989, EAT (unreported)*

The decision of the employer does not have to be perverse before a Tribunal will interfere, merely that it is outside the 'band of reasonable responses'. That is to say *no* reasonable employer could have taken that course.

**5.48**

In some extreme cases where the facts are basically agreed, the answer is obvious. If an employee is sent to prison for five years for setting fire to his employer's premises, a dismissal because of conduct would be patently fair. There would also probably be frustration (see paras. 2.34–46).

**5.49**   On the other hand if he was jailed for six weeks for non-payment of his wife's maintenance, it would probably not be fair to dismiss. What would have to be taken into account would be whether the job could be held open for him pending his release, as would seem likely. But, if this was the tenth time in two years when he had lost his liberty, there would come a stage when an employer might lawfully say, 'enough is enough'.

**5.50**

*BSC Sports & Social Club v. Morgan [1987] IRLR 391, EAT Treganown v. Robert Knee & Co. Ltd. [1975] ITR 121, QB*

It is what happens *up to* the date of dismissal (or an appeal: see paras. 5.110–111) that has to be considered and not what occurs afterwards. So if an employer dismisses an employee without giving the requisite or any notice, or paying money in lieu of notice (in breach of contract), or he fails to offer the employee a job that unexpectedly becomes available after the employee has left, then that is irrelevant.

**5.51**

*W Devis & Son Ltd v. Atkins [1977] ICR 662, HL Trico Folberth Ltd. v. Devonshire [1989] IRLR 396, CA*

Likewise, where an employer dismisses an employee for, say, redundancy and discovers later that he has been stealing during his employment, then if no true redundancy exists, the dismissal will be unfair. But compensation would be reduced to nil on the basis that he would only be entitled to an award that is 'just and equitable' (see para. 5.159(b)).

**5.52**

*Smith v. City of Glasgow Council [1987] ICR 796, HL*

Where an employer relies on several grounds, but fails to prove the important ones, the dismissal will be unfair where the remaining grounds do not warrant a dismissal.

### Express and Implied Terms

**5.53**   In deciding whether a dismissal is fair or unfair, a tribunal will generally have to find out the contractual position of the employee (see paras. 8.3–8). For instance, is there an express or implied term that he can be required to spend nights away from home? There may be a clause in his contract that stipulates this (an 'express term'), or it would be implied by the very nature of his job. This would arise in the case of a long-distance lorry driver.

**5.54**

*Jones v. Associated Tunnelling Co. Ltd. [1981] IRLR 477, EAT*

*Courtaulds Northern Spinning Ltd v. Sibson & anr [1988] ICR 451, CA*

The underlying principle applied, in ascertaining whether there is an 'implied term' in a contract, is

(i)  whether it is necessary to give the contract 'business efficacy', that is to say, to make the contract work in practice, *and*

(ii) whether it would probably have been agreed to by the parties, had they applied their minds to the question at the time, and been reasonable.

**5.55**

*UCATT v. Brain [1981] ICR 542, CA*

*Davies v. Jack Troth t/a Richards Transport Dec. 16, 1987, EAT (unreported)*

If such a driver was to refuse to undertake any long-distance trips involving spending nights away from home, a dismissal for this would, on the face of it, be fair; but the test to be applied where an employee refuses to obey a lawful instruction is whether the employer was acting reasonably in all the circumstances.

## Mutual Trust and Confidence

**5.56**

*B.B.C. v. Hearn [1977] IRLR 273, CA*

*Post Office v. Roberts [1980] IRLR 347, EAT*

Some terms are implied in every contract. There must be mutual trust and confidence. The test is as under:

". . . you have to look at the conduct of the party whose behaviour is being challenged and determine whether it is such that its effect, judged reasonably and sensibly, is to disable the other party from properly carrying out his or her obligations" (per Talbot J.).

**5.57**

*Bracebridge Engineering Ltd. v. Darby [1990] IRLR 3, EAT*

A female employee made a complaint that two supervisors had sexually assaulted her, but the employers failed to carry out an adequate investigation. This undermined the confidence of female staff. It was held that the complainant was entitled to leave and claim that she had been constructively dismissed.

**5.58**

*United Bank Ltd. v. Akhtar [1989] IRLR 507, EAT*

A bank sought to exercise their right to transfer a lowly paid employee from Leeds to Newcastle with one week's notice and with no relocation allowances. It was virtually impossible for him to comply. He resigned claiming that he had been constructively dismissed (see paras. 3.37–39) and that it was unfair. It was held that the employers were in breach of an over-riding implied obligation not to behave in a way likely to destroy or seriously damage the relationship of confidence and trust. There was a constructive dismissal by the employer and it was unfair.

**5.59**

*White v. Reflective Roadstuds Ltd. [1991] ICR 733, EAT*

On the other hand, where an employer, in the exercise of an unfettered right, transferred an employee to another department and this resulted in a loss of income, it was held that there was no *fundamental* breach. The employee was not entitled to leave. The 'reasonableness' test could not be imported through the back door.

**5.60**

*Moore v. C & A Modes [1981] IRLR 71, EAT*

Where a section leader with 20 years service in a retail store was dismissed for shoplifting in another shop, it was held to be fair. The trust necessary in the job was undermined.

**5.61**

An employee must serve his employer faithfully. If he secretly sets up a competitive business or passes his employer's secrets to another firm, then he may be dismissed without notice. Except on procedural grounds it would be most unlikely that any such dismissal would ever be unfair (see para. 10.24).

### Procedural Defaults

**5.62**

*Polkey v. A E Dayton Services Ltd. [1988] ICR 142, HL*

Where there has been a failure to comply with the Grievance or Disciplinary Procedures (which should be set out in writing in the contract – see paras. 9.38–44), or where there has been a breach of natural justice, then the employer may find a dismissal being castigated as unfair. The way in which procedural breaches can occur are considered at paras. 3.99–135.

**5.63**

It matters not that on a balance of probabilities, it would have made *no difference* had the correct procedure been followed or had there been no breach of natural justice. If there were facts known to the employer *at the time*, which justified the dismissal, and the breach was technical, the dismissal is likely to be fair.

**5.64**

*Sartor v. P & O European Ferries (Felixstowe) Ltd. July 9, 1990, EAT (unreported)*

*Fuller v. Lloyds Bank plc [1991] IRLR 336, EAT*

*Spink v. Express Foods Group Ltd. [1990] IRLR 320, EAT*

Minor breaches, provided they are not of major significance when considered 'in the round', will not turn a fair dismissal into an unfair one. In a marginal case it may be safer to start the disciplinary procedures again. This would be especially so where there has been a flaw which could not be cured on appeal, but that would be dependent on the employee appealing (see para. 3.150).

**5.65**

*Moore v. Sumner Products plc*

But where a dismissal is technically unfair, the compensation may be reduced to nil if the employee would certainly have been dismissed had the proper pro-

June 14, 1988, EAT
(unreported)

cedure been followed. If he *might* have been dismissed then some compensation should be awarded, the amount being governed by the degree of doubt.

**5.66**

McLaren v. National Coal
Board
[1988] ICR 370, CA

Where an employer relies on an employee's plea of guilty to a criminal offence to justify a dismissal he should know the basis upon which it was made. Except in rare circumstances, he should normally be afforded the opportunity of giving his side of the story. He may have pleaded guilty to avoid publicity or been badly advised by a lawyer, *and* have a cast iron defence to the charge.

**5.67**

Rumbelows Ltd. v. Ellis
June 15, 1988, EAT
(unreported)

An employee unambiguously admitted that he used a fraudulent parking voucher, and then put forward various explanations. It was held that the employer did not need to make an independent investigation to satisfy himself that he has forged the document. The dismissal for the forgery was fair.

**5.68**

John v. Rees & ors.
[1969] 2 AER 274, CD

The words of Sir Robert Megarry, Vice-Chancellor, should be borne in mind:

> "'When something is obvious' they may say, 'why force everybody to go through the tiresome waste of time involved in framing charges and giving an opportunity to be heard? The result is obvious from the start'. Those who take this view do not, I think, do themselves justice. As everyone who has anything to do with the law knows, the path of law is strewn with examples of open and shut cases, which somehow were not; of unanswerable charges which, in the event, were completely answered; of inexplicable conduct which was fully explained, of fixed and unalterable determination that, by discussion, suffered a change. Nor are those with any knowledge of human nature who pause to think for a moment likely to underestimate the feelings of resentment of those who find that a decision against him has been made without their being afforded any opportunity to influence the course of events."

**5.69**

Pritchett & Dyjasek v. J.
McIntyre Ltd.
[1987] ICR 359, CA

This does not always prove to be the case. An employer, who found that there had been a considerable loss of high grade metal at his factory, called in the police. They asked him not to disclose their presence while observations were kept on several employees. The employers, after making enquiries, were satisfied that two of their staff had manipulated samples to increase their bonuses and dismissed them without giving them the opportunity to state their cases. The dismissals were held to be fair in view of the need for secrecy and at the tribunal the employees were unable to put forward a satisfactory answer to the allegations.

**5.70**

Sanderson v. H K Clarkson
& Sons Ltd
Jan. 25, 1988, EAT
Whitbread & Co plc v. Mills
[1988] ICR 776, EAT

Normally speaking, there should be some procedure for appealing, but the fact that there is none does not, in itself, make a dismissal unfair. In a small business the dismissal decision may have been taken by the directors and there may not be someone more senior to whom an appeal could go. Sometimes, where there is no contractual right of appeal, it may be appropriate or even prudent to hold one.

## Mitigation

**5.71**

ECC International Ltd. v.
Mckenna & anr.
July 14, 1987, EAT
(unreported)

Care should be taken not to confuse mitigation with fairness to dismiss in dishonesty cases. Length of good service, the amount of money or value of goods involved, the loss of pension or other rights, and the circumstances of the appropriation are all relevant. But where the theft destroys the trust that must exist between an employee and his employer, then a dismissal will not be unfair. Although another employer might have taken another course of action in the light of the mitigation the dismissal does not become unfair.

## Blanket Dismissals

**5.72**

Monie v. Coral Racing Ltd.
[1981] ICR 109, CA

Molloy & Mundell v.
Kemps Contact Lenses Ltd.
July 30, 1986, EAT
(unreported)

Sometimes two, or more persons, in a group are suspected of being engaged in theft or in some dishonest activity. It may be impossible to pin down who is responsible or to establish how many are involved. If the matter is serious, then provided the employer has carried out a reasonable investigation, then the dismissals will not be unfair even if this might include an innocent person. The suspects must be given the opportunity to state their cases. Where any advances an explanation consistent with innocence, then he should not be dismissed otherwise it is likely to be unfair.

**5.73**

Whitbread & Co plc v.
Thomas & ors.
[1988] ICR 135, EAT

Parr v. Whitbread plc t/a
Threshers Wine Merchants
[1990] ICR 427, EAT

Where the activity relates to capability, e.g., stock losses caused by negligence or stupidity, then before the employer can dismiss both or all the employees, he must be satisfied on solid and sensible grounds at the date of dismissal that:

(a) the action, if committed by an individual, would warrant dismissal; and

(b) there must have been a full investigation and the proper procedures carried out; and

(c) he must believe on reasonable evidence that more than one person could have committed it; and

(d) the act must have been capable of having been done by the applicant as well as by those within the identified group,

then even though the applicant might be innocent, his dismissal would not be unfair.

## Employee facing Criminal Charges

**5.74** Difficulties often arise in cases where the employee is charged with stealing from his employer, and the trial may not take place for many months. Interviews with witnesses might be construed as an interference with the course of justice and consequently an employer's powers of investigation may be limited.

**5.75** If the evidence against the employee is very strong and the matter serious, then provided the employer carries out such investigation as is reasonable in the circumstances, then a dismissal is unlikely to be unfair, a suspension ought to be considered. There is, of necessity, a large 'grey' area in this field.

**5.76**

*Saeed v. Greater London Council (I.L.E.A.) [1986] IRLR 23, QBD Harris (Ipswich) Ltd v. Harrison [1978] IRLR 382, EAT*

In determining whether a dismissal is fair, the fact that an employee has been prosecuted for an offence connected with his work and subsequently acquitted is irrelevant.

"The function of the industrial tribunal is not to determine the employee's guilt or innocence of the crime alleged but to consider the behaviour of the employer . . . that is to say, whether they have shown . . . they acted reasonably in treating the employee's involvement in the alleged offences as a sufficient reason for dismissing him." (per Phillips J.)

**5.77**

*British Gas plc v. McCarrick [1991] IRLR 305 EAT*

On the other hand, where an employee pleads guilty in court to theft from his employer, then that fact coupled with conduct known to the employer that is consistent with dishonesty will be sufficient on which to base a dismissal. It does not matter if the employee protests his innocence afterwards, alleging he pleaded guilty to avoid possible imprisonment (but see para. 5.66).

### Dishonesty

**5.78**

*British Home Stores Ltd. v. Burchell [1980] ICR 303, EAT*

Not all dishonesty leads to the involvement of the criminal law. An employee found stealing from the till may often just be summarily dismissed. Before such action is taken, an employer:

(a) must have a genuine belief in the guilt of the employee, and

(b) that must be based on reasonable grounds, and

(c) that must have followed a reasonable investigation.

### Selection for Redundancy

**5.79** One of the greatest sources of dispute lies in cases involving selection for redundancy, especially where there is no laid-down procedure. If someone has to go, the employer has the invidious task of deciding who. How should he go about it?

**5.80** The most important thing to do is to reflect, weigh up the options and give everyone, so far as is possible (through their elected representatives if there are any), an opportunity to air their views.

**5.81**

*Polkey v. A E Dayton Services Ltd. [1988] ICR 142, HL*

If an employee is dismissed without any form of consultation, then it would be likely to lead to a finding of unfair dismissal even though it is shown that it was likely to have made no difference. It has to be proved, based on facts known to the employer at the time, that any consultation would have been 'utterly useless' or 'futile'.

**5.82**

*Leese v. Food From Britain Mar. 4, 1991, EAT (unreported)*

An instance of this defence being successful occurred where employers restructured their organisation in secrecy and within strict time limits. They had been pressurised to do so by those who provided their sole source of revenue. The job performed by a director was lost and he was selected for redundancy without any consultation. The evidence established there was no alternate position for him. It was held that these were exceptional circumstances and the dismissal was fair.

**5.83** Where an employer is contemplating making an

employee redundant he is bound to give his union, which it recognises for bargaining purposes (see paras. 15.113–119), the proposals and reasons in writing for making the person redundant (see paras. 4.53–66). But breach of this requirement does not, of itself, make a dismissal unfair.

**5.84** The best starting-off points is to ask for voluntary redundancies but if this does not provide sufficient candidates, then there must be compliance with any agreed formula (see para. 5.25). If there are none, the employer must decide who must go, weighing up the pro's and con's in each case.

**5.85** A good many employees can find reasons why someone else should have been selected in preference to themselves. The criterion applied by the tribunals is whether the person selected is within a band of reasonable responses whom the employer, in his discretion, might reasonably have selected. It is not whether the tribunal would have selected someone else.

**5.86**

*Walls Meat Co Ltd v. Selby*
*[1989] ICR 601, CA*

*Duncan v. Marconi*
*Command & Control*
*Systems Ltd. (Case B)*
*Oct. 14, 1988, EAT*
*(unreported)*

There is normally always a duty to consult each employee individually about a proposed redundancy. He should be given the opportunity to put forward suggestions how he could be retained in the employment. This applies even though the employer is implementing a formula agreed with the employee's union unless the numbers are so large that it would be impractical to carry out individual consultations.

**5.87**

*Dooley v. Leyland Vehicles*
*Ltd.*
*June 17, 1986, CS*
*(unreported)*

Where selection is made on the basis of a poor attendance record, an employer does not have to consider whether an employee's absences were due to an industrial injury sustained at work or mere malingering. Often it would not be practical to try to find out the reason. But the criteria for selection must be fair.

**5.88**

*Dick v. Boots The Chemist*
*Ltd.*
*June 25, 1991, EAT*
*(unreported)*

*MDH Ltd. v. Sussex*
*[1986] IRLR 12 3, EAT*

There is always a need to try to re-locate any redundant worker and failure to do so can result in a finding of unfair dismissal. It *must* be shown that the point had been considered *at the time* and there was no suitable alternate work available. Care should be taken not to assume that work at a more junior level would not be accepted. An employee may have lowered his sights. This duty usually extends to making enquiries at any 'associated company' (see paras. 3.153–161), but a failure to do so may not be fatal.

**5.89** The most difficult positions are likely to arise where questions of sex, marital status and race have to be taken into consideration. For instance, a married coloured girl is selected to go instead of a single white widower who has 3 children and a heavy mortgage. If the decision is taken on personal circumstances, or for humane reasons, and not based on competence, experience, reliability and so forth, then the dismissal is not only likely to be unfair but it will also be in breach of the Race Relations Act and the Sex Discrimination Act (see Chapters 11, 12 & 14).

## Divided Loyalties

**5.90**

*Dyer v. Inverclyde Ltd. Nov. 25, 1987, EAT (unreported)*

Sometimes a husband and wife are employed in the same business and one leaves to join a competitor. If the one who remains has access to confidential information that would be harmful to the business if disclosed to the rival, then, provided the risk is unacceptably high, it would be not unfair to dismiss.

**5.91**

*Coleman v. Skyrail Oceanic Ltd. t/a Goodman Tours [1981] ICR 864, CA*

On the other hand, where a woman was dismissed because she had married a man employed in a rival firm and there was concern about possible leakages, it was held to be no defence to a claim of discrimination on the grounds of sex (see Chapter 12). The dismissal was based on the assumption that men are less likely to be primary supporters of their spouses and children.

## Internal Appeals

**5.92**

It is not intended that disciplinary bodies should follow the procedures of ordinary courts of law, only that they should act fairly, and that includes giving *the appearance* of doing so. This is particularly important when considering the final stages of an appeal process, where there is often the risk of error.

**5.93**

*Rumbelows Ltd. v. Ellis June 15, 1988, EAT (unreported)*

A distribution manager dismissed an employee after an admission of forgery, for which various explanations were given. But as he was present at an appeal to the line manager and remained behind while the line manager deliberated, it was held to be unfair. It would give the impression of bias and undue influence.

**5.94**

*Whitbread & Co plc v. Mills [1988] ICR 766, EAT*

*Clark v. Civil Aviation Authority [1991] IRLR 412, EAT*

Sometimes there has been a procedural defect in the disciplinary procedure that would normally have made a dismissal unfair (see paras. 5.62–71). If an employee appeals against the dismissal and there is a proper investigation into the facts and a full hearing at which the employee can state his case, then that appeal can 'cure' the defect. It can turn the dismissal into a fair one. A mere review of the decision would *not* be sufficient.

**5.95**

*Stoker v. Lancashire County Council [1992] IRLR 75, CA*

A contract of employment provided a detailed disciplinary procedure with different tiers of appeal each performing precise functions. Breach of a stage turned an otherwise fair dismissal into an unfair one. The employee had been denied his contractual rights on his appeal. However, compensation was dealt with on the merits of the case (see para. 5.65).

## Sickness

**5.96**

Dismissals for sickness often cause trouble. It should be borne in mind that an employer is not the insurer of the good health of his employee. But he should take care not to cause its break-down by, for instance, bringing him into contact with injurious substances (see para. 15.1).

**5.97**

Where the employment is ended on the basis of genuine ill health, it is generally classified as a 'capability' dismissal (see paras. 5.21–22); where it is for malingering or similar reasons, it is a 'conduct' dismissal (see para. 5.23).

**5.98**

The distinction between the two is narrow and blurred, but it may affect the procedures to be used. In the latter case, the ordinary disciplinary procedures should be followed, and this applies where the dismissal is based on a mixture of both grounds.

**5.99**

*A Links & Co Ltd. v. Rose [1991] IRLR 353, CS*

But before an employee with a bad record for genuine sickness absences is dismissed:

(i)   he should be consulted about them but it is not essential to warn him of the possible consequences if they continue although it may be advisable to do so, and

(ii)  there should be a fair review of his case, obtaining independent medical advice where necessary, and

*Scott v. Secretary of State for Scotland July 14, 1988, EAT (unreported)*

(iii) the position should be discussed with him, especially concerning any medical opinion obtained, to see whether there is any chance of improvement;

and if the employers' needs for the work to be done outweigh the employee's requirement of further time to recover, then a dismissal will generally be held to be fair (see para. 5.139).

**5.100**

*Forth Ports Authority v. Lorimer Mar. 8 1991, EAT (unreported)*

An employer used disciplinary procedures against an employee who after the midday break returned to work very late and heavily intoxicated. The employers learnt that he had an underlying medical problem and made some perfunctory enquiries about it from his doctor. They dismissed him for gross misconduct. It was held to be unfair: it was not adequate to reach a conclusion without proper medical reports.

**5.101**

*International Sports Co Ltd. v. Thomson [1980] IRLR 340, EAT*

Where there are many minor and unrelated sickness absences, with some supported by medical certificates, it is not generally necessary for the employer to obtain independent advice before dismissing. But he must have warned the employee of the consequence of the absences continuing.

**5.102**

If necessary, medical advice should be sought and an employee should have the opportunity to rebut any opinions obtained. If, despite everything, there is little prospect of an improvement, he can be dismissed. It is first necessary though to consider whether any other post is available or likely to be available where ill-health would not be a problem.

## Natural Justice

**5.103**

*AMR Act 1988*

Employers should remember that they are required to have an employee's written consent to obtain medical reports on him from his medical practitioner. He *must* be told in writing what his rights are concerning the report, when the request for his permission is sought.

**5.104**

In nearly every case, there are always two sides to a story. It is essential that except in the most hopeless of cases the employee should be allowed to state his case before any decision is taken to dismiss.

**5.105**

*Polkey v. A E Dayton Services Ltd. [1988] ICR 142, HL*

Lord Bridge said:

". . . in the case of misconduct, the employer will not normally act reasonably unless he . . . hears whatever the employee wishes to say in his defence or in explanation or mitigation . . .".

**5.106**

*Morton v. City of Glasgow District Council*

Further, an employer must carry out a reasonable investigation to try to find out the truth before he reaches his final decision (see also paras. 3.117–150). If

**119**

Mar. 20, 1989, EAT
(unreported)
Stacey v. Babcock Power
Ltd.
[1986] ICR 221, EAT
he was misled over the position because the employee failed to inform him of an important fact, then that would not be fatal. The reasonableness test has to be applied from the moment of dismissal up to the time when the employee leaves (see para. 5.108).

**5.107** Every relevant aspect of a person's employment must be taken into account. When considering dismissing, it is essential to use the proper criteria, with fairness to the individual being in the forefront of any decision taken, and irrespective of the consequences. This may even mean on occasions that a trouble-maker has to be retained in preference to a hard-working and loyal member of staff.

**5.108** So if the employee has been dismissed with immediate effect, and not retained 'on the books', then the decision to dismiss must be judged on the facts known at that stage, unless there is an appeal.

Monie v. Coral Racing Ltd.
[1981] ICR 109, CA

**5.109** If the decision was patently correct on the information available when he was dismissed, but an appeal (even after the termination of the employment) disclosed fresh evidence that showed that an erroneous view had been taken, then an employer would be liable because

West Midlands Co-
operative Society v. Tipton
[1986] ICR 192, HL

> "the right of appeal . . . are necessary elements in the overall process of terminating the employment" (per Lord Bridge),

**5.110** Where the employee has been denied a contractual right to appeal or there has been a failure to operate an agreed procedure for appeals, then the same principle applies.

National Coal Board v.
Nash
The Times, May 7, 1986,
EAT

**5.111** The fact that the worker is appealing against one or more previous warnings, on which the employer partly relies in deciding to dismiss for a subsequent offence does not make a dismissal unfair. It is because he has been *warned* and was under that *warning* at the time of the commission of the subsequent misdemeanour that would be relevant. But the fact that they were under appeal would also have to be taken into consideration. If the appeal was due to be heard shortly after the disciplinary hearing, then the latter should be delayed.

Tower Hamlets Health
Authority v. Anthony
[1989] IRLR 394, CA

**5.112** If an employer decides to switch to outside contractors for economic or cost reasons, they do not have to justify those grounds or even show that they were beneficial.

Hodgkins v. CJB
Developments Ltd.
July 30, 1984, EAT
(unreported)

*Smith v. Lodge Bros (Funerals) Ltd. Oct. 19, 1989 EAT (unreported)*

A person was dismissed for a valid reason but the dismissal was held to be unfair because of a breach of procedure. The compensation was reduced to nil for contributory fault. It was the employee who had *caused* the dismissal. An employer's irregularities, although unfortunate, did not bring about the dismissal.

## Parity of Treatment and Penalties

**5.114** There is an implied term that an employer will not treat the employees arbitrarily, capriciously or inequitably.

**5.115**

*Murco Petroleum Ltd. v. Forge [1987] ICR 282, EAT*

The failure to give an employee an annual pay rise to which she had become accustomed and which was given to other staff, did not amount to a fundamental breach (see paras. 2.22–25). It mattered not that the employer behaved heartlessly: he had dealt with her case on its merits.

**5.116**

*Post Office v. Fennel [1981] IRLR 221, CA*

*Cowton v. British Railway Board Nov. 28, 1989, EAT (unreported)*

In deciding the appropriate remedy for misconduct the punishment awarded to other employees for similar offences in the same circumstances is a relevant factor to remember. It is always necessary to consider each case separately. If there are important distinguishing features, then failure to take them into account can be fatal.

**5.117**

*Whitbread & Co plc v. Allen & Bishop Jan. 17, 1989, EAT (unreported)*

*Procter v. British Gypsum Ltd. [1991] IRLR 7, EAT*

A disparity in treatment may be justified on the grounds that one person was young and led astray by a more senior employee, or one person had received several warnings whereas another had not. Where there had been a considerable increase in some particular type of trouble and employees had been warned to expect more severe punishment, then only those cases that occurred after that caution should be compared.

**5.118**

*Securicor Ltd. v. Smith [1989] IRLR 356, CA*

*Heald & ors v. National Coal Board Jan. 27, 1988, CA (unreported)*

But an employer is entitled to come to a decision based on facts known to him at the time, having made reasonable enquiries. This includes any findings and conclusions made by an appeal panel. If the dismissal was within the band of reasonable responses, it would not be unfair.

## The Duty of the Tribunal

**5.119**

*Scottish Midland Co-operative Society Ltd. v. Cullion [1991] IRLR 261, CS*

A tribunal hearing a case of unfair dismissal does not apply a critical or take a meticulous approach to decisions taken by employers. They generally hear the evidence that was previously before the employer and say to themselves:

> "Have the employers made adequate enquiries into the incident and was there credible evidence on which they might reasonably have come to view that they took? Was it within the band of reasonable responses for the employee to have been dismissed?"

**5.120**

*Linfood Cash & Carry Ltd.*
*v. Thomson*
*[1989] ICR 518, EAT*

*Morgan v. Electrolux Ltd.*
*[1991] ICR 369, CA*

A tribunal must *not* substitute their own views for that of the employer. At a disciplinary hearing the employer preferred the story given by one employee in preference to another. The tribunal having heard the witnesses took the opposite view. It was held that this was not relevant *unless* no reasonable employer could have held that belief.

**5.121**

*Co-Operative Wholesale*
*Society Ltd. v. Close*
*Oct. 31, 1989, EAT*
*(unreported)*

Further, in considering the penalty, the test to be applied is not whether a reasonable employer might impose a lesser punishment, but whether dismissal was a penalty that a *reasonable* employer might impose. Was it within the 'band of reasonable responses'?

**5.122**

*Moon & Ors. v.*
*Homeworthy Furniture*
*(Northern) Ltd.*
*[1977] ICR 117, EAT*

A tribunal does not apply the criteria of what they would have done in all the circumstances. They cannot tell an employer how to run his business and it is not their duty to take into account policy decisions even if they have brought about a redundancy situation. Lord McDonald put it in this way:

*Meikle v. McPhail*
*(Charleston Arms)*
*[1983] IRLR 351, EAT*

> "It may be as the tribunal suggest that the [employer] entered into the contract unreasonably if not recklessly . . . Many employees have to be dismissed as a result of incompetent business management, but this does not make the dismissal unfair."

## CONTRIBUTORY FAULT

**5.123**

*EP(C) Act 1978 (as*
*amended by E Acts 1980 &*
*1982) s.73(7A)(7B) & (7C)*

The Acts provides that in respect of:

(a) the *basic element* (see para. 5.159(a)), the amount shall be reduced:

    (i) 'where any conduct of the [employee] before dismissal, (or, where the dismissal was with notice, before the notice was given) . . . was such that it would be just and equitable to reduce [it] to any extent . . .', and/or

(ii) 'where [he] has unreasonably refused an offer [of reinstatement] . . . to such an extent as [the tribunal] considers just and equitable', and also

*EP(C) Act 1978 s.74(1)*

(iii) the amount of the compensatory award shall be such amount as the tribunal considers just and equitable in all the circumstances.

(b) the *compensatory element* (see para. 5.159(b)), the award shall be reduced

*EP(C) Act 1978 s.74(6)*

(i) "where . . . the dismissal was to any extent caused or contributed to by any action of the [employee], . . . by such proportion as [the tribunal] considers just and equitable", but

*Courtaulds Northern Spinning Ltd. v. Moosa [1984] ICR 218 EAT*

(ii) no reduction may be made where the employee was dismissed for taking part in industrial action during a dispute with the employer nor where he has contributed to his failure to be reinstated (see paras. 5.147–156), although, in the event a tribunal would probably have to take into account his failure to mitigate his loss (see paras. 2.76–84).

*T G W U v. Howard Oct. 10, 1991, EAT (unreported)*

*but*, where the dismissal is for trade union activities, no account may be taken of any conduct or action that relates to the employee's right to become or cease to remain a member of a trade union, whether or not his behaviour concerning it has been confrontational or 'bloodyminded'.

**5.124**

*Sulemanji v. Toughened Glass Ltd. [1979] ICR 499, EAT*

Thus, where a worker is habitually late in arriving for work, and the boss sees red one day and sacks him without any prior warning, then the dismissal would probably be unfair. The employee might be two-third's to blame for it. In such an instance, he would only recover one-third of his total compensation. On occasions, a tribunal will find that an employee is 100 percent to blame, and so he will recover nothing.

**5.125**

Although the wording in the Act differs for the two types of award, it has been held that in determining a

*R S P C A v. Cruden [1986] ICR 205, EAT*

reduction the tribunal should treat each in the same way, save 'in exceptional circumstances'.

**5.126**

*Walter Braund (London) Ltd. v. Murray [1991] ICR 327, EAT UD(I of CL) Order1991*

The reduction, if any, is made from the gross loss *before* taking into account any limit on the amount of the award. If the loss is, say, £30,000 and an employee is 50 percent to blame, the percentage reduction would be applied to the £30,000, e.g., making it £15,000. But only £10,000 could be awarded (see also para. 2.74).

**5.127**

*W Muir Ltd. v. Lamb [1985] IRLR 95, EAT*

What does not amount to contributory fault is a failure to use internal appeals procedure. It might be held to be a breach of duty to mitigate damages (see paras. 2.76–84), which would have the same effect.

**5.128**

*Parker Foundry Ltd. v. Slack [1992] IRLR 11, CA*

A failure by the employer to treat defaulters equally is not relevant at this stage, (see paras. 5.114–118); within reason, it is the employee's conduct *alone* that has to be considered in deciding whether an award should be reduced.

**5.129**

*Finnie v. Top Hat Frozen Food [1985] ICR 433, EAT*

In appropriate circumstances the performance of an employee caused by a lack of competence or his mental approach can be taken into account in determining contributory fault. For instance, if an employee is lazy, or does not try to improve, then a reduction would be warranted.

**5.130**

*Trico Folberth Ltd. v. Devonshire [1989] IRLR 396, CA*

If a person is dismissed for one reason that turns out to be misconceived, but there were valid alternate grounds to do so, then the dismissal would be unfair. The compensation could be reduced to nil where this would be just, based on contributory fault relating to those *other* grounds. Where the employer took the view that it would not be right to dismiss for those other grounds then there could be no reduction in the compensation.

### In Constructive Dismissal Cases

**5.131**

*Morrison v. Amalgamated Transport & General Workers Union (Case B) [1989] IRLR 361, CA*

*Holroyd v. Granure Cylinder Ltd. [1984] IRLR 259, EAT*

*Polentarutti v. Autocraft Ltd. [1991] ICR 757, EAT*

Even in constructive dismissal cases a tribunal may reduce an award where no reason for the dismissal has been advanced by the employer. There does not have to be a direct causal link between the dismissal and contributory fault only whether the dismissal was to any extent contributed to by the action of the employee. Further there do *not* have to be exceptional circumstances.

**5.132**

*Brown v. Rolls Royce (1971) Ltd. [1977] ITR 382, EAT*

*Warrilow v. Robert Walker Ltd. [1984] IRLR 304 EAT*

*Cullen v. Austin Rover Group Ltd., April 24, 1986, EAT (unreported)*

In deciding on the degree of fault, the tribunals employ a 'broad brush' approach to the whole employment record, and avoid legalism as much as possible. They consider whether there was any blameworthy, including 'bloody minded', conduct by the employee that was causative of his dismissal. The percentage reduction is applied in the same way as is set out in para. 2.75.

**5.133**

*EP(C) Act 1978 (as amended by E Act 1980) s.73(7B)*

Because of the wording of the Act (see para. 5.123(a)(i) above) if an employee commits some act warranting a reduction in compensation between a notice of dismissal and the dismissal, the *full* basic award still has to be paid.

**5.134**

*TeleTrading Ltd. v. Jenkins [1990] IRLR 430, CA*

*Polky v A E Dayton Services Ltd. [1988] ICR 142, HL*

It should be borne in mind that there can also be a reduction in compensation under the 'just and equitable' provisions (see para. 5.159(b)). That generally only can be made where the employer relies on conduct that was *not* known to him at the time of dismissal. This could occur where he dismisses him (unfairly) for being incapable of carrying out his job, but later discovers that he had been stealing.

**5.135**

*Post Office v. Benton & McLeish Mar. 24, 1988, EAT (unreported)*

*Chaplin v. H J Rawlinson Ltd. [1991] ICR 553, EAT*

An exception occurs in breach of procedure cases (see paras. 5.62–71), where all the information is known to the employer at the time. The reduction is then applied under the 'just and equitable' provisions, and that in appropriate cases can also reduce the compensation to nil. Further, there can be a reduction in compensation under *both* provisions.

## INSTANCES OF SUCCESSFUL UNFAIR DISMISSALS

**5.136**

*W. Weddel & Co. Ltd. v. Tepper [1980] ICR 286, CA*

Following observation of the employee who was handling meat in suspicious circumstances, the employers suspected him of dishonesty and resolved to dismiss him unless he offered a satisfactory explanation. When asked whether he had anything to say regarding the allegations that he was handling meat in an improper manner, he replied he had done nothing wrong. He was dismissed.

*Held*: failure to afford him a reasonable chance to clear his name was unfair and resulted in an unfair dismissal.

**5.137** Without any agreement, the buyer in a green-grocery

*Coleman v. Baldwin*
*[1977] IRLR 342, EAT*

business had the bulk and the most interesting part of his work removed from him, which left only humdrum duties.

*Held*: there was a fundamental breach of contract entitling the employee to leave and it was unfair because no attempt had been made to negotiate with him.

**5.138**

*Laughton & Hawley v.*
*BAPP Industrial Supplies*
*Ltd.,*
*[1986] ICR 634, EAT*

Employees were summarily dismissed on the grounds of gross breach of duty of loyalty when employers learnt that they intended to leave and set up a rival company.

*Held*: that as there was no evidence of a misuse of trade secrets or other confidential information, there was no breach of duty and the dismissals were unfair.

**5.139**

*East Lindsay District*
*Council v. Daubney*
*[1977] ITR 359, EAT*

Employee's contract was terminated because of ill-health. The employers relied on a statement from their medical officer saying he was unfit to carry out his duties and should be retired. No full medical report was obtained.

*Held*: that although a full medical report was not essential, it was incumbent on the employer to have adequate information. They must then discuss it with the employee so that he can have an opportunity to deal with any of the comments. The dismissal was unfair.

**5.140**

*Sutton & Gates (Luton)*
*Ltd. v. Boxall*
*[1979] ICR 67, EAT*

Electrician's work was satisfactory for four years, and then deteriorated. the employers found their business was being affected and, while he was away on holiday, they decided to dismiss him without giving him the opportunity to give any explanation.

*Held*: unless he was completely incapable, an operative should be warned that failure to measure up to the job will result in a dismissal. Failure to do so in this case resulted in the dismissal being unfair.

## INSTANCES OF CASES THAT FAILED

**5.141**

*Bouchaala v. Trusthouse*
*Forte Hotels*
*[1980] ICR 721, EAT*

Tunisian national had been dismissed because the employer had been informed erroneously by Dept. of Employment that he needed a work permit, which he did not have. The error did not afford the employer a defence on the grounds of statutory prohibition because none existed.

*Held*: the employer could reply upon 'some other substantial reason' and it was fair and equitable in the circumstances.

**5.142**

*Bailey v. B.P. Oil (Kent Refinery) Ltd. [1980] ICR 642, CA*

Employee certified himself sick in order to take a holiday in Majorca, but was seen out there by an assistant engineer. Disciplinary procedure leading to a dismissal was put in hand. The employers, in breach of an agreement, overlooked notifying the union representative about the intended dismissal.

*Held*: breach of procedural duty was only one of many matters to be taken into account. The dismissal was fair.

**5.143**

*Treganowan v. Robert Knee & Co. Ltd. [1975] ITR 121, QB*

An employee held views on some moral issues that caused offence to some fellow employees. She could have avoided causing the trouble and was dismissed. The events did not warrant dismissal without proper notice, which should have been six weeks.

*Held*: her dismissal for 'some other substantial reason' was fair. It was irrelevant that there was a breach of contract. That had nothing to do with the reason for the dismissal. She could recover the appropriate amount in the county court.

**5.144**

*Alidair Ltd. v. Taylor [1978] ICR, 445, CA*

A pilot damaged an aircraft very badly when landing. A Board of Inquiry set up by the employers concluded that the cause was lack of flying knowledge and error of judgment. The Board lacked independence but it was a fact finding body carried out within the principles of natural justice. The pilot was dismissed on the basis of the report.

*Held*: the dismissal was fair as the potential consequences of the smallest departure from the highest degree of skill could be disastrous.

**5.145**

*Power Packing Casemakers Ltd. v. Faust [1983] ICR 292, CA*

Employers requested employees to work overtime to complete an urgent order. Despite a threat of dismissal, three still refused to do it in order to bring pressure on employers concerning wage negotiations. Their contracts did not provide for compulsory overtime. They were dismissed.

*Held*: at the time of dismissal they were taking part in 'industrial action', and whether it was in breach of contract or not was irrelevant. The tribunal had no jurisdiction to adjudicate.

## TEMPORARY REPLACEMENT OF EMPLOYEES

**5.146**
*EP(C) Act 1978 s.61*

Where a worker is taken on temporarily as a replacement for a permanent employee who is away

(a) because a medical suspension under the Health & Safety at Work Act (see paras. 15.1–5), or

(b) a medical suspension under any other enactment, or

(c) for pregnancy or confinement (see Chapter 13),

(d) he/she is notified in writing at the time that the employment will be ended on the return of the permanent worker,

then if the replacement, after working for 2 years or more, is dismissed to allow for the permanent employee to return, it will be deemed to be on the grounds of *some other substantial reason* (see para. 5.20). Provided it is shown that the employer acted reasonably in the circumstances, it will not be unfair, (see para. 5.44–46).

## REMEDIES

**5.147**
*EP(C) Act 1978 s.69*

There are two options open to a dismissed employee:

(a) to seek reinstatement or re-engagement; or

(b) to claim compensation.

**5.148**
*EP(C) Act 1978 s.69(5)(b) & (6)(b)*

The power to order reinstatement or re-engagement is discretionary and is rarely exercised. Usually the employee does not want it for fear of being subsequently dismissed on good grounds. Generally no order is made if it would be impractical. Further where there has been contributory fault that would make it unjust to make an order, one will be refused.

**5.149**

Reinstatement means that the dismissed employee is returned to his old job on the same terms as before and with the same seniority etc., whereas re-engagement means being retained by the employer, but on different terms, which may be alternate work or less pay, loss of seniority, and so forth.

**5.150**

In deciding whether it is reasonably practical to take an employee back, a tribunal is required to 'take it into

Timex Corporation v.
Thomson
[1981] IRLR 522, EAT

Akram v. Lothian
Community Relations
Council
Oct. 12, 1988, EAT
(unreported)

account' as part of their general determination. *Prima facie*, is it correct? They do not have to come to a final conclusion. If the employer fails to comply, the onus then passes on him to prove that he has made genuine effort to comply but found that reinstatement was impractical.

**5.151**

Mabirizi v. National
Hospital for Nervous
Diseases
[1990] IRLR 133, EAT

Thus where employer established that they sincerely believed that trust and confidence had broken down, this was held to be a good reason for refusing to comply.

**5.152**

EP(C) Act 1978

If a permanent replacement has been taken on, the Tribunal must not take that fact into account unless the employer shows that:

(i)   it was not reasonably practical for the employee's work to have been done by anyone else other than a permanent replacement; or

(ii)  a reasonable time had elapsed before the employee indicated his wish to have his job back, and there was no reasonable alternate except to take on a permanent replacement.

**5.153**

Freeman plc. v. Flynn
[1984] ICR 874, EAT

Where a permanent replacement has been taken on before an order for reinstatement being made, an employer can escape liability by proving that they had made genuine efforts to find alternate employment but none was available. There is no duty to dismiss another employee to create a vacancy.

**5.154**

EP(C) Act 1978

Where an order is made for reinstatement the Tribunal will also specify any benefit, which includes loss of pay, which the employer will be required to reimburse. Where the order is for re-engagement the amount is discretionary. There is *no* limitation as to the sum specified.

**5.155**

O'Laoire v. Jackel
International Ltd.
[1990] ICR 197, CA

If the employer fails to comply with the order, the employee can apply to the Tribunal for an Additional Award (see para. 5.159(c)). He may not abandon his claim for reinstatement/re-engagement and seek to enforce the monetary award.

**5.156**

City & Hackney H.A. v.
Crisp
[1990] ICR 95, EAT

In making an award concerning back-pay following an order of re-engagement, the Tribunal may take into account any contributory fault (see paras. 5.123–135), but *not* a failure to mitigate.

## WHO PAYS THE COMPENSATION

**5.157**

*EP(C) Act 1978 (as amended by E Act 1982 s.7) s.76A(1)*

Normally speaking, it is only the employer who is responsible for paying any compensation ordered by the tribunal. Where an employee takes proceedings not only against his employer but also against a union and/or person(s) bringing pressure on his employer to dismiss him or where the employer has 'joined' the union and/or person(s) bringing pressure on him (see para. 3.179), then the tribunal will decide what percentage of the compensation (if any) should be paid by each party. This will be done based on blameworthiness.

**5.158**

*EP(C) Act 1978 (as amended by E Act 1982 s.7) s.76A(1)*

It should be borne in mind that an order for compensation can only be made against a party who is before the tribunal, e.g, a 'respondent' (see paras. 3.178–179). In every case the employer has to be made a 'respondent'. If the employee does not 'join' the union and/or person(s) bringing pressure (if there is one), the employer may do so.

## HOW COMPENSATION IS CALCULATED

**5.159**

*EP(C) Act 1978 (as amended by E Act 1982 s.5(2) & SD Act 1986 s.3(2)) ss.72(a) & 73(3)–(6)*

*EP(C) Act 1978 (as amended by E Acts 1980 & 1982) s.73*

*EP(C) Act 1978 s.71(5)*

Compensation falls into four parts:

(a) *The Basic Award*

(i) This is computed in the same way as the redundancy payment (see paras. 4.44–47) except there is no minimum age limit. It is subject to the same pro-rata reduction where the employee is approaching his/her 65th year and on the same basis as is set out in para. 4.49(a). Contributory fault (see paras. 5.109–114) is taken into account except (A) in redundancy cases (subject to the exception in (ii) below) and (B) where the employee unreasonably refuses an offer of full reinstatement, which is *deemed* to be a failure to mitigate (see paras. 2.76–84).

*EP (V of L) Order 1992*

The maximum in respect of dismissals (see paras. 3.64–73) up to April 1, 1992 is £5,940, and thereafter £6,150.

*UD (I of L of B & SA) Order 1992*

(ii) Where the dismissal is automatically unfair (see para. 5.7) the minimum award is £2,650 up to April 1, 1992 and thereafter £2,700 but this may be reduced for contributory fault (see paras. 5.123–135). This also applies in redundancy cases, although the proportional reduction can only be made to the difference between the normal basic award (calculated as in (i) above) and the £2,650/£2,700, if any.

*EP (C) Act 1978 (as amended by E Act 1982 sch.3 para.23) s.74*

*UD (I of CL) Order 1991*

(b) The *Compensatory Award*, an amount that is 'just and equitable in all the circumstances, up to a maximum of £10,000, having regard to the loss sustained by the complainant'. This consists of:

*Fentiman v. Fluid Engineering Products Ltd. [1991] ICR 507, EAT*

(i) the estimated loss of wages, net of tax and other deductions, up to time he obtained other employment or if his earnings are less than before, then up to the date of the hearing. Generally he needs not give credit for his earnings during the notice period, but the payment of salary in lieu of notice has to be taken into account; and

*Fougere v. Phoenix Motor Co Ltd [1976] IRLR 259, EAT*

*Ging v. Ellward Lancs Ltd. [1978] ITR 265, EAT*

*Morris v. Accro Co. Ltd. [1985] ICR 306, EAT*

*Addis v. Gramaphone Co. [1909] AC 488 HL*

(ii) the estimated future loss from the date of assessment; and this must take into account the personal circumstances and characteristics of the employee, e.g., his state of health, age but not the degree of 'unfairness' or the mental distress caused, or the manner of dismissal; and

(iii) the loss of any benefits, including pension rights, and expenses. Pensions can form a big item, raising the total award to well above the maximum award. It is extremely complicated, and where necessary, actuarial advice should be sought; and

*S H Muffett Ltd. v. Head [1987] ICR 1, EAT*

(iv) the loss of statutory rights (of usually about £100);

(v) any reasonable expenses incurred in consequence of the dismissal, e.g., costs incurred in seeking a new job, but *not* legal expenses;

*but*

*Holroyd v. Gravure Cylinder Ltd. [1984] IRLR 259, EAT*

all are subject to a pro-rate reduction for contributory fault (see paras. 5.123–135) together with a reduction for any failure to mitigate the loss. This would include a person removing himself from the labour market by taking a training course for 12 months (see paras. 2.76–84).

*James W Cook & Co. (Wivenhoe) Ltd. v. Tipper & ors. [1990] IRLR 386, CA*

If after a dismissal a firm closes down, the compensation cannot run beyond that point. It does not matter if it is proved that it would have been economically viable for the business to have continued.

*W Devis Sons Ltd. v. Atkins [1977] ICR 662, HL*

If an employee is dismissed on incorrect information, but the employer subsequently discovered grounds on which he could have validly dismissed, then although the dismissal might be technically unfair, the compensation can be reduced to nil. This is done on the basis of the 'just and equitable' provision.

*TBA Industrial Products Ltd. v. Locke [1984] ICR 228, EAT*

In arriving at the net amount, account will (generally) be taken of money paid in lieu of notice and/or of any ex-gratia payments (see paras. 2.70–75) and of any earning after the expiry of the notice period (see para. 3.10).

*EP(C) Act 1978 (as amended by E Acts 1980 & 1982) ss.71 & 76*

(c) There can also be an *Additional Award*, where the employer fails to comply with an Order for reinstatement or re-engagement, unless it was not practical for him to do so (*but* see paras. 5.138–156).

The Award works out as follows:

*EP (V of L) Order 1992*

(i) where the dismissal is unlawful under the discrimination Acts (Chapters 11, 12 & 14), then it shall not be less than 26 weeks' gross pay nor more than 52 with a maximum of £198 for each week's pay for dismissals (see paras. 3.64–73) up to April 1, 1992 and thereafter £205.

(ii) in any other case except where it is automatically unfair (as set out in para 5.7), not less than 13 weeks' gross pay nor more than 26 weeks' pay, calculated as in (i) above.

*Morganite Electrical Carbon Ltd. v. Donne [1987] IRLR 363, EAT*

In deciding the amount, the tribunal has to consider (i) the employer's conduct and (ii) the employee's loss. A deliberate refusal to take an employee back without any justification would warrant a figure at the top of the range. On the other hand, if the employee would have been away sick for much of the period or was not prepared to consider alternate employment, it would be appropriate to adopt an amount at the lower end.

(d) *A Special Award*

This is payable where:

*E Act 1982 s.5(3)*

(i)   the dismissal is automatically unfair (see para. 5.7), and

(ii)  where there is a redundancy situation, the employee selected for dismissal (because of union activities) has not:

    (a)  unreasonably refused an offer of suitable alternate employment, or

    (b)  unreasonably ended a trial period for a new job, or

    (c)  started work under a renewed or a different contract with his employer in consequence of an offer made before dismissal and the new contract starts within four weeks of the old one ceasing,

*and*

(iii) the employee seeks an order for either reinstatement or re-engagement, *and*

(iv)  the tribunal, in the exercise of its discretion (see paras. 5.147–156), refuses to make such an order, then, the compensation is calculated as follows:

*UD (I of L & BA & SA) Order 1992*

(v)   a week's gross pay (see paras. 3.101–105, but *without* an upper limit) is multiplied by 104, with a minimum of £13,180 and a maximum of £26,290 up to April 1, 1992 and thereafter £13,400 and £26,800 respectively.

Where an order for reinstatement or re-engagement is made, but not complied with, and the employer

*UD (I of L & BA & SA) Order 1992*

(vi)  *cannot* show that it was not reasonably practical to comply with it (see paras. 5.148–150), the compensation is increased to a week's gross pay (as in (v) above) multiplied by 156 with a minimum of £19,735 up to April 1, 1992 and thereafter £20,100 and with *no maximum*,

(vii) *can* show that it was not reasonably practical when the compensation is the same as in (v) above:

*and* in arriving at the amounts under (v) and (vi) above, the tribunal will:

(viii) make a reduction for contributory fault (see paras. 5.123–135) where appropriate, and this proportion may be greater than for the Basic Award, where the tribunal considers it 'just and equitable'. The amount may also be reduced if the employee has unreasonably refused an offer of full reinstatement.

**5.160**  Circumstances, where it might be 'just and equitable', could occur where, for instance, the employee has prevented an order from being complied with, or refused an offer of reemployment by an employer, but in coming to a conclusion on this aspect, no account must be taken of any breach or proposed breach of any requirement falling within para. 5.7(a),(b) or (c).

**5.161**
*Artisan Press v. Srawley & Parker [1986] ICR 328, EAT*

There must be strict compliance with the basic terms of an order for reinstatement. Where an employer, who purported to do so, but in fact gave two employees less favourable terms, it was held that that constituted a failure to reinstate in accordance with the law. It resulted in his having to pay the employees compensation that amounted in all to £38,147.

**5.162**
*EP(C) Act 1978 s.71(1) Artisan Press v. Srawley & Parker [1986] ICR 328, EAT*

Where there has been partial compliance relating to an ancillary matter, e.g., the employer was late in obeying an order or he failed to restore one of the employee's perks, the compensation is limited to that applicable in ordinary unfair dismissal claims, e.g., £10,000.

**5.163**
*EP (R of UB & SB) Regs. 1977 regs. 8 & 9*

If the worker has received unemployment pay or supplementary benefit during the time up to an order for compensation, the amount paid during this period will be deducted from the total award. The Department of Social Security will recoup the relevant sum direct from the employer and part of the award will be retained for a short while to enable this to be done. If the parties agree upon the figure for compensation, the recoupment regulations do not apply, and so it benefits employees.

**5.164**
*S H Muffett Ltd. v. Head [1987] ICR 1, EAT*

If a 35-year-old lorry driver who has been employed for ten years earning £150 per week (basic) and with a take-home pay of £125 (including allowances and overtime pay) was unfairly dismissed ten weeks before the tribunal hearing, and despite his best endeavours would not be able to get a comparable job until two weeks after the hearing, and he has, by his conduct, contributed by 20 per cent towards his own dismissal, then his compensation would work out as:

| | | |
|---|---|---|
| Basic Award 10 × £150 | £1,500 | |
| less 20% | 300 | |
| | £1,200 | £1,200 |
| | | |
| Compensatory Award | | |
| Loss to hearing 10 × £125 | £1,250 | |
| Loss up to obtaining new job | | |
| 2 × £125 | 250 | |
| | £1,500 | |
| less 20% | 300 | |
| | £1,200 | £1,200 |
| | | |
| Loss of statutory right, say, | £100 | |
| less 20% | 20 | |
| | £80 | £80 |
| Total | | £2,480 |

**5.165**   If the driver has lost anything in addition, for instance, the free use of a vehicle at weekends, or any other perks, or pension rights, then these will be added to his compensatory award. It would be subject to any reduction for contributory fault (see paras. 5.123–135) and any failure of an employee to mitigate his loss (see paras. 2.76–84).

## TIME LIMITS

**5.166**   A claim for compensation against an employer must
*EP(C) Act 1978 s.67(2)*   reach the tribunal within three months of the actual date of termination (see paras. 3.6473), except where the circumstances set out in para. 5.6 (e) apply, when it is 6 months.

**5.167**   It should be made as early as possible if reinstatement
*EP(C) Act 1978 s.70*   or re-engagement is sought, otherwise the opportunity may be lost (see paras. 5.147–156). A worker can make a claim as soon as he is given notice, but the hearing can only take place after his employment ceases.

**5.168**   The tribunal has power to entertain a claim beyond the three months, but the employee must prove that:

*EP(C) Act 1978 s.67(2)*

(a) it was not reasonably practical for him to have presented his claim within the three months, and

(b) that he did so within such further period as was reasonable (see paras. 3.79–86).

# CHAPTER SIX

# 'Action short of dismissal'

## GENERAL INFORMATION

**6.1** In 1971 the provision relating to 'action short of dismissal' was enacted. It was designed to protect an employee from a vindictive or an erring employer; but it has now done a full circle. It is of more benefit to him by affording him protection from the acts of fellow employees. He can get redress for loss and damage directly from a union, and/or person(s) bringing pressure on his employer to take action against him.

**6.2** 'Action short of dismissal' means any penalty imposed by an employer on an employee. It can be done in various ways: a failure to promote him, put in adverse reports on him, refuse to give him pay parity or permit him to have time off, threaten to dismiss him, refuse to give him overtime, put him on the worst jobs and matters of that kind.

**6.3** There is normally no prohibition against employers taking action of this kind: but where it is done against an employee *as an individual* for the purpose of:

*EP(C) Act 1978 (as amended by E Act 1982 s 10(4)) s.23*

(a) preventing or deterring him from or penalising him for, becoming a member of an independent trade union or taking part in its activities at 'the appropriate time' (see para. 5.7(B)), or

(b) compelling him to join or remain a member of a trade union, or of a particular trade union,

then it becomes unlawful.

**6.4** The provisions do apply to a person who *is seeking* employment where the reason for not taking him on is that he is considered a political activist or is likely to take part in trade union activities.

*Fitzpatrick v. British Railways Board [1981] IRLR 376, CA*

**6.5** The provision in 6.3(a) above may enable a person to rely on the Act where there is an inter-union dispute and the employer treats one set of workers differently from another. The union of the member who brings the complaint must be independent.

**6.6**

*National Coal Board v. Ridgway & anr. [1987] ICR 641, CA*

Members of the United Democratic Mineworkers Union were paid more than the National Union of Mineworkers, who alleged a breach of the provision set out in para. 6.3(a) above. It was held that as the employers' intention was to penalise the latter, it breached the section. The Act was designed to prevent an employee from being victimised for being a member of a particular (independent) union. Further, the action was taken against the employees as 'individuals' even though primarily directed against the union.

## PRESENT LIABILITIES

**6.7**

*E Act 1988 Sch 4 E Act 1990 s.1*

There are no defences available to an employer (or a person(s) bringing pressure: see para. 3.179) for any 'action short of dismissal'. From January 1, 1991 a refusal to take a person into employment where a closed shop exists because he is not a member of the, or a, union is unlawful.

## COMPLAINT TO TRIBUNAL, COMPENSATION AND TIME LIMITS

**6.8**

*EP(C) Act 1978 s.24*

If unlawful 'action short of dismissal' has been taken against an employee then he may make a complaint to the tribunal. The action must be taken within three months of the date of the action, or if that is not reasonably practical, then within such further period as is reasonable (but see paras. 3.79–85).

**6.9** If the tribunal finds the complaint well founded then:

(a) they must make a declaration to that effect, and

(b) they make an award of compensation for:

    (i) any financial loss,
    (ii) any other injury sustained, which includes a reasonable amount for frustration, hurt feelings, injury to health and so forth.

## INSTANCE OF CASE THAT SUCCEEDED

**6.10** Certain recognised unions, which did not include an

*Carlson v. The Post Office,*
*[1981] IRLR 479, EAT*

Association, had the right to distribute parking tickets outside a telephone exchange. The employee was refused a permit because he was not a member of one of the unions.

*Held*: this was capable of being 'action short of dismissal', if it was taken by the employer against him as an individual and if the refusal was done to subject him to a disadvantage for not being a member of an independent union.

## INSTANCE OF CASE THAT FAILED

**6.11**

*McCarthy v. Somerset C.C.*
*Feb. 29, 1981, EAT*
*(unreported)*

A lecturer who was also a trade union official was not promoted, and a lesser qualified person was put above her. She alleged that it was because, as a union official, she had expressed strong opposition to the course being taken by her employers.

*Held*: her failure to be promoted was due to her deeply held views which were inconsistent with a whole-hearted commitment towards the course.

## WHO PAYS THE COMPENSATION

**6.12**

*EP(C) Act 1978 (as*
*amended by E Act 1982*
*s.11) s.26A*

An employee is entitled to take proceedings against his employer and the union and/or the person(s) bringing pressure on the employer. It is then up to the tribunal to decide on the amount of compensation to be paid and how it should be split between the parties based on blameworthiness. It should be borne in mind that an order can only be made against a party who is before the tribunal, e.g., a named respondent (see paras. 3.178–183).

**6.13**

*EP(C) Act 1978 (as*
*amended by E Act 1982*
*s.11) s.26A(3)*

The employer must always be made a party to any proceedings (e.g., a 'respondent'), but the employee or the employer can 'join' the union and/or the person(s) bringing pressure.

## TIME LIMITS

**6.14**

*EP(C) Act 1978 s.24(1) & (2)*

A claim for compensation against an employer must reach the tribunal within three months of the action complained about, but a tribunal has power to hear a claim beyond this period, where the employee proves that:

(a) it was not reasonably practical for him to have presented his claim within the three months, and

(b) that he did so within such further period as was reasonable (see paras. 3.79–86).

# CHAPTER SEVEN

# Liability of unions and their officials for torts

## BACKGROUND

**7.1** The law has vacillated a great deal in the last two decades over the liabilities of unions, their officials and members for 'torts', that is to say, for loss and damage caused to others by their civil wrong-doing or unlawful acts.

**7.2** In the employment field, the problem generally manifests itself in the 'torts' of inducing or procuring a breach of an employment or of a commercial contract. It may occur by unlawfully interfering with a trade or a business or by intimidation or by a conspiracy to cause loss and damage to an employer. The action can be taken directly or indirectly.

**7.3**
*Lumley v. Gye*
*[1853] 118 ER 740 HL*

Thus where a union or a person (e.g., a shop steward) persuades employees in one company to stop providing services to another company with whom the union is in dispute, then they/he would have committed an actionable wrong. The employees in the first company would be breaking their contracts of employment with their employers. This would result in the first company being unable to supply services to the second company, in breach of their (commercial) contracts.

**7.4**
*Stratford & Son Ltd. v.*
*Lindley*
*[1966] AC 269, HL*
*Cornellia Tankers Ltd. v.*
*ITWF*
*[1976] ICR 274, CA*
*Read v. FSOS*
*[1902] 2 KB 732, CA*

Before liability can be established, it has to be shown that the action is unlawful. There must have been some pressure on employees to break their contracts to bring about a breach of a commercial contract, that the person inducing or procuring it knew (whether directly or inferentially) of the existence of such a commercial contract, and that would be a necessary consequence of his action. Further, it must be shown that loss was sustained as a result.

**7.5**
*Hadmore Productions Ltd.*
*v Hamilton*
*[1982] ICR 114, HL*

Unlawful interference with a trade or business could occur where there are commercial expectations. Thus even where there is no firm contract to supply services, but they are reasonably expected and the action is intended to frustrate these hopes, then unlawfulness is complete.

**7.6** Intimidation could occur where a person threatens to use violence or a union threatens employees with loss of union membership if they fail to comply with an unlawful union instruction with a view to causing damage to the employer or a third party. Usually a person(s) would be caught under the procuring or inducing breach of contract provisions (above) as well as for conspiracy to unlawfully cause loss and damage to the employer or any third party affected by this action.

**7.7**

*IR Act 1971*
*TULRA Act 1974*
*E Act 1980*
*E Act 1982*
*TU Act 1984*
*E Act 1988*
*E Act 1990*

Before 1971, the unions enjoyed almost complete immunity from actions for 'torts' but this became limited following the 1971 Act. The 1974 Act restored the protection for the economic torts, but not for other types of tort. This protection has now been eroded by further legislation and there is now only very restricted immunity.

**7.8** The present legislation is more in line with that in other major industrialised nations. As the subject has strong political undertones, there is likely to be a further see-sawing in the position; but to what extent is a matter of conjecture.

**7.9** Union officials and members of unions have never enjoyed the same measure of protection as unions, but few employers tended to take action against them. It would have a limited effect especially where very heavy losses were being sustained. There would be the risk of further inflaming the situation. The employer needed to be able to bring proceedings against the union not only by obtaining an injunction against it, but also to have recourse to its funds.

**7.10** If a party (a 'tort-feasor') is liable for damages to another arising out of a 'tort', then even though others were responsible for part of the loss, the party would be liable to pay the whole amount to the victim. He could seek a contribution from his fellow 'tortfeasors' to the extent to which they were responsible.

**7.11** The loss and damage recoverable is that which would normally flow from the 'tortious act'. Thus, if a person negligently injures another who is under a contract to undertake a lucrative three months singing tour of

America, and is prevented from going, then he would be entitled to compensation not only for the injuries he has sustained, but also for his net financial loss.

## THE CURRENT POSITION

**7.12**

*Dimbleby & Sons v. National Union of Journalists [1984] ICR 386 HL*

The law has been described as a 'legislative maze'. It is extremely complicated not least because the provisions are to be found in several Acts and because of the circuitous route by which liability is determined.

**7.13** A union is 'vicariously' liable in accordance with the normal 'common law' rules and under the statutory provisions for the acts of its officials and union members in certain circumstances.

## WHEN LIABILITY ARISES

**7.14**

*Heaton's Transport Ltd. v. TGWU [1972] ICR 308, HL General Aviation Services (UK) Ltd. v. TGWU [1985] ICR 615, HL*

The position at 'common law' lacks certainty and depends on the law of agency. This in turn requires consideration of the rule book of the union, and of any express or implied authority that a union official or member may have for taking any action. The current position may not be properly recorded.

**7.15**

*E Act 1982 s. 15(2)*

Under the 1982 Act, it is provided that all:

> "acts shall be taken to have been done by the union if it was authorised or endorsed by a responsible person."

**7.16** Such an act will be treated as so 'authorised or endorsed' if it comes from:

(a) the principle executive committee;
(b) a person with power to authorise or endorse the acts complained of;
(c) the president or general secretary, or equivalent;
(d) a full time officer of the union or a committee to whom he regularly reports unless:

*E Act 1982 s. 15(3)–(7)*

> (i) he was prevented by union rules, or his action is repudiated by the principle executive committee, president or general secretary 'as soon as reasonably practical' and

> (ii) the official or the committee is notified in writing immediately of the repudiation, and

(iii)  no act inconsistent with the repudiation occurs,

*E Act 1990 s.6*

but from January 1, 1991, the list of 'authorised persons' has been widened to include any other Committee or official of a union, whether or not employed by the union. A Committee is defined as any group constituted in accordance with union rules.

**7.17**  There will be prima facie liability for a Committee or any member of a group, e.g., a shop steward, who off their/his own bat decide to call a strike. It matters not whether that group or individual has authority to take the action.

**7.18**  An official of an union was given authority by an 'authorised person' to go ahead with a strike upon the failure of further negotiations. He acted within that delegated power. It was held that because there was a close relationship between the two, then immunity was not be lost.

*Tanks & Drums Ltd. v. TGWU [1991] IRLR 372, CA*

**7.19**  The only way a union can avoid liability is to make an open disavowal of the act of the group or official. This should be communicated to the victim of the unlawful action. Additionally, the union must give to each member of the group or to the official a notice in the following terms:

*E Act 1990 s.6(5A)*

"Your union has repudiated the call (or calls) for industrial action to which this notice relates and will give no support to unofficial industrial action taken in response to it (or them). If you are dismissed while taking unofficial industrial action, you will have no right to complain of unfair dismissal."

**7.20**  A union that fails to take the appropriate action will be liable for damages that flow from the 'tort' committed by the group or individual.

**7.21**  Immunity can be preserved in the following circumstances, namely, where

*TULR Act 1974 (as amended by TULR (Amendment) Act 1976 s.3(2) & E Act 1982 s 14) s 13*

(a) the action relates to *interferences with contracts of employment*; and

(b) the action is done '*in contemplation or furtherance of a trade dispute*'; and

(c) it does not involve certain types of '*primary*' or '*secondary action*'; and

TU Act 1984 (as
amended by E Act
1988 sch.3
para.5(8)(c))
s.10(1)-(3)

TULR Act 1974 (as
amended by E Act 1980)
s.15(1) sch.3 para.12 &
sch.4) s.15

E Act 1988 s.10(1)

(d) the action taken has the '*support of the members under a secret ballot*';

and

(e) any *picketing* is carried out in a lawful manner; and

(f) the action *does not induce a breach of statutory duty*, nor

(g) is the action is designed to bring about *union membership.*

## (a) Interference with Contracts of Employment

**7.22** The nub of the immunity relates to an indirect attack upon an employer by means of breaches of the contract of employment. This is usually done by taking part in strikes, part withdrawal of labour, 'blacking' of goods, and other forms of industrial action, thereby preventing or hindering the employer from meeting his obligations under business or commercial contracts with his clients. Immense damage can be done on occasions.

**7.23** Employees may take the action on their own initiative, or they may be persuaded to do so by others, and it can be for a variety of purposes. What is lawful now is very limited. Elaborate formulas have to be used to find out whether there is, or is not, immunity.

## (b) 'In contemplation or furtherance of a trade dispute'

**7.24** 'In furtherance of a trade dispute' means that there must be some dispute between *a worker and his employer* relating wholly or mainly to one or more of the following matters:

Mercury Communications
Ltd. v. Scott-Garner
[1984] ICR 74, CA

(a) terms and conditions of employment;
(b) engagement or non-engagement, termination or suspension of employment;
(c) allocation of work;
(d) discipline;
(e) membership or non-membership of a union;
(f) facilities for officials of unions;
(g) machinery for negotiation or consultations, including recognition issues.

**7.25** If there is a dispute outside the United Kingdom then action taken in support of that dispute comes within the definition so long as it is likely to affect the employees of the company in this country concerningany one of the matters set out in para. 7.24 (a)–(g) above.

**7.26** For instance, if employees of an firm with international connections, who work in Coventry, 'black' goods going to America to give support their fellow workers there who are on strike in order to obtain an additional week's holiday, and the employees over here feel that this will help them to get another week's holiday for themselves, then that action would be lawful.

**7.27**

*General Aviation Services (UK) Ltd v. TGWU [1985] ICR 615, HL Conway v. Wade [1909] AC 506, HL*

Fear of job losses can come within the section because it relates to 'the termination of employment', but it must be genuinely based on 'something definite and of real substance'.

**7.28** A 'worker' means an employee, or former employee whose employment was terminated in connection with the dispute.

**7.29**

*News Group Newspapers Ltd. & ors. v. SOGAT '82 & ors. [1987] ICR 181, QBD Associated British Ports & ors. v. Transport and General Workers Union CA (but overturned by HL on another point) [1989] ICR 557*

Where there is interference with a contract by unlawful means, e.g., by nuisance, or violence or even intimidation through threats being made to employees, then the immunity is lost.

### (c) 'Primary' and 'Secondary Action'

**7.30** 'Primary action' occurs where some action is taken by an employee directly against his employer, which is at the core of the dispute. Thus, this would happen if employees acted on union instructions to 'go-slow' in support of a wage claim.

**7.31**

*E Act 1982 s.17*

'Secondary action' occurs where a person induces another to break or interfere with a contract of employment, or threatens that his own or another's will be broken or interfered with, where the employer is not involved in the dispute.

**7.32**

*E Act 1990 s.4*

Except where there is lawful picketing (see paras. 7.45–48), all forms of secondary actions are unlawful. So staff are restricted to try and induce drivers of a supplier not deliver goods to their employer and similar action.

### (d) 'Support under a secret ballot'

**7.33** Immunity from actions for tort will also be lost unless

TU Act 1984 ss.10(1)-(5) &
11(3)-(11)
the union has held a secret ballot, conducted in the specified manner, of all those entitled to vote. A majority of those voting must favour the action.

**7.34**

TU Act 1984 (as amended
by E Act 1988 s.17) s.11(1)
Separate ballots have to be conducted at each place of work. All members who are entitled to vote must be allowed to participate and there must be a majority in favour of action at *that* workplace before it is taken.

**7.35**

Monsanto plc v. Transport
& General Workers Union
[1987] ICR 269, CA
Secretary of State for
Scotland v. Scottish Prison
Officers Association & ors.
[1991] IRLR 371, CS
These requirements apply to industrial action as well as to strikes, and there must be a specific unequivocal question relating to each. The *instructions* to take the action must be taken within four weeks of the ballot otherwise it will be unlawful. It does not matter that the action is taken beyond the period provided it relates to those instructions.

**7.36**

Post Office v. Union of
Communications Workers
[1990] ICR 258, CA
A temporary suspension of action while negotiations take place would not affect the validity of the ballot. But if the industrial action ceases because the union decide to change tactics, say, by mounting a public relations campaign, then a fresh mandate must be obtained before resuming industrial action.

**7.37**

E Act 1990 s.8
If during the four week period a court prohibits the industrial action and the order subsequently either lapses or is discharged, an application can then be made to the same court within eight weeks of the ballot for a direction that the time lost under the order should be disregarded when adding up the four weeks.

**7.38**

TU Act 1984 s.11
London Underground Ltd
v. National Union of
Railwaymen
[1989] IRLR 341, QBD
A union put four matters to its members and asked whether they were prepared to take strike action. It was held that the ballot was invalid. There was no 'trade dispute' in respect of three of them; if there had been one concerning all, it would have been lawful.

**7.39**

TU Act 1984 s.11(1)
Those union members who

> 'it is reasonable at the time of the ballot for the union to believe will be called upon in the strike or other industrial action to act in breach of, or inter-fere with, their contracts of employment',

Presho v. D.H.S.S.
(1984) ICR 463 HL
must be allowed to vote. This includes those union members who are indirectly interested in the outcome of the dispute.

**7.40**

Those eligible to vote must be supplied with a voting paper, and so far as is reasonably practical, be allowed to vote without interference or constraint, in secret and without direct cost. The results must be fairly and accurately counted and the results made known to those entitled to vote.

**7.41**

*TU Act 1984 s.11
British Railway Board v.
National Union of
Railwaymen
[1989] ICR 678, CA*

A complaint by an employer that a union had failed to give an *opportunity* to all its members to vote did not invalidate the ballot. The union was able to prove that they had taken steps, so far as was reasonably practical, to circulate all their members. Further, what failure there was would not have affected the result. It would be unlawful if a person called on to strike had been denied the right to vote, in the sense of being wrongly disqualified.

**7.42**

*TU Act 1984 s.11(2)*

Failure to comply with these requirements nullifies the procedure and will result in the union losing its immunity.

**7.43**

*Falconer v. N.U.R. &
A.S.L.E.F.
[1986] IRLR 331, County
Court*

A union instructed its members to take industrial action without a prior ballot. This resulted in expense to a ticket-holder who was unable to travel home by rail. It was held that the union must indemnify him for his loss because they had unlawfully induced a breach of contract between British Rail and the traveller.

**7.44**

*E Act 1990 s.7*

All the voting papers must specify the names of individuals who are authorised to call industrial action in the event of a vote in favour. Indemnity will be lost if anyone else, e.g., a shop steward, instructs members of a union to take industrial action.

### (e) 'Lawful Picketing'

**7.45**

*TULR Act 1974 (as
amended by E Act 1980
s.15(1) sch.3 para.12 &
sch.4) s.15*

Picketing is only lawful where it is done by a person in contemplation or furtherance of a trade dispute at or near his place of work. It must be for the purpose of peacefully obtaining or communicating information or peacefully persuading another person to abstain from working.

**7.46**

An official of the union is covered where he takes part in a picket provided he does it in a lawful manner and is representing his members at the time.

**7.47**

*J & R Kenny Cleaning
Services (a firm) v.
Transport & General
Workers Union
The Times, June 15, 1989,
CA*

Several employees were made redundant as a result of the employer losing a cleaning contract for a building. They picketed the premises. It was held to be unlawful because there had to be a 'trade dispute' between the employer and those picketing. Their action in picketing was directed at the company who got the new contract who was not their former employer.

**7.48**

*Thomas v. NUM (South Wales Area) [1985] IRLR 136, ChD*

Unreasonable harassment of employees on the public highway as they go in and out of work constitutes a 'tort'. It matters not whether it is done by weight of numbers, intimidatory conduct or even physical obstruction. Where the union had encouraged large numbers to attend, they were held vicariously liable for the consequences.

### Code of Practice

**7.49**

*Code of Practice Picketing Secy. of State Dec. 7, 1980*

A Code of Practice produced by the Secretary of State recommends that the number of pickets should be limited to six at each entrance. There should be consultation with the police, and there should be no interference with essential services. No disciplinary action should be taken against a union member for crossing an unauthorised picket line, or one manned by member(s) not at their place of work.

### (f) *Where the action induces a breach of statutory duty*

**7.50**

*Meade v. Haringey L.B.C. [1979] ICR 494, CA Barretts & Baird (Wholesale) Ltd. v. Institute of Professional Civil Servants [1987] IRLR 3, QBD*

It would seem that where there is a requirement for the employer to carry out certain statutory duties then any attempt to persuade employees to stop doing their jobs can constitute action that is outside the protection of the s. 13 immunity. But it must be shown that the action *did* prevent compliance with the statutory requirements and not merely made it more difficult.

### (g) *Action designed to bring about union membership*

**7.51**

*E Act 1988 s.10(1)*

Immunity is lost where one of the reasons for taking industrial action is that the boss employs or intends to employ non-union labour or members not of a particular union. Where its purpose is to pressurise employers into treating non-union members or members not of a particular union less favourably, the result is the same.

## STRICT COMPLIANCE

**7.52**

*Shipping Company Uniform Inc. v. International Transport Federation & Anr. [1985] ICR 245, QB Metropolitan Borough of Solihull v. N.U.T. [1985] IRLR 211, ChD*

If there is a failure to comply at any stage with any of the technical requirements of the Acts, then the union will find itself liable. They should dissociate themselves from the action, especially if taken against the rules or directions. Even if they do, they may still be caught on occasions by factors outside their knowledge.

**7.53**

*Conway v. Lindley*
*[1965] AC 269, HL*
*Torquay Hotels Co. Ltd.*
*v. Cousins*
*[1969] 2 Ch. 106, ChD*
*Norbrook Laboratories*
*Ltd. v. King*
*[1984] IRLR 200, CA*

Political and sympathy strikes are no longer immune, nor are wildcat strikes or those called by a union official out of spite. Furthermore, any grievance must be communicated to the employer first. Demarcation strikes are also no longer immune because they are not between an employee and his employer.

**7.54**

*Express Newspapers Ltd.*
*v. McShane*
*[1980] ICR 42, HL*

But motive, e.g., hatred of an employer, does not remove the immunity, *provided* the purpose comes within the provisions. The person taking the action though must honestly and genuinely believe that his objective is likely to be achieved by the action.

**7.55**

*Dimbleby & Sons v.*
*National Union of*
*Journalists*
*[1984] ICR 86 HL*

A newspaper group was in dispute with some printers and switched their work to a non-union printer. An instruction by a journalist union, which was itself in dispute with an 'associated employer' (see paras. 3.153–161) of that non-union printer, to its membership, to 'black' all work sent to the printer was ruled to be unlawful.

**7.56**

An attempt to insert terms into the contracts between the journalist and the group that they did not have to provide work to be used by the non-union printer and thereby create a 'primary' dispute over 'terms and conditions of employment' failed. It did not come within the strict definition, e.g., the dispute was not 'wholly or mainly' related to it (see para. 7.24).

## LIMIT ON DAMAGES

**7.57**

*E Act 1982 s.16*

The maximum amount of damages that may be awarded against a union depends on its size. The figures apply in respect of all actions against a union except for personal injury or a breach of duty arising out of a property dispute. The maximum applies to each case against a union.

| Total Membership | Maximum Damages |
| --- | --- |
| less than 5,000 | £10,000 |
| 5,000–24,999 | £50,000 |
| 25,000–99,999 | £125,000 |
| 100,000 or more | £250,000 |

## TIME LIMITS

**7.58**   Proceedings have to be started within six years of the breach complained of, otherwise they will be 'statute-barred'.

# CHAPTER EIGHT

# A contract under the 'Common Law'

## GENERAL INFORMATION

**8.1**  The 'common law' has evolved over the centuries from decisions given by the judges on different facts. A great body of 'case law' has been created and this remains the corner-stone of our law today. Up to 1963, the law governing contracts of employment was almost exclusively derived from this source.

**8.2**  Although statutes concerning employment create new rights and obligations, and in doing so alter the 'common law', a lot of the concepts of the 'common law' still have to be applied. The problem that generally arises is the meaning to be attached to various words and phrases, and this frequently leads to litigation.

**8.3**  A contract of employment usually arises in this way. When an employee applies for a job, the boss usually specifies the terms and if they are agreed, then a contract of employment is concluded. If the employer has accepted various stipulations made by his prospective employee, e.g., that he will not work away from home or that he must be allowed to use the company car for his own purposes in non-working times, then they too are incorporated into the contract.

**8.4**  Many terms have to be implied in a contract of employment. There are two main circumstances where this occurs, namely they

(a) they are so obvious that it would be otiose to specify them;

(b) they are necessary to give business efficacy to the contract. The relationship in a particular case is such that it could not really work without them.

**8.5**

*Liverpool C.C. v. Irwin [1977] AC 239, HL Sim & ors. v. Rotherham Metropolitan Borough*

So it was held that teachers had a professional obligation to co-operate in the running of a school during school hours, in accordance with the time-table and other administrative requirements. They were also

*Council & ors.*
*[1986] ICR 897, ChD*

constrained to carry out directions given to them from time to time, provided that they were reasonable.

**8.6**

*Scally & ors. v. Southern and Social Services [1991] ICR 771, HL*

Terms had been negotiated with a representative body, which conferred valuable rights on an employee, but before he could benefit from them he had to take certain action. He knew nothing about them and could not reasonably be expected to be aware of them. It was held that there was an *implied* duty on the employer to take reasonable steps to draw them to his attention. Failure to do so entitled him to compensation for the loss that followed.

**8.7**

*Courtaulds Northern Spinning Ltd v. Sibson & anr. [1988] ICR 451, CA*

In deciding what terms should be implied (see para. 5.53–55), concerning mobility of employment where a contract is silent on the point, it has been held that an employer can move an employee from one site to another, *for any reason*, provided it is reasonably within daily reach of his home.

### Conflict between Express & Implied Terms

**8.8**

*Johnstone v. Bloomsbury Health Authority [1991] ICR 269, CA*

Sometimes an express term appears to conflict with a term implied by law. Where there is a conflict the general rule is that the express term prevails. But courts have ruled otherwise where justice demands it. An express term gave discretion to the employer to order an employee to undertake overtime. He was required to work long hours which was having an effect on his health. It was held that the implied provision, that an employer must exercise a duty of care for the safety and health of his employer, over-rode what had been agreed.

## TERMS TO BE IN WRITING

**8.9**

Many terms in a contract of employment have to be put into writing (see paras. 9.15–45). This enables each side to know exactly what has been agreed, thus narrowing the areas of dispute.

**8.10**

It should be borne in mind that people's memories are notoriously fickle when recollecting terms that go against their cases. Consequently it is better to have as much as possible committed to writing.

## WHAT IS A BREACH OF CONTRACT

**8.11**   A 'breach of contract' arises when one side or the other breaks a term of contract. For instance, the employee who has arranged with the employer that he should not be required to work away from an agreed site except in emergencies, cannot be sent away unless a genuine emergency exists. So if the boss sends him to another place out of spite when another worker was available,then that would be a breach of contract.

## CONSEQUENCE OF A BREACH

**8.12**   A 'breach of contract' gives rise to a 'common law' cause of action that entitles the aggrieved party to claim various rights including recovery of any damage sustained by him.

**8.13**   The precise terms of a contract of employment are important because the nature of the remedy depends on the extent and seriousness of the breach.

**8.14**   If the breach goes to the root of the contract, i.e., it is very important, then the innocent party is entitled to treat the contract as at an end (see paras. 2.44–54) and sue for any loss suffered. But he is obliged to mitigate his damages (see paras. 2.76–84).

**8.15**

*Wadham Stringer Commercials (London) Ltd. & Anr. v. Brown [1983] IRLR 46, EAT*

It is not necessary for the conduct of a party to be culpable. For instance, an employer might be under a mis-apprehension that an employee could be required to spend nights away from his home whereas his contract might stipulate the contrary. An attempt to force him to go off on an overnight trip could amount to a fundamental breach entitling him to leave the employment and sue for breach of contract. In such a situation, neither the circumstances inducing the breach, nor the circumstances that led the employee to accept such repudiation, are relevant.

**8.16**   If a male manager is guilty of disreputable conduct, such as assaulting his female secretary, then this again would be a fundamental breach entitling her to leave and sue for her loss.

**8.17**   An employee who secretly sets up a competitive business, or who uses his employer's confidential information to work against his interests, is guilty of gross misconduct and may be summarily dismissed.

**8.18**

*Laws v. London Chronicle (Indicator Newspapers) Ltd [1959] 1 WLR 698, CA Blythe v. Scottish Liberal Club [1983] IRLR 245, CS*

One act of disobedience or misconduct can justify a summary dismissal where it is of such a nature as to show that the employee is repudiating the contract or one of its essential conditions. The secretary of a club that was being closed down refused to attend two committee meetings, in the mistaken belief that he was not obliged to do so. It was held that his employer was entitled to summarily dismiss him because he was deliberately refusing to carry out important duties.

**8.19**

If the breach is not serious, the contract continues and the aggrieved can only sue for damages. In practice, the worker (if he is the victim) does not take proceeding, if he wishes to retain his job. The employer very rarely sues his employee. To do so would be counter-productive and in any event he generally has other means of resolving the problem.

**8.20**

*Miles v. Wakefield Metropolitan D.C. [1987] ICR 368, HL*

Where a person is an 'office-holder' and he has failed to perform part of his statutory duty, by for instance engaging in 'go-slow' or other industrial action, then his employers (or the body responsible for paying his salary), may make a pro-rate deduction from his stipend, provided they have not acquiesced in his action.

**8.21**

*Wilusznskiv v. Tower Hamlets London Borough Council [1989] ICR 493, CA*

An employee refused to perform the full range of his duties. He was told by his employers that until he did he would not be required to work and would not be paid. It was held that the employers were entitled to withhold the *whole* of his remuneration, even though he voluntarily attended for work and carried out a substantial part of his duties. But it was necessary for the employers to show that they did not exercise any of the normal controls associated with an employer/employee relationship.

## ACTING IN GOOD FAITH

**8.22**

An important implied term relates to the duty of an employee to act in 'good faith'. But it is established that there is no requirement that he should disclose his own past misconduct, whether it occurs before the contract or during it, even though a relationship of trust exists.

**8.23**

*Sybron Corpn v. Rochem Ltd. [1983] ICR 801, CA*

But there is a duty:

"to inform against other fellow servants [even] if by so doing so you inevitably incriminate yourself

**155**

... [but this] depends on the contract and on the terms of employment of the particular servant. He may be so placed in the hierarchy as to have a duty to report either the misconduct of his superior as in Swain v. West (Butchers) Ltd., [1936] 3 AER 261 or the misconduct of his inferiors, as in this case" (per Stephenson L.J.).

**8.24**

*Horcal Ltd. v. Gatland [1984] IRLR 288, CA*

Where a person is in a 'fiduciary' relationship with his employers, that is to say, the nature of his job requires him to act in the utmost good faith, then he must disclose any breaches of the contract made by himself when negotiating a further agreement. This might apply where he was settling the terms of a 'golden handshake' package.

**8.25**

*Sinclair v. Neighbour [1966] 3 AER 988, CA*

A betting office manager borrowed £15 from the till of his shop to place a bet at another shop, putting in an IOU. He had replaced the money before his employers found out about it. It was held that because he knew that his employers would not have agreed to it, and although it was not necessarily dishonest, nevertheless it was inconsistent with the continuance of the confidential relationship between them. The employers were entitled to summarily dismiss him.

## IMPLIED DUTY OF CONFIDENTIALITY

**8.26**

In every contract of employment there is an implied duty of confidentiality. Employees may not pass over trade secrets and other confidential information to outside parties. Those in breach may be injuncted from doing so.

**8.27**

*Dalgleish & ors. v. Lothian & Borders Police Board [1991] IRLR 422, Ct.S*

A similar duty lies on the employer not to disclose to third parties information provided to them in confidence by their employees. This can extend to the names and addresses of employees that had been given solely in the course of the employer-employee relationship.

## WRONGFUL DISMISSAL

**8.28**

Wrongful dismissal usually occurs where a person is dismissed with insufficient notice or where there has

*Jones v. Lee & Anr.*
*[1980]*
*ICR 310, CA*

been a breach of certain procedural requirements contained in the contract of employment.

**8.29**

*Dietman v. Brent LBC*
*[1988] IRLR 299, CA*

A local authority dismissed a social worker without a disciplinary hearing on the grounds that an independent panel of enquiry had stated, in a report, that she had been 'grossly negligent' in the supervision of a child under her care. It was held that she had been wrongly dismissed. It was a pre-requisite to dismissal under her contract of employment that there should be a hearing. Further, she had been denied the right to put forward any mitigating factors.

**8.30**

*Reg. v. Secretary of State,*
*ex p Benwell*
*[1984] ICR 723, DC*

So too, where an employer sacked a prison officer but failed to comply with certain statutory duties laid down in the Code of Discipline, it was held that a purported dismissal was void.

**8.31**

*Boston Deep Sea Fishing &*
*Ice Co. v. Ansell*
*[1888] 39 ChD 339, CA*

In considering whether a dismissal is wrongful an employer is entitled (contrary to the position under the statutory law) to rely on any facts he discovers after the dismissal so as to justify it.

**8.32**

*Wadham Stringer*
*Commercials (London) Ltd.*
*& Anr. v. Brown*
*[1983] IRLR 46, EAT*

It is not necessary that a party should intend to breach the contract of employment; suffice that he does. So if the contract is silent on what notice (at common law) should be given to an employee, and he is dismissed with, say, three months notice, but a court finds that a reasonable period is six months, then the employer will be liable.

**8.33**

*Decro-Wall International*
*SA v. Practitioners in*
*Marketing Ltd.*
*[1971] 2 AER 216, CA*

Where there has been a wrongful dismissal, the employee can choose whether to accept it or not. If he declines to do so and is able to carry on working, then the contract subsists, but he is only entitled to his salary while he works.

**8.34**

*Gunton v. Richmond-*
*upon-Thames B.C.*
*[1980] ICR 755, CA*

If he is prevented from doing so, then there arises a duty to 'mitigate' his loss (see paras. 2.76–84). That in practice would mean an obligation to seek work elsewhere. Once he enters other employment, he puts it out of his power to perform his duties under the original contract, and consequently will be:

> "taken to have accepted his wrongful dismissal as a repudiatory breach leading to a determination of the contract of service" (per Buckley L.J.).

**8.35**

*Shove v. Downs Surgical*
*plc.*

Damages can be very high on occasions. A contract provided for notice of 30 months for a chairman of a company. He was summarily dismissed, and it was held

*[1984] ICR 32, Q.B.*

to be wrongfully. His total award for loss of salary and other fringe benefits, after taking into account his duty to mitigate (see paras. 2.76–84), came to £84,300.

**8.36**

*Reg. v. Greater Manchester C.C., ex.p. Greater Manchester Residuary Body*
*July 14, 1987, C.A. (unreported)*

Some contracts come to an end by operation of law, by for instance a winding-up order or by an Act of Parliament. Employees are not entitled to notice, or money in lieu of notice. So when the Greater Manchester Council was abolished by the Local Government Act 1985, employees were debarred from relying on their contractual severance scheme that provided for a payment in lieu of notice.

## THE RIGHT TO DISMISS

**8.37**

Because, at common law, an employer does not have to give reasons for, or justify a dismissal, he is (generally) immune from any claim. But he must give the requiredlength of notice and comply with any express or implied procedural requirements laid down in the contract of employment.

**8.38**

*Reg. v. Birmingham C.C., ex p NUPE & Ors.*
*The Times, April 24, 1984, DC*

Thus where the decision to dismiss and offer new contracts was taken by the Chief Education Officer and approved by the Education Committee, it was held that the decision was void. The Education Officer had no power to dismiss, and the error was not put right by the Committee confirming the decision.

**8.39**

*Reg. v. Hertfordshire C.C. ex p. NUPE & Ors.*
*[1985] IRLR 258, CA*

Employers in the public sector are likely to be in a different position to ones in the private field. In making a decision, they must consider all pertinent matters, omitting all irrelevant collateral considerations. It must be one to which a reasonable employer could come.

**8.40**

*Jilley v. Transfleet Services Ltd.*
*Jan. 16, 1981, EAT (unreported)*
*Wilson v. Racher [1974] ICR 428, CA*

An employee guilty of gross misconduct may be dismissed without notice. He is not entitled to money in lieu. There is no statutory definition of 'gross misconduct' but it can cover grave acts of dishonesty or violence, habitual drunkenness, working for a competitor or otherwise seriously damaging his employer's interest. It also extends to gross incompetence by a skilled man, and to instances where the employee's conduct is seriously insulting or insubordinate.

## THE RIGHT TO SUSPEND

**8.41** Sometimes a contract expressly or impliedly empowers an employer to suspend an employee for various reasons. There may be a complaint that needs investigation, and it may be wise to keep the person away from work. Sometimes, the contract entitles the employer to suspend as a form of punishment.

**8.42** Normally speaking, an employee must be paid his wages in full unless the contract of employment makes provision to the contrary. There has to be strict compliance with all the procedural requirements.

**8.43** So an Education Authority, which had statutory power to suspend staff on the grounds that they were medically unfit, was not entitled to put a teacher on half pay. They had failed to follow strictly the formal requirements laid down in the Conditions of Service for Schoolteachers.

*Whitley v. Harrow London Borough Council, The Times, Mar. 29, 1988, QB*

## INJUNCTIONS RESTRAINING DISMISSAL

**8.44** The High Court has power to make an order of 'specific performance' of contracts or of 'prohibition' in certain employment cases. It is rarely used where it would have the effect of ordering an employer continue to employ someone against his will. A failure to comply would amount to contempt of court, leading on occasions to dire consequences.

**8.45** Where there is still mutual trust and confidence, or the applicant can be relied upon to carry out his duties properly, and there is a 'workable situation', then a court may injunct an employer from terminating an employee's contract of employment pending the full trial.

*Wadcock v. London Borough of Brent [1990] IRLR 228, HC Dietman v. London Borough of Brent [1988] IRLR 299, CA*

**8.46** Where an employee was dismissed with insufficient notice by an employer who was reluctant to do so but who had bowed to organised industrial pressure, it was held that as the employer was willing to reemploy him and it was practical to do so, a declaration could be made nullifying the effect of the notice until there was a full trial on the issues.

*Hill v. C.A. Parsons & Co. Ltd. [1971] 3 AER 1345 CA*

**8.47** In rare instances, even where trust and confidence are lost, a Court may still grant an order. Thus where an employer was in breach of contract in dismissing a

*Robb v. London Borough of Hammersmith & Fulham*

**8.48**

senior employee who was on suspension on full pay at the time, an order was made to restore the position. It enabled him to pursue rights that he would otherwise have lost.

*[1991] ICR 514, QBD*

An offer of employment 'subject to satisfactory references' usually means adequate in the eyes of *the* employer, and *not* of *a* reasonable employer. The person would never become an employee until accepted by the employer, so no question of an injunction would arise.

*Wishart v. National Association of Citizens Advice Bureaux Ltd. [1990] IRLR 393, CA*

**8.49**

A *tribunal* has power to order reinstatement or re-engagement (see paras. 5.147–156), but a breach of the order can only lead to a limited financial penalty plus perhaps some costs. The employer cannot be forced to take the employee back.

## VARIATION IN TERMS OF EMPLOYMENT

**8.50**

If an employer wishes to vary the terms of employment against the wishes of an employee he can do so at *common law* without exposing himself to an action for damages provided he does so in a proper manner.

**8.51**

Thus if a manager is entitled to six months' notice, then an employer can give him notice of dismissal to come into effect six months later. An offer of reem-ployment, for instance, at half his existing salary could be made. There would be no wrongful dismissal. But it could be unfair (see Chapter 5).

**8.52**

If he does not wish to take this course, then he must either show that there is an express or implied agree-ment within the contract of employment to make a variation. If there is no power, and the employee leaves in consequence to a change forced on him, the employer will be liable to pay damages for any loss sustained by him.

*Miller v. Hamworthy Engineering Ltd. [1986] ICR 846, CA*

**8.53**

What an employer cannot do is to give notice to 'vary' a contract. He can only give the appropriate notice to dismiss the employee and offer new terms to come into effect after the notice period. The option is given to the employee to accept the new terms or cease to be employed.

*Rigby v. Ferodo Ltd. [1988] ICR 29, HL*

**8.54**

A Local Authority tried to substitute essential car user

*Keir & Williams v. Hereford & Worcester CC [1985] IRLR 505, CA*

allowances given to two employees under their contracts of employment. Instead of driving their own cars on official business they had to use transport from a pool instead. The court declared the move unlawful under the contract. It was of no effect.

**8.55** Provided variations can be imposed within the scope of the contract, the employer who makes any is immune from a claim for damages.

**8.56** Taxmen refused to use computers for collecting PAYE. It was held that although a new skill was required to operate the machines, it did not go beyond the existing contract. Their consent was not necessary.

*Cresswell v. Board of Inland Revenue [1984] ICR 508, ChD*

> "It can hardly be considered that to ask an employee to acquire basic skills . . . is something the slightest bit esoteric or even nowadays unusual" (per Walton, J).

**8.57** Furthermore, it was held that the employers were entitled to suspend without pay those who refused to operate the computers. The legal principle of 'no work, no pay' applied when they were being required to carry out a lawful requirement.

**8.58** Employers retained the right in the contracts of employment with their staff to amend their rules 'from time to time'. They introduced a non-contributory life scheme,but subsequently revoked it. It was held this fell within the powers conferred on them under the contracts and so was immune from interference by the courts.

*Cadoux v. Central Regional Council [1986] IRLR 131, CS*

**8.59** If an employer varies the terms in breach of contract, then the employee must choose what course he wishes to follow. He can leave the employment and claim damages for wrongful dismissal, or compensation for an unfair 'constructive dismissal' (see paras. 3.35–43). Or he can seek a declaration (from the courts) that the purported variations are unlawful and unenforceable against him. Alternatively he can claim damages for any loss sustained because of the employer's breach.

*Rigby v. Ferodo Ltd [1988] ICR 29, HL Miller v. Hamworthy Engineering Ltd. [1986] ICR 846, CA*

**8.60** If he does nothing but carries on working as normal, he will be deemed to have 'affirmed' the contract, and will be bound by the new terms. The acceptance of salary may be evidence of an affirmation. This can be rebutted by evidence that it was accepted 'without prejudice' to his other rights (see para. 2.55–65), or

*Bliss v. SE Thames Regional Health Authority [1987] ICR 700, CA*

where he has indicated that he does not agree to the variation and takes some action to establish his rights. However, he must act *promptly*.

**8.61**

*Robertson v. British Gas Corporation [1983] ICR 351, CA Gibbons v. Associated British Ports [1985] IRLR 376, QBD*

Sometimes an employee's contract of employment incorporates some terms which are contained in collective agreements with a union. If the employer recognises that union for the purposes of collective bargaining (see para. 15.113–116) but subsequently withdraw it, then those terms will still bind the employer and employee.

## COMPENSATION FOR BREACH OF CONTRACT

**8.62**

As already indicated the effect of a wrongful dismissal is to give rise to a claim for damages (see para. 8.12). This is assessed on the basis of the difference between what the employee would have earned during the period when he was entitled to work, and he has earned (or it is anticipated he will earn). The amount is always subject to a duty to mitigate any loss by seeking alternative employment (see paras. 2.76–84).

**8.63**

*Gothard v. Mirror Group Newspapers Ltd. [1988] ICR 729, CA*

Where money is paid 'in lieu of notice', it may be either gross or net, at the whim of the employer. Although it may be expressed to be a payment based on what the employee would have earned had he worked out his notice, nevertheless it is a payment to ward off a claim for breach of contract, i.e., it is a settlement figure. It is only where judgment is given for a breach of contract-that it has to be net. Perhaps surprisingly the employer does not have to account to the Revenue for the notional tax deducted.

**8.64**

*Addis v. Gramophone Co. [1909] AC 488 HL*

The measure of damages is not generally affected by the motive of the employer, except where there was an intention to avoid making a payment to comply with statutory obligations. But the fact that the employee was dismissed in a harsh and humiliating manner, does not entitle him to obtain compensation for his injured feelings. Nor is it relevant that it made it more difficult for him to obtain alternate employment, although this would be taken into account when considering whether he has made adequate steps to mitigate his damages.

**8.65**

*Withers v. General Theatre*

Where a person is deprived of publicity that would have had the effect of enhancing his reputation, he is

*Corpn.*
*[1933] 2 KB 536, CA*

entitled to damages to cover this. Thus an actor was held to be entitled to recover damages when he was wrongfully prevented from appearing at a music-hall. But he could recover nothing for his injured feelings.

**8.66**

*Bailey v. Bullock*
*[1950] 66 TLR 791, KB*

Damages are recoverable for substantial inconvenience and discomfort arising from a breach of contract.

## TIME LIMITS

**8.67** Claims must be brought within six years of the breach otherwise they become 'statute barred'. An extension can be obtained in certain limited circumstances.

# CHAPTER NINE

# Contracts of employment

## GENERAL INFORMATION

**9.1**

C of E Act 1963, now EP(C) Act 1978 (as amended by E Act 1982 sch.2 para 8 & sch.4) s.1–6

In 1963 Parliament passed the first of a number of statutes which regulate the minimum notice that has to be given to every employee. The period depends on his length of service (see para. 3.10). These rights and duties apply to an employee, irrespective of age, who has a qualifying period of service of not less than one month.

**9.2** They also require the employer to serve on his employee, within 13 weeks, certain written terms (see paras. 9.15–45) of the contract of employment. Fresh particulars also have to be given where there are changes (see para. 9.10).

**9.3** Although it is usually good practice to include all the fundamental terms in the written particulars, it is not often done. Oral terms are just as binding as those in writing but the difference is that whereas a document speaks for itself, a dispute over any terms agreed verbally requires adjudication, and as such it lacks certainty.

**9.4** For instance, a worker might allege that his boss promised him the use of a car at weekends. If the boss disputes that, a tribunal would have to decide whose recollection was correct – which is not an easy matter, especially where it is one person's word against another's.

**9.5** Although a contract of employment is not expected to have the same sort of precision and clarity as a lease or a will, nevertheless some care ought to be taken in formulating it. Quite expensive consequences can follow from a failure to be reasonably definite.

**9.6** For instance, before it can be ascertained whether a dismissal was wrongful (at common law) or unfair (under the statute), the rights and obligations of each party have to be ascertained. This depends on what was agreed under their terms of contract. Was the steel erector restricted to a radius of 100 miles of Birmingham, or could he be sent anywhere in the British Isles? If he was sacked for refusing to go to Bodmin, the question of what he could be required to do would be crucial in deciding whether he was in breach of his contract of employment.

**9.7** The employer is required to serve the contract on the employee but it is not necessary for all the relevant documents to be given to him. Suffice for him to know where they can be found.

**9.8** Frequently, various terms are agreed with a union, or with some other body. It would be sufficient if the actual contract stated that both parties would be bound by such-and-such an agreement. That agreement must be reasonably accessible to the employee, e.g., in an office, or at a work's canteen.

**9.9**

*W E Cox Toner (International) Ltd. v. Crook [1981] ICR 823, EAT*

It is obviously better that an employee's signature is obtained on a copy of the agreement, because that will prove that he has received it. Even if he were to refuse to sign a copy, he is still likely to be bound by the terms. If he continues to work for any length of time, he will (generally) be taken to have 'affirmed' it (see paras. 2.51 & 3.48).

**9.10** Any alteration in the written statement must be notified to the employee in writing within one month of the change. This may be done by a written reference to some other document, e.g., "the new rates of pay have been agreed in writing with your union and may be seen on the canteen notice-board".

**9.11**

*Gascol Conversions Ltd. v. Mercer [1974] IRLR 155, CA*

It should be borne in mind that even if the main terms of a contract are set out in writing, it does not mean that they are conclusive if there is a dispute about any. They are very persuasive and in the absence of strong evidence to the contrary, they are likely to be binding.

## WHO IS EXCLUDED

**9.12** Certain categories of employees are excluded from these provisions, the main ones being as under:

*EP(C) Act 1978 s.144(1)* (a) certain merchant seamen and fishermen;

*s.141(1)* (b) those who work outside Great Britain (see paras. 3.93–100);

*ss.138 (1)&(5) & 139(1)*

(c) Crown servants and those who work in the national health service and in the House of Commons;

*EP(C) Act 1978 (as amended by E Act 1982 sch.2 para. 8(4)) s.5A*

(d) certain part-time workers (see paras. 3.27–0);

*E Act 1989 s.13(3)*

(e) the Disciplinary Rules and Grievance Procedures (see paras. 9.38–44) do not apply, from February 26, 1990, to workers where there are less than 20 employees (together with those in an 'associated employer' (see paras. 3.153–161).

**9.13** The written particulars have to be served on a worker whose spouse is the employer.

**9.14** For the minimum notice provisions, the following are

*P(C) Act 1978 s.2(2)* also excluded:

(a) generally those on fixed term contracts,

*EP(C) Act 1978 (as amended by E Act 1982 sch.2 para.3(2) & (3)) s.49(4)&(4A)*

(b) those who have worked for less than three months after being engaged for a fixed period of one month or, for a specific task of three months or less;

*EP(C) Act 1978 s.49(5)*

(c) those whom the employer has the right to summarily dismiss, e.g., those guilty of gross misconduct.

## WHICH WRITTEN TERMS HAVE TO BE INCLUDED

**9.15** The following particulars must be included in the written terms that have to be served.

### (a) *The name of the employer and of the employee*

**9.16** This is not just a formality – a lot can depend on it. It

*EP(C) Act 1978 s.1(2)(a)* enables the identity of the employer to be known, so that, if the necessity arises, the proper party can be sued. For instance, if the employer is stated to be H.G. Jones, then Mr Jones will be personally liable for any claim or debt. If it is stated to be H.G. Jones Ltd., then only the limited company can be responsible and not their directors. A former employer (to the immediate past one) can also be liable in certain circumstances.

### (b) *The job title*

**9.17** This is important as it enables each party to see the scope of the work normally done. Accordingly, if the employer requires flexibility, he must say so. It is desirable to provide that in some circumstances there can be a change of job. Although it is not obligatory to provide a full job specification, it is probably desirable to do so, perhaps in a separate document.

**9.18** If a job title is very restrictive, an employee might refuse to do something outside what a person in that occupation normally does on the grounds that he is not contractually bound to do so. A dismissal for that refusal is likely to be unfair as well as wrongful.

**9.19** The scope of what an employee can be required to do is also important in equal pay, discrimination and redundancy cases.

**9.20**

*Cowen v. Haden Ltd. [1983] ICR 1, CA*

A divisional contract surveyor could be required to undertake all duties within the scope of his 'capabilities'. He was dismissed because the job of 'divisional contract surveyor' ceased to exist. It was held that his dismissal on the grounds of redundancy was unfair because there were other jobs available which he was 'capable' of doing.

### (c) *Date of commencement of employment*

**9.21**

*EP(C) Act 1978 (as amended by E Act 1982 sch.2 para.8(1)(a)) s.1(2)(b) & (c)*

This effects such matters as the qualifying period of employment required to bring certain proceedings, the amount of redundancy pay (see paras. 4.44–47) or the basic award (see para. 5.159(a)) payable in unfair dismissal cases.

**9.22** In giving the date of commencement, the statement must show whether any previous employments count towards the period of 'continuous employment' (see paras. 3.23–36). The date does not have to be the one on which the employee actually commences work but when he becomes an employee (see para. 3.24).

**9.23** For instance, if the business had been bought by the present employer, and the employee came with it, then there will have been continuity, and this must be reflected in the dates provided.

### (d) *Scale of remuneration and intervals when paid*

**9.24**

*EP(C) Act 1978 s.1(3)(a) & (b)*

If an employee is dismissed, certain calculations are made on the basis of the basic pay, plus what constitutes compulsory overtime, cost of living allowances and so forth (see paras. 3.101–106). Travel allowances are not included in the basic pay, so it is important to spell out everything clearly.

**9.25** If the employee leaves because he alleges that the agreed amount is not being paid to him, the written-terms should be able to prove who is right.

### (e) Normal hours of work

**9.26**
*EP(C) Act 1978 s.1(3)(c)*

Hours of work are often important. Generally pay is based on it. If it is alleged that the employee was always late arriving, or early in leaving the written statement of hours will clearly establish what was agreed.

**\* 9.27**
*Martin v. Solus Schall [1979] IRLR 7, EAT*

If overtime is compulsory, this should be recorded, otherwise it could lead to a dispute, and perhaps a claim. It is better to rely on an express written term rather than an implied one, even if the nature of the job is such that overtime is essential. If it is obvious to all, usually it will be inferred, but there may be some exceptions.

### (f) Holiday entitlement and holiday pay

**9.28**
*EP(C) Act 1978 s.1(3)(d)(i)*

This can be important where there may be conflicting interests, e.g., the employer wants the employee to work in holiday periods, or close down his factory at certain times of the year. An employee with children home from school may want to take holidays at special times.

**9.29** If the employer is flexible on dates, but requires a certain length of notice, the period should be stated in the written terms. A great many small employers keep a chart showing holiday arrangements for staff in different departments. An employee will know whether a time that he wants will be feasible.

### (g) Particulars of any pension or pension scheme

**9.30**
*EP(C) Act 1978 s.1(3)(d)(iii)*

This is often a complex subject, and the full particulars are not easily incorporated into the written contract. It will usually suffice to deal with it in general terms, referring to other documents which will set out the terms in detail.

**9.31** If there are no pension rights, then the contract *must* say so. Failure to do so may result in a lot of trouble to the employer (see para. 9.49).

### (h) Terms and Conditions re incapacity due to injury or sickness

**9.32**

*EP(C) Act 1978 s.1(3)(d)(ii)*

If there are no terms or conditions relating to pay or other benefits during absences due to sickness or injury,then the contract *must* say so. Failure to comply can turn out to be extremely costly (see para. 9.49).

**9.33**

Many employers like to keep the matter within their discretion and make an ex-gratia payment. Sometimes they provide the difference between what benefits the worker receives from the State and what he would have earned.

**9.34**

It is desirable to include details about notification procedures and certification rules.

### (i) The Period of Notice

**9.35**

*EP(C) Act 1978 s.1(3)(e)*

This must be not less than that provided for under the existing legislation (see para. 3.10). Where an employee gives in his notice, then the period must be not less than one week.

**9.36**

If the minimum period of notice is not given by an employer then the employment will be deemed to carry on until the end of the statutory period for certain limited purposes (see paras. 3.10–14). This does not apply where the employer is entitled to summarily dismiss for misconduct.

**9.37**

*Robert Cort v. Charman & Sons [1981] ICR 816, EAT*

Frequently employers provide for a longer period of notice in respect of their senior employees than is required by statute. If the employee is dismissed without being given the additional agreed period of notice, the contract will only carry on until the end of the statutory period (see para. 3.10). An employee could sue at common law for breach of the agreement, but the amount would probably not be sufficiently large to warrant such a claim, especially as he is under a duty to mitigate his damages (see paras. 2.74–84).

### (j) Disciplinary Rules and Procedure

**9.38**

*EP(C) Act 1978 s.1(4)(a)*

The rules should lay out the standard expected, but they should not be too compendious as this only leads to endless arguments. A lot of the matters will be inferred. It may be convenient to adopt the ACAS Code of Practice (see para. 3.165).

**9.39**

To have a basic structure aided by practice and com-

*John Walker & Sons Ltd. v. Walter, Jan. 19, 1984, EAT (unreported)*

mon sense is probably the best, but if there are particularly important matters, e.g., punctuality, or drunkenness, then these should be specifically spelt out together with the possible consequences of a breach and the reasons why.

**9.40** For instance, if a manufacturing process requires 5 employees to be in attendance, and the loss could be fairly substantial if any one person is absent then this should be stated. An employee should be warned that if he is habitually late then he is likely to lose his job.

**9.41** It is important to make provision for the employee to be allowed to be represented by a fellow worker, or union official when he is being disciplined. When a hearing is being arranged, it is desirable to remind him of his rights to be represented. Many an employee is unable to put his case forward in the best manner.

**9.42** Frequently, claims are brought on the grounds of a failure by the employer to comply with a procedural requirement. A breach does not automatically result in a finding of unfair dismissal. It may depend upon whether the beach is serious or merely a technical and whether the result would have inevitably been the same on the information available (see paras. 5.62–64 & 5.142).

*Polkey v. A E Dayton Services Ltd. [1988] ICR 142, HL*

### (k) *Grievance Procedure*

**9.43** There should be some outlet to enable an employee who has a grievance to give vent to his feelings. If there are none, then trouble can be expected. The grievance procedure is designed to provide a forum in which the employee can get the trouble off his chest.

*EP(C) Act 1978 s.1(4)(b)*

**9.44** The procedure for invoking it should be set out. In particular the person to whom he can complain should be identified, and in the event of his not obtaining any satisfaction, to whom he can go at a higher level.

### Alteration of Written Terms

**9.45** If any particulars of employment, which are required to be in writing, are altered, then written notification of them must be given to the employee within 1 month of the change.

*EP(C) Act 1978 s.4*

## REMEDIES FOR FAILURE TO SUPPLY PARTICULARS

**9.46**

*EP(C) Act 1978 s.11(1)-(7)*

If an employer fails to supply the employee with a statement containing the obligatory information, the employee can refer the matter to the tribunal. The tribunal has power to determine what particulars should have been given. Where the particulars have been supplied but are alleged to be wrong, the tribunal can confirm, amend or substitute other terms.

**9.47**

*Construction Industry Training Board v. Leighton [1978] IRLR 60, EAT*

An employer is also entitled to refer the matter to the tribunal. The particulars as found by the tribunal will bind each party as if they had been included in the written statement. What the tribunal cannot do is to interpret the meaning of an agreement. If the parties disagree as to what a term means, they must seek their redress in the ordinary civil courts.

**9.48**

In exercising its powers, the tribunal will not re-write or amend a binding contract. It will merely direct an amendment or substitution of particulars where there is an error or omission. It cannot make any monetary award.

**9.49**

*Mears v. Safecar Security Ltd. [1982] ICR 626, CA*

The first task of the tribunal on a reference to it, is to ascertain whether there were any express written or oral terms. If not, then they must decide whether a term can be implied in all the circumstances which may include any deducible from the subsequent acts of the parties. If that fails to provide the answer and there are no factors pointing either way, then the term most favourable to the employee must be adopted. In the last resort a tribunal will have to

"invent them for the purpose of literally writing them into the contract" (per Stephenson L.J.).

**9.50**

For instance, if an employee claims sickness pay during a lengthy absence, and there is nothing about it in the contract, then the employer will probably find himself liable to make the payment.

**9.51**

*Boothferry B.C. v. Boyle Dec. 19, 1984, EAT (unreported)*

The tribunal is entitled to hear oral evidence from each side as to what they understood the position to be, and, if necessary, what they intended.

## AMENDMENT OF THE CONTRACT

**9.52**

A contract of employment can always be changed,

provided that there is an agreement to it. For instance, if the wages paid to an employee were unilaterally reduced from £200 per week to £150, then in all probability the employee would not agree. If the employee carried on working and accepting a payment of £150 each week for a lengthy period, then he will be deemed to have 'affirmed' the contract.

**9.53**

*Robertson v. British Gas Corporation [1983] ICR 351, CA*

On the other hand, the employer can (usually) impose a variation provided he complies with the necessary common law requirements (see paras. 8.50–61). Under *statutory* law, if the alteration is serious and the employee objects to it, then he can leave and claim he has been 'constructively dismissed' (see para. 3.37).

**9.54**

*Berriman v. Delabole Slate Ltd. [1985] ICR 546, CA*
*Ellis v. Brighton Co-operative Society Ltd. [1976] IRLR 419, EAT*
*Evans v. Elemeta Holdings Ltd. [1982] ICR 323, EAT*

The dismissal will be unfair unless the employer can bring himself within a permissible ground (see para. 5.20). In this situation, it is usually possible to resist a claim on the grounds of 'some other substantial reason', where the change is made for sound business reasons. It will be necessary to show that there had been adequate consultation with an employee and every effort made to accommodate his objections or difficulties.

## TIME LIMITS

**9.55**

*EP(C) Act 1978 s.11(9)*

If an employer has left the company, an application for particular of his terms must be made within three months of the termination of the employment. There is *no* power of extension.

**9.56**

*EP(C) Act 1978 s.122*

Where an employer has gone bankrupt, the worker may recover his compensation from the Department of Employment. The Department has a statutory obligation to discharge some of the employers' debts like holiday pay, or payment in lieu of notice. Where the terms have not been set out in the written statement, the tribunal may have to determine them before a payment is made.

**9.57**

Sometimes a union wishes to establish a right on behalf of their membership. Where the contracts of all the employees are silent on a point, an employee will be selected to bring a test case. The ruling will cover every other employee.

# CHAPTER TEN

# Covenants restricting employment

## GENERAL INFORMATION

**10.1**    Sometimes an employer must risk letting his staff know about confidential matters relating to his business. Should the employee leave, then he could to use this information and it could have a most serious effect.

**10.2**    To protect his position, the employer will often obtain from his employee, at the time he is taken on, a covenant. That will give an undertaking that when he leaves he will not compete with the business, either by setting up a competitive company or work for another employer in a similar type of work.

**10.3**    It is usually for a limited period and within a stated area. This is known as a 'restraint of trade'. Such a covenant will only be enforceable if it is shown to be reasonable as between the parties, *and* that it is in the public interest.

*Spencer v. Marchington*
*The Times, Feb. 1, 1988,*
*HC*

**10.4**    An employer must prove that it is reasonable in area and time in order to reasonably protect his business. A claim that it is not in the public interest must be proved by the employee.

**10.5**    The principle was enunciated by Lord MacNaughten in this way:

*Maxim-Nordenfelt Gun Co.*
*v. Nordenfelt*
*[1894] A.C. 535, HL*

"The public have an interest in every person's carrying on his trade freely: so has the individual. All interferences with the individual liberty of action in trading, and all restraints of trade of themselves, if there is nothing more, are contrary to public policy, and therefore void. That is the general rule. But there are exceptions: . . . It is sufficient justification . . . if the restriction is reasonable . . . in reference to the interests of the parties concerned, and reasonable in reference to the interests of the public, so . . . as to afford adequate protection to the party in whose favour it is imposed, while at the same time it is in no way injurious to the public."

## WHEN AN INJUNCTION WILL BE GRANTED

**10.6**

*Herbert Morris Ltd. v. Saxelby [1916] 1 AC 688, HL*
*Roger Bullivant Ltd & ors v. Ellis & ors [1987] ICR 464, CA*

In considering the interests of the parties, the covenant must be necessary to protect some trade secret or to prevent some personal influence being exercised over customers to entice them away. It must be for no longer than is necessary to prevent the employee from enjoying the unfair advantage that he had obtained from the acquisition of the information.

**10.7**

*John Michael Design plc v. Cooke & Foley [1987] ICR 445, CA*

Once it is established that the restraint in favour of a firm is reasonable then an injunction will be granted (subject to judicial discretion). It matters not that the customer has indicated that he no longer wishes to trade with the company but intends to deal with the ex-employee instead.

**10.8**

*Rex Stewart Jeffries Parker Ginsberg Ltd v. Parker [1988] IRLR 483, CA*

Where an employer *wrongly* dismisses an employee, he will be unable to enforce a restrictive covenant, because he cannot take advantage of his own wrong. If the employee brings about his own (premature) dismissal he will still be bound by the covenant (see para. 3.60).

**10.9**

*General Bill Posting v. Atkinson [1909] AC 118, HL*

But if an employee is entitled to and does leave the employment because of the conduct of the employer (i.e., 'constructive dismissal: see paras. 2.50–54) then the employer loses his right to enforce any restrictive covenant that he may have against him.

### The 'Blue Pencil' Test

**10.10**

*Attwood v. Lamont [1920] 3 KB 571, CA*

The general rule is that where a covenant is too wide, then an attempt to enforce it in the courts will fail. But where it is possible to apply the 'blue pencil' test, e.g., deleting parts leaving the rest intact without the necessity of rewriting it, and the remaining part is separate and not part of a single covenant, it will be enforced.

**10.11**

*Office Angels Ltd. v. Rainer-Thomas & anr [1991] IRLR 214, CA*

If a covenant is capable of being construed as giving a wider protection than was intended or is necessary, then it will fail entirely. The 'blue pencil' cannot be applied.

**10.12**

So where an employee covenanted not to engage in

Attwood v. Lamont
[1920] 3 KB 571, CA
Ronbar Enterprises Ltd. v.
Green
[1954] 2 AER 266, CA

several different businesses, it was held not to be severable into part that could be enforced and parts ignored. To do so would require some of the terms to be rewritten. But where an outgoing partner covenanted not to engage in similar work or compete with the partnership, it was held that the covenant was severable. The latter term was effective.

**10.13**

A & D Bedrooms Ltd. v.
Michael & Hyphen Fitted
Furniture Ltd.
March 8, 1983, CS
(unreported)

Sometimes the principle can act very harshly where the harm is likely to be great. An interior designer with fiveyear's experience in the furniture business covenanted not to work in a similar job in the U.K. for 12 months following her leaving the company. 'Untold damage' could be done to the employer by disclosure of confidential pricing and certain other information if she joined a competitor. It was held to be an appropriate case to injunct her from doing so.

**10.14**

Dairy Crest Ltd. v. Pigott
[1989] ICR 92, CA

Each case has to be considered on its own particular facts and previous authorities are usually of little help in deciding what is *reasonable*. They do not bind the judge.

## WHERE COVENANTOR IS VENDOR OR SHAREHOLDER

**10.15**

Systems Reliability
Holdings plc v. Smith
[1990] IRLR 377, ChD

Where a business is acquired on terms that the former owners or shareholders (whatever the size of their holding or whether they are employees as well) agree to a restriction on their future activities to protect the goodwill of the undertaking, different considerations apply.

**10.16**

A wider restrictive covenant will be upheld provided:

(i) it is legitimate for the purchaser to protect those interests, and

(ii) the protection is no more than necessary.

**10.17**

Allied Dunbar (Frank
Weisinger) Ltd. v.
Weisinger (Case B)
[1988] IRLR 60, ChD.

Generally, the parties are the best judges of what is reasonable between them, and what price, in particular, should be paid for the restrictions. The Court will shy away from trying to apply any sort of doctrine of 'proportionality', e.g., to establish whether the price is too low for the restriction.

## APPLICATION OF THE PRINCIPLES

**10.18**

*Fitch v. Dewes*
*[1921] 2 AC 158, HL*

A solicitor's articled clerk agreed with his employers not to practise as a solicitor within seven miles of a stated place for an unlimited period. It was held that the covenant was reasonable. A person who had served in that position must have got a knowledge of the affairs and clients of the business. That put him in a position of being able to impair gravely the goodwill of his employer's practice.

**10.19**

*Marion White v. Francis*
*[1972] 1 WLR 1423, CA*
*Cantor Fitzgerald (UK) Ltd.*
*v. Wallace & ors.*
*July 31, 1991, QBD*
*(unreported)*

A distinction has to be drawn between two categories of employees. Firstly, those who have direct dealings with clients and enhance the goodwill of the business through their skill and personality. The employer has anidentifiable proprietary interest in that goodwill that he can protect. Secondly, where the employee operates on a highly personalised basis and has acquired a reputation for efficiency, integrity and trustworthiness. Those qualities attach themselves to him and not to the business. The employer would have no proprietary interest that could be made the subject-matter of the restrictive covenant.

**10.20**

*WAC Ltd. & ors. v.*
*Whitlock*
*[1990] IRLR 22, CS*

Careful wording of a restrictive covenant is vital. Terms prohibited shareholders of a company from carrying on in business in competition with that firm for two years after they ceased to hold any shares. It was held that a former shareholder could not be restrained from becoming an employee of a company in competition. The covenant would apply only where he was setting up or operating his own firm.

## INDIRECT RESTRAINTS OF TRADE

**10.21**

*Bull v. Pitney-Bowes Ltd.*
*[1966] 3 AER 384, QBD*

The same general principles apply to indirect restraints. An employee was required by his employers to join a pension scheme, a rule of which provided that should he become employed in any activity in competition or detrimental to the employers' interests then he would be liable to forfeit his rights under the scheme. It was held that the doctrine of restraint extended to those affected by indirect means. On the facts, it was unreasonable and therefore void.

**10.22**

*Kores Mnfrg. Co. Ltd. v.
Kolok Mnfrg. Co. Ltd.
[1958] 2 AER 65, CA
Eastham v. Newcastle
United Football Club Ltd.
[1963] 2 AER 139, ChD*

Two companies that were near each other and manu-
factured similar products agreed that neither would
take any person who had been employed by the other
without consent until after a period of five years. The
restraint was held to be void as it extended to all
employees whether they possessed confidential information or not. Furthermore it was not limited to the
period when the companies were situated near each
other. Although the employee would not be a party to
such an agreement, he could apply for a declaration
that such an agreement was void. This was on the
grounds that it interfered with his right to seek
employment.

## EQUITABLE RESTRAINTS

### While employment subsists

**10.23**

*Wessex Dairies Ltd. v.
Smith
[1935] 2 KB 80, CA*

It is an implied term that an employee must faithfully
serve his master, and quite often it is expressly so stated
in the contract of employment. An employee maynot
make out a list or memorise the names of clients *before*
leaving for use later on. This would amount to a breach
of this duty and would expose him to an action.

**10.24**

*Hirac Ltd. v. Park Royal
Scientific Instruments Ltd.
[1946] 1 Ch. 169, CA*

Provided that the relationship of employer/employee
still exists then the worker can be restrained from
setting up his own firm or working for a competitor.
This may not be done though where the effect of such
an order will be to force him to continue working for
the employer as an alternative to starving.

**10.25**

*Evening Standard Co Ltd.
v. Henderson
[1987] ICR 588, CA*

The production manager of a newspaper gave only
one month's notice of resignation instead of 12 months
as required under his contract of employment. He
intended to work for a competitor. It was held that the
employers were entitled to an order restraining him
from joining the other firm for the 12 months, as they
had refused to accept the (ineffective) notice (see para.
1.26) and they were prepared to pay him his salary for
the 12 months although not requiring him to work.

**10.26**

*Provident Financial Group
plc & anr. v. Hayward
[1989] ICR 160, CA*

But where no work was to be provided ['Garden
Leave'] and the employee joined or proposed to join a
competitor during the notice period, it was held that
the employer could rely on the employee's breach of
obligation of good faith to restrain him. It had to be
proved that the period was not excessive and some

harm was going to be sustained by the employer as a result of the use of trade secrets or confidential information when working for the rival. The remedy of damages for breach of contract was always open to the employer.

**10.27**

*In re A Company [1989] ICR 449, ChD*

Although an employee can be restrained during (and after) employment from disclosing confidential information, he will not be injuncted from informing bodies established under an Act of Parliament or the Inland Revenue of irregularities. It would be against public policy to do so and it matters not whether the employee is acting out of malice.

### After employment ends

**10.28**

Sometimes an employer overlooks or is unable to obtain a covenant from an employee restricting him from using confidential information, and after he leaves, he uses the information that he has obtained whilst employed.

**10.29**

*Faccenda Chicken Ltd. v. Fowler & anr. [1986] ICR 297, CA*

Even without such a covenant, the employee can be restrained from setting up in competition (or using information) in appropriate circumstances. There is an implied term in every contract of employment that afteran employee leaves he will not use or disclose information of such a high degree of confidentiality as to amount to a trade secret. But he is entitled to approach freely and canvas his former employers' customers, suppliers or other contacts, as this does not amount to a 'trade secret'.

## HOW ENFORCEABLE

**10.30**

These rights and duties are only enforceable in the ordinary courts.

**10.31**

Usually proceedings take the form of an application for an interlocutory injunction, i.e., for an order for a temporary ban until the full trial takes place. This generally has the effect of disposing of the action because there is usually a delay of a year or more. By that time the problem will probably have resolved itself.

**10.32**

In deciding whether to grant such an injunction, the court applies the 'balance of convenience' test, e.g.,

*American Cyanamid v.*
*Ethicon Ltd.*
*[1975] AC 396, HL*

(a) whether there is a serious issue to be decided, and

(b) whether damages would provide an adequate remedy to the employer, and

(c) whether the employer would be in an adequate position to compensate the employee for any damages should he lose at the full trial;

but it does *not* decide upon the relative strength of the cases unless

*Lawrence David Ltd. v.*
*Ashton*
*[1989] ICR 123, CA*

"the action cannot be tried before the period of restraint has expired, or [it] has run a large part of its course, that the grant of the interlocutory injunction will effectively dispose of the action . . ." (per Balcombe, L.J.).

**10.33**

*Lansing Linde Ltd. v. Kerr*
*[1991] ICR 428, CA*

Where it is necessary to assess the likely outcome of proceedings it is nevertheless undesirable that there should be a prolonged preliminary battle, effectively proving the case at the interlocutory stage.

## TIME LIMITS

**10.34**    The six year rule applies, after which a claim becomes 'statute barred'.

# CHAPTER ELEVEN

# Equal pay and sex discrimination

## GENERAL INFORMATION

**11.1**  The Equal Pay Act 1970, as amended, together with the Sex Discrimination Acts 1975 and 1986, and the Equal Pay (Amendment) Regulations 1983 have been enacted to try to prevent discrimination against women that is not based on some justifiable reason.

**11.2**  Behind the legislation lies Article 119 of the Treaty of Rome, and Regulations and Directives made under the Treaty (see paras. 1.29–41). The result has been that this subject has become increasingly complicated and uncertain. The draftsmen of our legislation in following Directives are

*McGrath v. Rank Leisure Ltd.*
*[1985] ICR 527, EAT*

"required to patch new Flemish broadcloth upon the fine weave of our domestic law . . . do[ing] the minimum damage to either fabric" (per Waite J.).

**11.3**  The European Community law is drawn in very wide and sweeping terms, and the European Court of Justice (see paras. 1.81–83) decides whether there has been a transgression of the Treaty on the facts of each case. The result is that there is now evolving a 'case law' similar to our own common law (see Chapter 8).

**11.4**  As the European Law takes precedence over our own (see para. 1.29), it is always necessary to consider not only our own statutes and case law, but also the Treaty and decisions made under it. But the European Law must be clear before an English statute should be construed to conform to it.

*Shields v. E. Coombes (Holdings) Ltd.*
*[1978] ITR 473, CA*
*Roberts v. Tate & Lyle Food & Distribution Ltd.*
*[1983] ICR 521, EAT*

**11.5**  The European Court has emphasised that there is a duty laid on national courts not to follow domestic legislation where it conflicts with European law. It is not necessary to wait until the law has been changed by legislative or constitutional means.

*Nimz v. Freie und Hansestadt Hamburg*
*[1991] IRLR 222, ECJ*

**11.6**  An added complication is that the European law does not divide the subject of equal pay and sex discrimination quite as explicitly as is done by our two Acts. A

*Secretary of State for Scotland & Greater Glasgow Health Board v.*

*Wright & Hannah*
*[1991] IRLR 187, EAT*
claim under Article 119 of the Treaty of Rome may be brought direct, where nothing in UK legislation covers the point.

## EQUAL PAY

**11.7**  So far as the Equal Pay Act and the Sex Discrimination Act 1975 are concerned, there is no over-lapping of the rights and duties arising out of them. The distinction between them, which is very important when considering which Act applies in a particular case is that the Equal Pay Act is concerned with instances where an employee (of any age):

*EqP Act 1970 (as amended)*
*s.1(2)*

(a) of one sex receives less favourable treatment than one of the opposite sex in respect of pay received under a contract with the same or an 'associated employer' (see paras. 3.153–161); or

(b) is treated less favourably than an employee of the opposite sex regarding a term in the contract of either. This would arise, for instance, where a man's contract entitled him to the benefit of a car for his own use, whereas a woman's contract precluded such a right, or omitted any reference to such an entitlement,

*provided*

(c) the work they are doing is:

*s.1(4)*
   (i) the same, or

   (ii) of a broadly similar nature and the differences are not of practical importance, or

*s.1(5)*
   (iii) rated as equivalent under a 'job evaluation scheme', or

*EqP (A) Regs. 1983 Reg.2*
   (iv) the work is rated as of equal value.

**11.8**
*EqP Act 1970 (as amended)*
*s.1(5)*
*Bromley & ors. v.*
*H & J Quick Ltd.*
*[1988] ICR 623, CA*

A 'job evaluation scheme' is a study that has been undertaken to evaluate in terms of effort, skill, responsibility, decision and so on, the demands made on a worker, and to compare them with others in an undertaking or group of undertakings.

**11.9**
*EqP Act 1970 (as amended)*
*s.2A(3)*
*Bromley & ors. v. H & J*

The scheme itself must be prepared in an analytical way and exclude any favourable treatment to either sex, that is to say, it

*Quick Ltd.*
*[1988] ICR 623, CA*
*EEC Directive 75/117*

'must be based on the same criteria for both men and women and so drawn up so as to excludeany discrimination on grounds of sex'

**11.10**

*Pickstone & ors. v.*
*Freemans plc.*
*[1988] ICR 697, HL*
*Avon County Council v.*
*Foxall & ors.*
*[1989] ICR 407, EAT*
*EqP Act 1970 (as amended)*
*s.2A(1)(a)*

If no members of the opposite sex are employed on similar work, and/or *no* job evaluation study has been carried out, or if a non-discriminatory one is in existence and does not show that the applicant's job has been rated as equal to a named comparator, then the employee may apply to the tribunal for an order that an independent expert may be appointed to carry out a work valuation.

**11.11** The procedure is quite elaborate. A tribunal goes through several steps. They must decide:

*EP (A) Regs. 1983 Reg.3*
*Leverton v. Clwyd*
*[1989] ICR 33, HL*

(a) whether there are 'no reasonable grounds for determining that' her work is of each value to a male comparator (or vice versa), e.g., is it a hopeless case? If the claim will fail, it will be dismissed at this stage; if not, and

*Reed Packaging Ltd. v.*
*Boozer*
*[1988] ICR 391, EAT*

(b) the employer raises the defence of 'genuine material factor', then that matter will be considered at a preliminary hearing; if the allegation succeeds, the case will stop; if not,

(c) the tribunal must refer the claim to an independent expert for a report. After he has gone through several formalities his report is filed in the tribunal.

*Sheffield Metropolitan*
*District Council v. Siberry*
*& anr. (Case A)*
*[1989] ICR 208, EAT*

(d) When it is accepted by the tribunal, the findings of fact set out in the report are *binding* in the sense that no *new* evidence may be introduced to contradict them. It does not prevent the parties from making submissions on them.

*Tennants Textile Colours*
*Ltd. v. Todd (Case B)*
*[1989] IRLR 3, CA*
*(Northern Ireland)*
*Aldridge v. British*
*Telecommunications Ltd.*
*[1989] ICR 720, EAT*

(e) A full hearing will take place at which the parties may present their expert's reports. The recommendations made by the independent expert have no special status and are not binding. They will be considered by the tribunal which may accept or reject them.

**11.12**

*London Borough of*
*Barking & Dagenham v.*
*Camara [1988] ICR 865,*
*EAT*

It should be borne in mind that the onus of proof (see paras. 2.14–19) remains on the applicant throughout. An independent expert's report which is favourable to the employee does not shift the burden of proof on to the employers.

**11.13** The expert in preparing his report must consider all

*Bromley & ors. v. H & J Quick Ltd.*
*[1988] ICR 623, CA*

the information supplied, any representations made to him and prepare a summary. Each party is then entitled to comment on the report. The expert must summarise those comments and give his conclusions, (i) taking no account of the difference of sex and (ii) acting fairly always. He should follow an analytical approach, in the sense of describing the process of dividing a physical or abstract whole into its constituent parts.

**11.14** Each side is fully entitled to obtain their own expert's report and present evidence to the tribunal. In the end the tribunal will have to decide, in the light of *all* the evidence submitted, whether or not the claim is substantiated.

**11.15**

*EqP Act (as amended)*
*s.1(2)(C)*
*Pickstone & ors. v.*
*Freemans plc*
*[1988] ICR 697, HL*

Even if a person of the opposite sex is employed in the same capacity and place as a complainant and earns the same, the latter may nevertheless make a complaint that another worker of the opposite sex is performing work of equal value, in another area of operations and is paid more. It matters not how the disparity arises, whether for historical reasons or otherwise.

**European Law**

**11.16** Article 119 of the Treaty of Rome provides:

'men and women should receive equal pay for equal work',

and pay is described as being

'the ordinary basic . . . wage and any other consideration, whether in cash or in kind, which the worker receives, whether directly or indirectly, in respect of his employment . . . [and] pay for the same work at piece rates shall be calculated on the basis of the same unit of measurement [and] . . . that pay for work at the time rates shall be the same for the same job':

they have been amplified by Directive 117 (see paras. 1.30–41) which states that the principles of equal pay mean

'for the same work or for work to which equal value is attributed, the elimination of all discrimination on the grounds of sex with regard to all aspects and conditions of remuneration. In particular, where a job classification system is used . . .

**183**

it must be based on the same criteria for both men and women . . . and exclude any discrimination'.

**11.17** Many of the arguments turn on whether a difference in pay is justified, and the extent to which such extraneous circumstances as market forces, red circling, business efficiency, union pressure, shift working and so forth provide a defence.

**11.18**

*Sun Alliance & London Insurance Ltd. v. Dudman [1978] ICR 551, EAT*

The European Court (see paras. 19.48–51), in general, tends to take a more robust view, sweeping aside historical circumstances as providing a valid defence. Our own courts are more cautious, although they will intervene where there is a perpetuation of past discrimination, often unintentional. Where there is underlying discrimination, the effect of which can clearly be seen, they will generally ensure that there is a remedy.

**11.19** Indirect discrimination that affect women's pay is an area that is likely to be a fertile ground upon which claims can be successfully brought. This is especially so if there is a big disparity between the earnings of men and women.

**11.20**

*Enderby v. Frenchay Health Authority & anr. [1991] ICR 382, EAT*

But the mere fact that there is a substantial difference in pay made to two groups of workers, one predominantly male and the other female, both doing work of equal value and where there is the same access to both jobs, is not, *in itself*, sufficient to establish discrimination. It is necessary to prove (i) a factor that caused the disparate effect and, which (ii) was tainted by gender preferment.

**11.21** So if a job is particularly arduous, involving great hardship, which attracts more men than women, then *prima facie* it would be unaffected by discrimination. If there were extraneous factors which made the position impossible for women because, for instance, it could not be combined with looking after children, then there could be unintentional *indirect* discrimination.

**11.22**

*Nimz v Freie und Hansestadt Hamburg [1991] IRLR 222, ECJ*

The European Court has ruled that where, as a result of a collective agreement, it was shown that the part-timers, predominantly women, received substantially less than full-timers, mainly men, as a result of increments relating to hours of work per week, then it was discriminatory. It had to be justified objectively. If there was no good cause for the difference, then there would have to be parity of pay.

**11.23**

*McKechnie v. UBM Building Supplies (Southern) Ltd. [1991] ICR 710, EAT*

A private severance payment for a woman, aged 61, was inter alia calculated in accordance with statutory retirement provisions. It was held to be discriminatory. A man in identical circumstances would get more 'pay'.

## The Effect of the Law from the E.E.C.

**11.24**

*Defrenne v. Sabena [1976] ICR 549, ECJ*

The matter is complicated for the reasons set out in paras. 1.29–41. As the European Law is particularly concerned with discrimination in pay and conditions, it is always necessary to consider it in respect of any employment problem. The European Court has held that Article 119 may be directly relied upon by any employee.

**11.25**

*Murphy & ors. v. Bord Telecom Eirann [1988] ICR 445, ECJ*

The ban against discrimination under Article 119 applies where a person of one sex does work of greater value than a person of the other sex but is paid less. The work has to be carried on in the same establishment or service, and it may be either in the public or private sector.

**11.26**

It follows that if women are doing work of greater value but are paid *the same* there would still be discrimination. There would have to be some difference to reflect the higher value of their work. It would seem that the *extent* of the differential, except where it is only nominal, would not be subject to judicial interference either under Article 119 or our indigenous law.

**11.27**

*Rummler v. Dato-Druck GmbH [1987] ICR 774, ECJ*

Where a job classification system is used, it is permissible to take into account objectively the degree of strength or physical hardship required on a job although this might adversely affect women as a whole. But the scheme, taken in the round, must be evenly balanced by taking into account all aptitudes that normally favour women as well, and so be fair to both sexes.

**11.28**

*Hayward v. Cammell Laird Shipbuilders Ltd. [1988] ICR 464, HL*

Different terms, some more favourable and some less, applied to a female canteen worker, whose work had been adjudged to be of equal value to that of a male painter, a thermal engineer and a joiner. It was held that she could rely on our domestic legislation that gave her greater rights than under Article 119 of the Treaty of Rome. Each of the 'terms' of one sex (within the meaning of the Equal Pay Act) had to be compared with similar terms of the opposite sex. It mattered not that the value of the complete package was the same in each case.

**11.29**

*EqP Act 1970 (as amended) s.1(3) Leverton v. Clwyd CC [1989] ICR 33, HL*

But it would be open to an employer to argue that the better perks enjoyed by a woman constitute a genuine material factor (see para. 11.42) justifying a pay differential, but the defence *must* be raised at the outset of the proceedings.

## THE ESSENCE OF THE EQUAL PAY ACT

**11.30**

*EqP Act 1970 (as amended) s.1(1)*

The basic concept of the Act is that it requires that every term in a woman's (or man's) contract of employment must not be less favourable than that in a man's (or woman's) contract. This is achieved by writing 'an equality clause' into every contract. Any term in the contract that is inconsistent with it has no effect and any favourable term that is omitted will be deemed to be included.

**11.31** In deciding whether any term is less favourable, a comparison must be made with a member of the opposite sex who is employed by the same or any 'associated employer' (see paras. 3.153–161).

**11.32** It does not matter whether the two employees who are being compared, work on the same premises or even in different parts of the country. Where they work far apart there will be a risk that any comparison may not be realistic.

**11.33**

*EqP Act 1975 (as amended) s.1(2)(c) & (6)*

But where two employees, who are being compared, work at *different* establishments, they must have common terms and conditions of service, either generally or for employees of the class being considered.

**11.34**

*Leverton v. Clwyd County Council [1989] ICR 33, HL*

A qualified nursery nurse sought to compare her worth with 11 male comparators doing work ranging from caretakers to clerks. They were employed at *other* establishments for the same employer, but under different contractual terms. It was held that she could bring herself within the section. She and her comparators were bound by the same 'Purple Book' terms of employment that set out the relevant scales.

**11.35** But the claim was defeated because the difference in the annual pay was due to a 'genuine material factor' (see paras. 11.29 & 11.42) namely, she worked for fewer hours each week and had longer holidays.

**11.36**

*McCarthys v. Smith (No.2) [1980] ICR 672, CA*

Under the Community law, a comparison may not only be made with a fellow employee of the opposite sex in the same undertaking, but also with a predecessor in the job. The tribunal will have to take into account the length of the time gap and whether there has been a change of economic circumstances.

**11.37**

In order to come within the provisions it is not necessary to show that there was an intention by the employer to discriminate: merely that the effect was discriminatory. The equality clause:

*Jenkins v. Kingsgate Ltd. [1981] ICR 715, EAT*

"operates to counteract all discrimination whether direct or indirect . . . : it looks at the effect . . . not whether they are expressed in overtly discriminatory words or with any particular intention" (per Browne-Wilkinson, J.).

**11.38**

*Kowalska v. Freie und Hansestadt Hamburg [1990] IRLR 447, ECJ*

An 'indirect' discriminatory effect concerning pay arose where a provision in a collective agreement had the effect of favouring men. They were mainly full-time workers as opposed to women who were mostly part-time. Only full-time workers were entitled to a severance payment on retirement. The European Court ruled that the provision had to be justified *objectively* on grounds other than sex.

**11.39**

*Barber v. Guardian Royal Exchange Assurance Group [1990] ICR 616, ECJ*

The European Court has further ruled that, as a party can rely on Article 119 direct, national legislation will not provide protection for any breach, where a provision has a more adverse effect against women (or men). It would have to be proved that the requirement was justified on objective grounds unrelated to sex (see paras. 11.22).

**11.40**

*Handels-og Kontorfunk-tionaerernes Forbund i Danmark v. Dansk Arbejdsgiverforening [1989] ICR 74, ECJ*

Statistical evidence that prima facie indicates that there is discrimination in pay between men and women in a firm generally (and not between *a* man and *a* woman) will pass the burden of proof. The European Court has ruled that it is for the employer to show that the disparity is attributable to such facts as better job performance, and not to irrelevant factors such as higher training that is not necessary for the position.

**11.41**

*Reg. v. Secretary of State for Social Services & ors., ex p. Clarke & ors. [1988] IRLR 22, QBD*

The mere fact that an employer is complying with a statutory regulation and has no power to depart from it, is not enough, in itself, to raise a defence where it is claimed that a requirement in that regulation is in breach of the European law. The provisions in the regulations and those that have come about as a result of consultations or agreements between various interested parties must have been screened to eliminate discrimination.

## HOW CAN LIABILITY FOR EQUAL PAY BE AVOIDED?

**11.42**

*Rainey v. Greater Glasgow Health Board [1987] ICR 129, HL EqP Act 1970 (as amended) s.1(3)*

Once an employee has established a *prima facie* case of discrimination concerning pay or any other term in the contract, the employer can only escape liability if he can prove that the variation *is* due to a genuine material factor, which is not a difference of sex.

**11.43**

*McGregor v. GMBATU [1987] ICR 505, EAT*

In an ordinary *equal pay* claim, the employer *must* prove that the genuine material difference applies, but in an *equal value* allegation, he need only show that it *may* be a defence.

**11.44**

It may be shown, for instance, that the higher pay reflects longer service, which applies equally to both sexes and that it is not affected by past discrimination. It may relate to experience or because the employee is or was being overpaid for some special reason (see para. 11.53). This is sometimes called 'red circling'. It would have to be shown that the lesser salary would be paid to any successor to the job, whether male or female.

**11.45**

*Rainey v. Greater Glasgow Health Board [1987] ICR 129, HL Bilka-Kaufhaus GmbH v. Weber von Hartz [1987] ICR 110, ECJ*

A tribunal is entitled to look beyond the 'personal equation'. It may consider the economic factors connected with the efficient running of the business provided they are objectively justified. The European Court has put it this way. It is up to the employer to show that

> "the means chosen for achieving that objective correspond to a real need on the part of the undertaking, [and] are appropriate with a view to achieving the objective in question and are necessary to that end".

**11.46**

*McPherson v. Rathgael Centre and Northern Ireland Office [1991] IRLR 206, CA Northern Ireland*

This defence was not open to an employer, who having set salary levels that he later discovered were discriminatory, continued to pay at those rates. He did so without any justification apart from being advised to do so. It seems that if the comparator occupied a key position and it would cause immense harm should he leave then the employer could have relied on that fact.

## TO WHOM DOES IT APPLY?

**11.47**

*EqP Act 1970 (as amended)*
*s.11(2)*

Any worker, whether an employee or one who works under a contract to execute personally any service or labour (see para. 11.99), full or part-time, including those serving a Minister of the Crown or employed in a government department, or in statutory bodies, or office holders, and irrespective of age or length of service, are covered by the Act unless:

*SD Act 1975 s.10*

(a) the work is wholly or mainly outside Great Britain (see para. 3.93–100); but in the case of a person employed on ships registered in Great Britain, or on aircraft or hovercraft registered in the United Kingdom, the exclusion applies only where the work is done *wholly* outside Great Britain or its territorial waters;

*EqP Act 1970 (as amended)*
*s.1(9)*

(b) The is a member of the armed forces;

*EqP Act 1970 (as amended)*
*s.(1)(b)*

(c) the provision relates to pregnancy or childbirth;

*EqP Act 1970 (as amended)*
*s.6(1A)(a) SD Act 1986, ss.7*
*& 8*

(d) there are special statutory exceptions, such as under the Factories Act 1961, where there are, for instance, restrictions on women working on certain lead processes;

*EqP Act 1970 (as amended)*
*s.6(1A)(a)&(b)*
*Roberts v. Cleveland AHA*
*[1979] ICR 558, CA*
*Duke v. GEC Reliance Ltd.*
*[1988] ICR 339, HL*

(e) the provision relates to death or retirement (and *not* in consequence of them), but not regarding access to a membership of an occupational pension.

**11.48**

*Bilka-Kaufhaus GmbH v.*
*Weber von Hartz*
*[1987] ICR 110, ECJ*

Article 119 (see para. 11.16) has been held by the European Court of Justice to cover benefits made under a contractual scheme that supplements the State pension. The exclusion of part-timers to the scheme, which mostly affected women, was indirect discrimination against them, and breached the Article. To escape liability it was necessary to show that the scheme was based on objectively justified factors unrelated to any discrimination on the grounds of sex.

**11.49**

*Barber v. Guardian Royal*
*Exchange Assurance*
*Group*
*[1990] ICR 616, ECJ*
*Rinner-Kuhn v. FWW*
*Spezial-Gebaudereinigung*
*[1989] IRLR 493, ECJ*

The European Court has also held that benefits, including a (private) pension and redundancy pay, which were received by a prematurely dismissed man were 'pay' within the meaning of Article 119. If the value of them depended on different ages for men and women, then that would be discriminatory. However, redress could only be obtained in respect of claims from May

19, 1990. It has also been ruled that the German equivalent of statutory sick pay is 'pay' within the Article.

**11.50**
*Roberts v. Birds Eye Walls Ltd. [1992] IRLR 19, CA*

An employer contracted out a private occupational scheme under which a person's statutory old age pension was deducted from the sum. The rate was otherwise the same for each sex. It was held to be discriminatory against women as they were adversely affected between the ages of 60 and 65 years.

## INSTANCES OF SUCCESSFUL EQUAL PAY CASES

**11.51**
*Sorbie v. Trust House Forte Hotels Ltd. [1977] ITR 85, EAT*

A waitress did identical work to a waiter who was paid more than her, but who was given the title of 'banqueting supervisor'.

*Held*: the waitress was entitled to equal pay because the equality clause applied.

**11.52**
*Arnold v. Beecham Group Ltd. [1982] ICR 744, EAT*

A female's job as a catering supervisor was classed as Grade 2 under a job evaluation study. A man's job as a vending supervisor was also classed as Grade 2. Management and unions agreed the boundaries of the grades, but there were substantial objections from the staff to the scheme.

*Held*: as the job evaluation scheme had been accepted by both sides, although not implemented, her job had been rated as equivalent to the man's. Consequently she was entitled to a declaration in her favour.

## INSTANCES OF EQUAL PAY CASES THAT FAILED

**11.53**
*Methven v. Cow Industrial Ltd. [1980] ICR 463, CA*

A female sought equality with a man who was performing the same clerking job as her although he was being paid more. Employers established that the man had been put into the job because of age and ill-health but his previous income and status had been preserved.

*Held*: the difference was due to a material different, viz. the protection of the man's income and position that had nothing to do with sex.

**11.54**
*Capper Pass Ltd. v. Allan [1980] ICR 194, EAT*

A female canteen worker sought equality with a male worker. He was required to work shifts (for which he was entitled to extra pay) and was responsible for stock control and handling money: he was also largely unsupervised.

*Held*: the man, who got a productivity payment that the women did not, was not on 'like work' for the purposes of the Equal Pay Act.

## SEX DISCRIMINATION

**11.55**

*Garland v. British Rail Engineering Ltd. [1982] ICR 434, HL*

There are two parallel provisions that affect this subject; the law imported from Europe, and, that which arises from our own Acts of Parliament (see paras. 1.28–41).

**11.56**

*Pickstone & ors. v. Freemans plc [1982] ICR 867, CA (but upheld in House of Lords on different grounds).*

This leads to considerable complication. It is always necessary to look at the European law where there is a doubt whether our own law covers the situation, or whether the European law over-rides it (see paras. 1.29 & 11.4).

### European Law

**11.57** Article 2(1) of Directive 76/207 provides;

". . . the principle of equal treatment shall mean that there shall be no discrimination whatsoever on the grounds of sex either directly or indirectly by reference in particular to marital or family status":

and this is amplified in Article 5:

"Application of the principles of equal treatment with regard to working conditions, including the conditions governing dismissal, means that men and women shall be guaranteed the same conditions without discrimination on the grounds of sex."

**11.58**

*Burton v. BRB [1982] 3 WLR 387, ECJ*

Where the Directive requires legislation to be passed by a Member State, it cannot be directly relied upon by an employee in the private sector. Only those employed in an organ of the State can sue on it (see para. 1.34–35).

**11.59**

*Commission of European Community v. Kingdom of Belgium [1991] IRLR 393, ECJ*

Where a measure adversely affects one sex, mostly women compared to the opposite sex, mostly men, this would amount to *indirect* discrimination. But it would *not* be a violation of European law if it was shown

(a) that the scheme was intended to achieve an appropriate policy,

(b) the means adopted were likely to achieve that objective and

(c) the discriminatory effect was unavoidable.

## Discrimination under Sex Discrimination Acts

**11.60**
*SD Act 1975 ss.1 & 2*

There are two kinds of discrimination, *direct* and *indirect*. The Acts, with certain exceptions, applies equally to men and women (and also to married persons: see Chapter 12). It is, of course, primarily directed towards the protection of women. References made hereafter to 'women' apply equally to 'men'.

### *Direct* Discrimination

**11.61**
*SD Act 1975 s.1(1)(a)*

*Direct* discrimination arises where an employer or prospective employer treats a woman less favourably than he treats or would treat a man on the grounds of sex. This can be established by what is said or can be inferred from all the circumstances.

**11.62**

In determining whether there is *direct* discrimination, e.g., whether there is in truth any difference in treatment of a woman compared to a man, it may be necessary in certain cases to discover the underlying reason for the action.

**11.63**
*Berrisford v. Woodward Schools (Midland Division) Ltd [1991] ICR 564, EAT*

An unmarried matron at a girl's school became pregnant and was dismissed because she declined to marry the putative father or leave voluntarily. A man who would cause a female to become pregnant would be given a third option, he could give up the relationship. It was held that it was not discriminatory. It was the continuing evidence of extra-marital activity that was *the reason* for the dismissal and the same treatment would be accorded to both sexes.

### Indirect Discrimination

**11.64**

*Indirect* discrimination occurs where the same requirement or condition is applied to both sexes (see also paras. 14.6–14), but

*SD Act 1975 S.1(1)(b)*

(i) the ability of one sex to comply with it is considerably smaller proportionally than the other sex;

(ii) it is not justified irrespective of sex;

(iii) that it is a detriment to the person complaining because she cannot comply with it.

**11.65**

*James v. Eastleigh Borough Council [1990] ICR 554, HL*

*Reg. v. Birmingham City Council ex p. Equal Opportunities Commission [1989] IRLR 173, HL*

The distinction between direct and indirect discrimination can sometimes be difficult to discern. The test for the former propounded by Lord Goff is:

". . . would the complainant have received the same treatment from the [employer] but for his or her sex",

e.g., where there is not necessarily an intention to discriminate but where that is the effect of action, or inaction, taken or not taken, by an employer. But there can be indirect discrimination that does not offend against the law because, for instance, it is justified.

**11.66** It would seem that where a condition or requirement is imposed with the express *intention* of, say, excluding women from a job, then that would be direct discrimination. The defence of justification could not then be put forward.

**11.67**

*EqP Act 1970 (as amended) s.5(3)*

Furthermore, in both types of discrimination like must be compared with like, where it is appropriate. A single woman's position must be compared with that of a single man or a group of women (of which an employee forms part) with a similar group of men (see para. 14.5 & 14.14).

**11.68**

*Bain v. Bowles & ors [1991] IRLR 356. CA*

This provision may not be relied on where an employer fears that the *consequence* of not taking discriminatory action might be very serious, e.g., the possibility of sexual harassment of young girls. That there would be little risk were women to have contact with boys was not a legitimate comparison.

### Ingredients of *Indirect* Discrimination

**11.69**

*Pearse v. City of Bradford Metropolitan Council [1988] IRLR 379, EAT*

In determining whether there is *indirect* discrimination it is necessary to establish the 'pool' from which the comparison is made. Generally the 'pool' must be relevant for the job. It should be restricted to those who are not only qualified to apply for a post, but possess some particular speciality where this is required and is necessary.

**11.70**

*Bullock v. Alice Ottley School [1991] ICR 838, EAT*

To make a comparison it is not permissible to allow staff to be subdivided into small units. A school made domestic staff, mostly women, retire at 60 but permitted gardeners and maintenance staff, mostly men, to stay on until 65. It was held that the employers had discriminated against a female who was compulsorily retired at 60 because her position should have been compared to the whole staff.

**11.71** An employer seeking to rely on the defence of justification is entitled to show that there are

*71Rainey v. Greater Glasgow Health Board [1987] ICR 129, HL*

"objectively justified grounds which are other than economic, such as administrative efficiency in a concern not engaged in commerce or business" (per Lord Keith).

**11.72** There must be a real need for the measures adopted and they must be both appropriate and necessary. It has been held that if the method of carrying out a scheme allows for the most economic and efficient use of available resources, being targeted at those most in need within a priority group, then although the effect might be discriminatory this would be 'justifiable'.

*Bilka-Kaufhaus GmbH v. Weber von Hertz [1987] ICR 110, ECJ Cobb & ors. v. Secretary of State for Employment & anr. [1989] ICR 506, EAT*

**11.73** A female teacher was required under her contract to coach badminton after school hours. When she adopted a child she was unable to continue with this duty, and her pay was then reduced to take account of this. A complaint of sex discrimination failed because her employers established that the requirement was objectively justifiable when the discriminatory effect of the duty was balanced against their reasonable needs.

*SD Act 1975 s.1(1)(b)(iii) Briggs v. North Eastern Education & Library Board [1990] IRLR 181, CA Northern Ireland*

**11.74** What is not permissible is to take a decision that is based on wider social issues, however commendable or reasonable they may be. Only those necessary for the business of the employer are protected. A member State is entitled to make legislative provisions that have a discriminatory affect on one sex, where the social and economic policies behind them justify such a course.

*Greater Manchester Police Authority v. Lea [1990] IRLR 372, EAT Reg. v. Secretary of State for Employment, ex p. Equal Opportunities Commission & anr. [1991] IRLR 483, QB*

**11.75** Detriment is a very wide term and can encompass such acts as a supervisor subjecting an employee to discriminatory abuse providing it amounts to putting a person 'under a disadvantage'. Generally it is limited to matters about which a *reasonable* employee could justifiably complain. An employer though should have regard to the feelings of an employee whom he knows to be particularly sensitive.

*Ministry of Defence v. Jeremiah [1980] ICR 13, CA Wileman v. Minilec Engineering Ltd. [1988] IRLR 144, EAT*

**11.76** What a person cannot do, in seeking to prove that she has suffered 'a detriment', is to try to obtain enhanced rights where they are not available to anyone of either sex in her grade. A claim that the refusal to provide

*Clymo v. Wandsworth London Borough [1989] ICR 250, EAT*

them, because of her personal circumstances, is discriminatory will fail.

## Pregnancy

**11.77**

*Hayes v. Malleable Working Men's Club [1985] ICR 703, EAT*

It is now established that a pregnant woman can compare herself with a hypothetical 'sick' a man, whose circumstances are similar regarding absence.

**11.78**

*Dekker v. Stichting Vormingscentrum voor Jong Volwassenen Plus [1991] IRLR 27, ECJ*

The European Court has also ruled that there would be a breach of the principle of equality of treatment under the Equal Treatment Directive (see para. 11.16) if a female was refused employment on economic grounds because of her pregnancy. That there was no male candidate for the job was irrelevant. The main reason for the decision not to employ her related to a factor that applied exclusively to women, e.g., pregnancy, and relying on that *fact* was direct discrimination.

**11.79**

*Webb v. Emo Air Cargo (UK) Ltd. The Times, Dec. 30, 1991, CA*

But our courts have held that where employers can prove that they would have refused employment to a man who would have been absent from work for a similar period, through sickness for instance, then they would escape liability.

**11.80**

*Handels-og Kontorfunk-tionaerernes Forbund i Danmark v. Dansk Arbeijdsgiverforening [1991] ICR 74, ECJ*

The European Court has also ruled that it was not discriminatory to dismiss a female who after returning from maternity leave was repeatedly absent through-sickness, the origin of which lay in the childbirth. It was proved that the employers would have dealt with men in the same way who were similarly absent from work through sickness from other causes.

## Victimisation

**11.81**

*SD Act 1975 s.4*

There can also be discrimination by way of victimisation. This arises where a person is treated less favourably because he has brought proceedings or given evidence or information under this Act or the Equal Pay Act, or done something connected with these two Acts. This does not apply where the alleged victim makes a false allegation or one not in good faith (see paras 14.15 & 14.40).

**11.82**

*Cornelius v. University College of Swansea [1987] IRLR 141, CA*

If the reason for the action is to penalise a person who is conceived to be a trouble-maker, it would be caught, provided that the underlying reason related to helping someone in connection with the Acts.

## WHEN IS IT UNLAWFUL?

**11.83**   It is unlawful for an employer to discriminate against a person on the grounds of sex, in respect of employment at an establishment in Great Britain:

*SD Act 1975 s.6 Brennan v. Dewhurst [1984] ICR 52, EAT*

(a) regarding the arrangements made for recruitment for jobs. This could occur where a woman is 'filtered out' by a junior manager at an early stage of the interviewing process, even though the actual decision is made by someone at a more senior level, and in the event no one was ever appointed;

(b) in the terms on which he offers the person that employment, e.g., by offering a male book-keeper, for instance, four weeks holiday a year, but only offering a female one two weeks;

(c) by refusing or deliberately omitting to offer that employment to one sex. This might occur where an employer requires written applications on company forms, but he declines to provide any for one sex;

(d) in the way he affords access to promotion, transfer or training, or to any other benefits, facilities or services;

(e) by dismissing the person, or subjecting her to any other detriment.

**11.84**   Problems often arise over questions put to candidates at interviews. If they are gender stereotyped and have a demoralising effect on the person so that her (or his) performance is undermined, then that in itself can be a detriment, amounting to discrimination. But there is nothing to prevent a prospective employer from exploring difficulties in the job to assess whether the interviewee will be able to cope with them.

*Simon v. Brimham Associates [1987] ICR 596, CA Woodhouse v. Chief Constable of West Yorkshire Police July 27, 1990, EAT (unreported)*

**11.85**   The ramifications of the word 'detriment' in (e) above are extensive. A female teacher felt obliged to move to another school because of sexual harassment by two male colleagues during her duties. It was held that this amounted to a detriment. This arose too where an employer refused to allow a woman with small children to work part-time, where it could have been done at small expense and without causing great disruption.

*Porcelli v. Strathclyde D C [1986] ICR 564, CS Home Office v. Holmes [1984] ICR 678, EAT*

**11.86**   A male employee was alleged by two women cleaners

*Balgobin & anr. v. London Borough of Tower Hamlets [1987] ICR 829, EAT*

working in the same department to have sexually harassed them. He was suspended. At a disciplinary hearing, the allegation was unproved and he was returned to his old job. An allegation was made that it was discrimination to allow him back. A tribunal found that the claim of the earlier sexual harassment was substantiated (although unknown to the employers). But it ruled that it was not discrimination to permit the employee to return. The Act made it necessary to look at the treatment and not *at the consequence* of that treatment. The man would have been allowed back whether the fellow employees were women or a man complaining of homosexual advances by the male employee.

## WHEN IS LIABILITY EXCLUDED?

**11.87**

*Beets-Proper v. F Van Lanschot Bankiers N V [1986] ICR 706, ECJ*

The State is entitled to fix difference ages at which men and women may draw their State pensions but *not* at which they may be compulsorily retired.

**11.88**

*Roberts v. Tate & Lyle Industries Ltd. [1986] ICR 371, ECJ*

An employer provided redundancy terms, under which men and women could both receive a cash payment or an early retirement pension at the age of 55. This meant that women received it five years, and men ten years, earlier than their State pensions. It was held that this was not discrimination. Both sexes were entitled to the same rights, and as the State *was* entitled to discriminate in fixing the age of retirement for each sex, that aspect had to be disregarded (but see para. 11.65).

**11.89**

*SD Act 1975 s.7 Timex Corporation v. Hodgson [1982] ICR 63, EAT*

Discrimination on the grounds of sex is allowed in respect of recruitment, promotion, transfer or training, or to a dismissal or subjecting a person to a detriment or denying him/her access to benefits, facilities or services, *provided* it is based on a 'genuine occupational qualification'.

**11.90**

*SD Act 1975 s.7(2)(a)*

A 'genuine occupational qualification' could arise for 'reasons of physiology', e.g., a man would normally take the part of a male actor, and a woman would model female clothes.

**11.91**

A job might require great strength, or be dangerous, but it would be unlawful to refuse a job to a woman on the grounds that she is a woman. It would be permissible to decline to take her on because, she, as an individual, is unsuitable. Hence women may join the fire service.

**11.92**

*SD Act 1975 (as amended by SD Act 1986 ss.1(2)) & 7(2)(b) Sisley v. Brittania Security Systems Ltd [1983] ICR 628, EAT*

Where a job involves working or living in a private home that is likely to entail a degree of physical or social contact with a person of the opposite sex residing there, or knowledge of intimate details of such a person's life, and where there might be reasonable objection, then discrimination is permissible.

**11.93**

*SD Act 1975 (as amended by E Act 1989 s.3(3)) s.51*

It is also permissible where there might be a breach of statutory requirements (like under the Factories Act 1961) but it only applies to legislation passed after 1975, except where the Acts relate

(a) to pregnancy or maternity, or

(b) to special circumstances causing risks specially affecting women, eg. processes involving the use of lead, or in certain pottery work, or exposure to ionising radiation, and

(c) to an appointment in single sex educational establishments.

**11.94**

*SD Act 1975 s.7(2)(g)*

Where the act might cause offence to foreigners, then the Act does not apply. So women can be excluded from jobs where the work is partly carried out in countries where there are different customs concerning women.

**11.95**

*SD Act 1975 s.48*

In certain limited instances, positive discrimination is allowed by a training body. It may limit one sex access to facilities for training, to redress any imbalance that existed during the previous 12 months.

**11.96**

*SD Act 1975 ss.19, 43–5, 52 & 85 SD (A) Order 1987*

The provisions do not apply to the armed forces and to the various cadet corps, to ministers of religion, to charities, sport, insurance, or acts done to safeguard national security. A certificate from the Secretary of State that an act was done for national security purposes is now no longer conclusive of that as a fact.

**11.97**

*SD Act 1975 s.51 Hampson v. Department of Education & Science [1990] ICR 511, HL*

Where a discriminatory act is carried out pursuant to any enactment or statutory instrument or pursuant to a condition or requirement imposed by a Minister of the Crown under an enactment, then it must be show to be reasonably necessary (see para. 14.32).

## TO WHOM IT APPLIES

**11.98**

*SD Act 1975 s.10*

The Act applies to a person of any age and irrespective of length of service but not where the person is employed wholly or mainly outside Great Britain (see paras. 3.93–100). Persons employed on ships registered in Great Britain, or on aircraft or hovercraft registered in United Kingdom and operated from Great Britain are also protected unless their work is wholly outside the territorial waters (see para. 14.25–27).

**11.99**

*Quinnen v. Hovell [1984] ICR 525, EAT SD Act 1975 s.82(1) Mirror Group of Newspapers Ltd. v. Gunning [1986] ICR 145, CA*

A person who is employed under a contract personally to execute any work or labour is also protected. A female had a contract under which she undertook to perform various services and to pay for supplies. She was not required to attend at the place where the operations were carried out. It was held that the relationship was outside the scope of the Act.

**11.100**

*SD Act 1975 ss.9 11–6, 18, 20*

It applies to contract labour, e.g. those persons who are supplied by employment agencies, to partnerships, to trade unions and employers' organisations, to professional and trade bodies, to qualifying and vocational training bodies, to the Employment Service Agency, and the Training Service Agency. It also applies to the police (but with some limited exceptions) and to the prison service, and to qualifying and vocational training bodies. Midwifery is included.

**11.101**

*SD Act 1975 s.39–1 Simon v. Brimham Associates [1987] ICR 596, CA*

Those who unlawfully give instructions to discriminate are caught by the Act, as well as those who carry out such instructions, even in good faith. So too are those who pressurise other to do so.

**11.102**

*SD Act 1975 s.41*

Employers and principals are liable for the unlawful acts of discrimination committed by their staff and agents during the employment. It matters not whether it is to their knowledge or not, unless they can prove that theyhave taken such steps as were reasonably practical to avoid such incidents occurring.

**11.103**

*Balgobin v. London Borough of Towers Hamlet [1987] ICR 829, EAT*

It is not generally sufficient to prove that the acts were unexpected. The frailties of human nature are such that some positive action should have to been taken to limit the chances of it happening. There should be proper supervision and an equal opportunities policy with adequate training of supervisors in it. Where complaints are made, especially of harassment, they should be energetically investigated.

**11.104**
*SD Act 1975 s.42*

Aiders of others who breach the Act are also liable provided it is done knowingly. It is a defence to prove that the person acted on the statement of that other and that it was reasonable for him to rely on it.

**11.105**
*SD Act 1975 ss.37 & 38*

It is unlawful to make a condition that results in an act of discrimination, or to publish an advertisement that indicates an intention to discriminate.

**11.106**
*SD Act 1975 s.85*

Acts done by a Minister of the Crown, or a government department, or acts done on behalf of the Crown by a statutory body or a person holding a statutory office comes within the ambit of the Act.

**11.107**
*SD Act 1975 s.63(2)*

The tribunal does not have power to adjudicate where there is a complaint of discrimination by a qualifying body relating to a decision by that body. But there must be a statutory right of appeal from a decision.

## INSTANCES OF SUCCESSFUL DISCRIMINATION CASES

**11.108**
*Grieg v. Community Industry [1979] ICR 356, EAT*

A young girl applied for a job with an organisation aimed at alleviating unemployment amongst juveniles. She was not allowed to join a particular activity because she would be the only girl in a group of men and certain emotional problems were anticipated.

*Held*: even though the motives were honourable, it was still discrimination.

**11.109**
*Steel v. Union of Post Office Workers [1978] ICR 181, EAT*

Women were allowed to become 'full-time post persons' following the Act. Before that they could only be 'temporary full-time'. Walks and rounds were allocated based on service as 'full-time post persons'.

*Held*: because the allocation was based on length of service it was discriminatory. Women were not given an equal chance. It is did not matter what title was given to the length of service.

## INSTANCES OF CASES THAT FAILED

**11.110**
*Noble v. David Gold & Sons (Holdings) Ltd. [1980] ICR 543, CA*

Women did the lighter work in the employers' warehouse that handled books and magazines. The heavier work was done by men. The women themselves made it clear that the heavier work was too much for them.

When the lighter work fell off, three women were made redundant.

*Held*: the work of the men and women was different. There was no discrimination, and nor were the women who were left entitled to equal pay.

**11.111**

*Rice v. Fon-A-Car [1980] ICR 133, EAT*

Taxis were owned and maintained by the driver but run by a firm to whom the owner paid a weekly sum in return for business. Driver obtained permission to employ a relief driver for his night shift but, when the firm learned it was a woman, they told him to dismiss her, which he did.

*Held*: the driver did not supply contract labour nor provide services for the purpose of finding employment for women, and consequently the Act did not apply.

## PROVING DISCRIMINATION

**11.112**

*Owen & Briggs v. James [1982] IRLR 502, CA*

It is sufficient for the purpose of proving a case that the racial factor was *an important part of* a persons' decision or action. It does not that it was the *sole* reason.

**11.113**

*SD Act 1975 s.74*

It can be extremely difficult to prove discrimination and sometimes suspicions are ill-founded. A questionnaire has been prepared by the Secretary of State, obtainable from any Department of Employment, which can be served on the employer. In it the aggrieved can ask any relevant questions to elicit information to see whether there has been discrimination.

**11.114**

By careful questioning it is possible to determine whether there is discrimination (whether intentional or not), and an aggrieved will be able to decide whether to institute proceedings.

**11.115**

*SD Act 1975 s.74(2)(b)*

The employer is not bound to answer the questionnaire. Failure to do so will probably result in an adverse inference being taken against him in any proceedings in the tribunal. An uninformative or evasive reply is likely to have a similar effect.

**11.116**

*SD (Q & R) Order 1975 para. 5 Williams v. Greater London Citizens Advice Bureau [1989] ICR 545, EAT*

A questionnaire must be served within three months of the alleged act of discrimination, or, within 21 days of an Originating Application being served (see paras. 18.8–12). A Chairman (or a tribunal) has power to extend the 21 days, and this will generally be granted where a reasonable explanation for the delay is given.

**11.117**

*Carrington v. Helix Lighting Ltd. [1990] ICR 125, EAT*

In appropriate circumstances, a further questionnaire may be served with leave. This will normally be given where the information sought is not available in existing documents so that an order for Discovery or Inspection (see paras. 18.26–33) would not be apt.

## THE EQUAL OPPORTUNITIES COMMISSION

**11.118**

*SD Act 1975 s.53*

The Commission is charged with the duty of eliminating unlawful discrimination, and it is armed with several powers to enable it to carry it out.

**11.119**

*SD Act 1975 ss.57, 67, 68*

*Firstly*, it may conduct formal investigations into cases where it believes that conduct by an employer contravenes the Acts. If it does find a default it may issue a 'non-discrimination notice' requiring the employer to cease the discrimination or the discriminatory practice alleged. An employer who receives such a notice must either comply with the requirement or appeal to the tribunal within six weeks against any of the requirements. He can also apply to the High Court for a Judicial Review (see para. 1.64–66).

**11.120**

*SD Act 1975 s.68(2)&(3)*

Where the tribunal finds that a/the requirement(s) to be unreasonable because it or they are based on an incorrect finding of fact or for any other reason, it will quash it or part of it. It may also substitute any other requirement.

**11.121**

*SD Act 1975 s.73*

*Secondly*, it alone may seek a declaration from the tribunal that an employer, in the employment field, is engaging in discriminatory practices, or an advertisement by him is discriminatory, or that he has instructed another, over whom he has control, to discriminate, or he is pressuring another to discriminate.

**11.122**

*SD Act 1975 s.75*

*Thirdly*, it may help an individual in preparing and/or presenting her case where a question of principle is involved, or where it would be unreasonable to expect that person to do so herself having regard to the complexities or other difficulties involved.

### Code of Practice

**11.123**

The Commission has produced a Code of Practice

setting out the steps that should be taken to eliminate discrimination. It gives guidance on how employees at all levels should be instructed on how to prevent the Acts being contravened, and what measures should be taken to promote equality of opportunity.

## REMEDIES

**11.124**  On a complaint being made to the tribunal, there are three courses open:

*EqP Act 1970 (as amended) s.2(1A)*

(a) it can declare what are the rights of the complainant and the employer; in *Equal Pay Act* cases, not only can both sides apply for an order, but also the Secretary of State can do so where it appears to him that a woman (or a man) has a claim for equal treatment but it is not reasonable to expect her (or him) to make a complaint;

*EqP Act 1970 (as amended) s.2(5)*

(b) in *Equal Pay Act* cases, it can award arrears of remuneration, e.g., the difference between what has been received and what should have been received, up to two years before the proceedings were instituted and/or any damages for the same period, e.g., the value of a car which had been given to a man but denied to a woman;

*SD Act 1975 s.65(a)&(b) Bradford City Metropolitan Council v. Arora [1991] ICR 226, CA Alexander v. Home Office [1988] ICR 813, CA*

(c) in *Sex Discrimination* cases, it can award compensation for injury to feelings. The amount has to be kept moderate and calculated on the same basis as in defamations cases. A sum of around £500 to £3,000 would be appropriate.

Exemplary damages may be awarded where a respondent:

(i) is exercising a governmental function, or

(ii) where they are motivated by money, or

(iii) the award is authorised by statute.

*SD Act 1975, s.66(3)*

*but* the power to award any compensation does not arise if the discrimination is *indirect and* there was no intention to discriminate.

*s.65(c)*

(d) it can make a recommendation that the employer take certain action within a specified period, as appears practical to avoid the effect of the discrimination.

**11.125**

SD Act 1975 s.65(2) UD(I of CL) Order 1991

The maximum amount of compensation for discrimination is £10,000. This is the same as for claims relating to unfair dismissal (see para. 5.159(b)) and if proceedings are also brought under those or any of the other employment Acts at the same time, the total award cannot exceed this figure.

**11.126**

Damages for loss of earnings, prospective loss of earnings and injured feelings and other losses are included in the compensation.

**11.127**

SD Act 1975, s.65(3) EP (C) Act 1978 (as amended by E Act 1982 s.5(1)) s.71 & 76

Failure to comply with a recommendation without reasonable justification can result in a further award of compensation being made, or the existing award being increased (see also para. 5.159(c)).

# TIME LIMITS

## In Equal Pay Cases

**11.128**

EqP Act 1970 (as amended) s.2(4) British Railway Board v. Paul [1988] IRLR 20, EAT

An application may be made during the employment and it would appear without limitation of time after its termination, although no compensation can be recovered in respect of losses sustained prior to two years from the date of the issue of the Originating Application. Only one application concerning the same complaint may be made, unless a later application refers to different matters.

**11.129**

EqP Act 1970 (as amended) s.2(3)

If proceedings are initially taken in the County Court and the question of the operation of the equality clause arises, the case can be stopped and referred to the tribunal for a decision. The Secretary of State is also empowered to refer a case to the tribunal. There is no time limit on such referrals.

## In Discrimination Cases

**11.130**

SD Act 1975 s.76(1) Lupetti v. Wren's Old House Ltd. [1984] ICR 348 EAT Barclays Bank plc v. Kapur & ors. [1991] ICR 208, HL

An application by an individual must be made to the tribunal within three months of the matter complained of, or, if it is a continuing discrimination, then at any time. A dismissal that is alleged to be discriminatory continues up to the date the employee leaves the employment, so the time limit starts from then.

**11.131**

The time limit is six months when the Commission

SD Act 1975 s.76(4) makes a complaint. There is no limit where it relates to an application to obtain a decision whether a contravention has occurred.

**11.132**

*SD Act 1975 s.76(5)*

Where a claim is outside the period, a tribunal has power to adjudicate if, in all the circumstances, it considers it 'just and equitable' to do so (see para. 3.87–88).

## When Time Starts to Run

**11.133**

*Barclays Bank plc v. Kapur
[1991] ICR 208, HL*

Where there is a continuing disability during the employment, the detriment only stops when the same rights are granted to all. Time runs from then. An example would be the refusal to grant the same pensions rights to certain groups of employees for a time. There is no such thing as acquiescence.

**11.134**

*Amies v. Inner London
Education Authority
[1977] ICR 308, EAT
Sougrin v. Harringey
Health Authority
[1991] IRLR 447, EAT*

But where a person was denied promotion because of discrimination, then although the effect of it continues, nevertheless it has been held that this is a one-off situation. Proceedings must be taken within three months of the event.

# CHAPTER TWELVE

# Discrimination against married persons

## GENERAL INFORMATION

**12.1**

*SD Act 1975 s.3*

The Sex Discrimination Act 1975 provides that it is unlawful to discriminate against a *married* person of either sex in the same way as applies between men and women (that is dealt with at para. 11.83). This can be done in two ways:

(a) on the ground of the marital status, the employer treats that person less favourably than he would treat a unmarried person of the same sex, or

(b) he applies to that person a requirement or condition that he applies or would apply equally to an unmarried person but:

    (i) the proportion of married persons who can comply is considerably smaller than the proportion of unmarried persons of the same sex who can comply, and

    (ii) which is not justifiable (see paras. 11.64–6) irrespective of the marital status of the person to whom it is applied; and

    (iii) it is to that person's detriment because he cannot comply.

**12.2**

*SD Act 1975 s.5(iii)*

It is not possible to cross over the sexes and make a comparison between a married man and a single woman or a married woman and a single man.

**12.3**

*SD Act 1975 ss.6(3)(a)&(b)
& s.48*

The same defences as in sex discrimination (see paras. 11.87–97) are available to an employer and in particular, in respect of direct discrimination ((a) above) that being a married person is a 'genuine occupational qualification'.

## WHEN IT IS WRONG TO DISCRIMINATE

**12.4**  In deciding whether there is discrimination, a distinction has to be drawn between whether the decision was taken because the person was married or whether somebody else was a better candidate for a job, or for promotion, or whatever is the complaint. In the case of a married woman, no consideration must be given to the likelihood that she might leave to have children.

**12.5**
*Hurley v. Mustoe*
*[1981] ICR 490, EAT*

A married woman with several young children applied for a job as a waitress but was refused because the proprietor thought there was a strong risk that she might absent herself frequently. Her children might be ill or there might be difficulty with baby-sitters. It was held to be discrimination. The employer was equating this 'person' with all women with young children. He should have reached a decision on her previous employment record. Had her former employers found her to be reliable?

**12.6**
*Kidd v. DRG (UK) Ltd.*
*[1985] ICR 405, EAT*

Part-time workers in a factory were selected for redundancy before those employed full time. It was alleged that this was indirectly discriminatory against married women. They were more likely to have children to look after, and so be prevented from working full time. It was held that for proportional purposes their position should be compared with single women with children. There was no statistical evidence to support the proposition that their position was more adversely affected.

## INVESTIGATING ACTS OF DISCRIMINATION

**12.7**
*SD Act 1975 s.53*

The services of the Equal Opportunities Commission are available to help in investigating alleged acts of discrimination (see paras. 11.118–122) and the questionnaire can be used (see paras. 11.113–117).

## REMEDIES AND TIME LIMITS

**12.8**
*SD Act 1975 s.76*

These are the same as in sex discrimination (see paras. 11.124–127).

# CHAPTER THIRTEEN

# Maternity rights

## PROTECTION AGAINST UNFAIR DISMISSAL

**13.1**

*EP(C) Act 1978 s.33 E Act 1980 s.11–3*

Up to 1975, there was no special protection afforded to women who had to give up their jobs as a result of pregnancy. Parliament then gave them the right to return to their old employment after the birth of their child provided that they complied with certain formalities. These rights were subsequently incorporated in the 1978 Act that was later amended in some technical respects by the 1980 Act.

**13.2**

*Lavery v. Plessey Telecommunications Ltd. [1982] ICR 373, EAT [1983] ICR 534, CA*

The provisions have been heavily criticised for:

"being of inordinate complexity exceeding the worst excesses of a taxing statute . . . We feel no confidence that, even with the assistance of detailed arguments from skilled advocates, we have now correctly understood them . . ." (per Browne-Wilkinson J.).

so, consequently, if a case is complicated, then it may be necessary to obtain expert advice.

**13.3**

*EP(C) Act 1978 s.60*

If an employer dismisses an employee, with more than two years' continuous service at the time of dismissal (see paras. 3.64–73), because, or mainly because, she is pregnant or any other reason connected with her pregnancy, that would be automatically unfair, unless:

(a) she was incapable, at that time, of doing the work she was employed to do, or

(b) there was some statutory prohibition against her continuing to do it,

*and*, in either case,

(c) he fails to offer her:

    (i) a new job, which is available at that time, and

    (ii) that is suitable and appropriate to her in all the circumstances, and

    (iii) the terms he offers her are no less favourable, *and*

(d) if he proves that there was no suitable alternative, he must establish that the dismissal was fair and equitable in all the circumstances (see paras. 5.44–45).

**13.4**

*Elegbede v. The Wellcome Foundation Ltd. [1977] IRLR 383 IT Grimsby Carpet Co Ltd. v. Bedford [1987] ICR 975, EAT*

An employee was suffering from hypertension brought on by pregnancy and was dismissed. This was held to be a reason connected with pregnancy. As the employer could not bring himself within one of the defences, it was unfair. Post-natal depression or miscarriage could be a reason connected with pregnancy and thus provide protection to an employee.

**13.5**

*Del Monte Foods Ltd. v. Mundon [1980] ICR 694, EAT*

It is necessary for the employer to be aware of the pregnancy before he can be liable. An employer was unaware that a member of staff was pregnant, which made her absenteeism worse, and she was dismissed for repeated absences. It was held that these special provisions did not apply and the dismissal was fair.

## TIME OFF FOR ANTE-NATAL CARE

**13.6**   These provisions are considered at paras. 15.38–40.

## FORMALITIES NECESSARY FOR RIGHT TO RETURN TO WORK

**13.7**

*EP(C) Act 1978 (as amended by E Act 1980 sch. 2) s.33(3)(b)*

A woman who has been continuously employed for 2 years immediately prior to the 11th week before the expected date of confinement, is entitled to have her job back following the birth, provided:

*EP(C) Act 1978 (as amended by E Act 1980 s.11(1)) s.33*

(a) she gives notice to her employer in writing at least 21 days before the absence began, or if that was not reasonably practical, as soon as reasonably practical thereafter, that she will be absent because of pregnancy but intends to return to work; she must also give the expected week of confinement;

*EP(C) Act 1978 s.33(5)*

(b) she produces for inspection, if requested by her employer, a certificate from her doctor or mid-wife that gives the expected date of confinement;

*E Act 1980 s.11(2)*

(c) if asked by her employer in writing made not less than seven weeks after the expected date of confinement, she confirms in writing within 14 days after receipt of the request or if that is not reasonably practical, then as soon as reasonablypractical thereafter, her intention to return to work;

E Act 1980 s.11(1)

(d) she gives written notice to her employer at least 21 days *before* the date she intends to return. The date must be not later than 29 weeks after the beginning of the week when the birth occurred.

**13.8**

Secretary of State for Employment v. Ford & Sons (Sacks) Ltd. July 17, 1986, EAT (unreported)

In calculating whether there is the two year qualifying period, the relevant final date is mid-night between the Saturday and Sunday *before* the beginning of the week when the infant is due, and work backwards from then.

**13.9**

EP(C) Act 1978 s.47(2)

Both parties are entitled to delay the return to work beyond the 29 weeks by a further four weeks. The employer can do so for any reason provided he specifies it. The employee may only do so by providing a doctor's certificate stating that she will be incapable of work on the notified date of return.

**13.10**

A certificate may only be issued once and this even applies if the first certificate is issued well within the 29 week period and the second one covers a return within the 33 weeks. However, there is nothing to prevent a woman from turning up for work and then going sick immediately, and so preserving her employment.

### Loss of rights

**13.11**

Lavery v. Plessey Tele-communications Ltd. [1983] ICR 534, CA Institute of Motor Industry v. Harvey The Times, Jan. 16, 1992, EAT

In respect of para. 13.7 (a) and (d) above, a failure to comply with the requirements will be fatal, and the employee will lose all her rights. Further, she cannot claim that she has been constructively dismissed based on the failure to reinstate her in her job. There would be no obligation on her employer to do so, until she has exercised her statutory right of giving notice of her intention to return.

**13.12**

Nu-Swift International v. Mallinson [1979] ICR 157, EAT

If a mother cannot make up her mind and does not send in her notice in time, then she loses her rights. If she was too ill, that would come within this saving clause, but ignorance is not generally an acceptable reason.

**13.13**

Secretary of State for Employment v. Cox [1984] IRLR 437, EAT

But where a woman, who has not complied with the requirements, has a miscarriage and is able to return to work within 26 weeks, then she can rely upon para. 9(1)(d) and (2) of schedule 13 to the 1978 Act that preserves her continuity where the absence is on account of pregnancy, and not for any other reason (e.g., a resignation, or a dismissal).

**13.14** Often, the position on whether the contract still exists has to be implied. The retention of the P.45, or the employee's name being kept on the pay-roll and similar acts are all indicative of the contract of employment continuing.

## FAILURE TO ALLOW TO RETURN

**13.15**

*EP(C) Act 1978 ss.43(3) & 56*

If the employee complies with all the formalities, then a failure or refusal to allow her to return to work will be deemed to be a 'dismissal' by the employer.

**13.16**

*EP(C) Act 1978 s.45 & sch.2 paras.2(1) & (2)*

It will then have to be shown that the 'dismissal' was fair and equitable in all the circumstances (see paras. 5.44–45) *but* where it arises out of a redundancy, there is a duty on the employer to offer alternative employment either within his own firm, a successor or with an 'associated employer' (see paras. 3.153–161), if there is a suitable available vacancy, and failure to make an offer will result in the dismissal being unfair.

**13.17**

*Community Task Force v. Rimmer [1986] ICR 491, EAT*

If suitable alternative work is available then it may not be qualified by considerations of what is economic or reasonable, or by terms imposed by third parties. The employee will only be entitled to the ordinary compensation (see para. 5.159(a)(i), (b) and (c)).

**13.18**

*EP(C) Act 1978 sch.2 para.2(2) sch.2 para.2(1)*

Thus if there is a suitable vacancy that had been overlooked, then the employee will be entitled to compensation. Even if he can bring himself within the provisions, he would still have to show that the dismissal was fair and equitable in the circumstances.

### Interruption of work

**13.19**

*EP(C) Act 1978 s.47(5)*

If there is an 'interruption of work' due to industrial action or for some other reason, and it is not reasonably practical to expect the employee to return on the notified date of return, then she is entitled to delay her return until it is settled. She must return as soon as reasonably practical thereafter.

**13.20**

*EP(C) Act 1978 (as amended by E Act 1980 s.11(3), s.47(6) & (7)*

If the interruption occurs during the 29-week period and no notice has been given, then the employee can return to work at any time within 28 days from the end of the interruption. She must still give 21 days notice within that first week otherwise it will not be in time. The 28 days period can be extended by the employee for a further four weeks on medical grounds.

**13.21**

EP(C) Act 1978 s.45(1) & (2)
Edgell v. Lloyds Register of
Shipping
[1979] IRLR 463, IT

Upon her return to work, the terms and conditions must be no less favourable than those that would have been applicable had she not been absent because of pregnancy, but the actual job need not be precisely the same. A girl was reallocated different duties within her job description and her capacity and nature of work remained the same. It was held that there was no breach of duty by the employer.

**13.22**

E Act 1980 s.12

If it is not reasonably practical for the employer to allow the employee to return to her old job for a reason other than redundancy, e.g., because of a reorganisation in the firm, then the employer must prove that he, or an 'associated employer' (see paras. 3.153–161) offered her alternative employment that was suitable and appropriate to her in the circumstances, which she accepted (but left after a period) or that she unreasonably refused it.

## SMALL EMPLOYERS

**13.23**

Special protection is given to small employers who often find it difficult to cope with a long absence by an employee.

**13.24**

E Act 1980 s.12

If there are not more than five employees, counted together with those with any 'associated employer' (see paras. 3.153–161) at the time the employee left, and it is not reasonably practical (see paras. 3.79–86) for the employer to permit her to return to her old job, or for him or any 'associated employer' to offer her alternative work that is suitable and appropriate to her in the circumstances, and that are on terms that are not less favourable, then the employer will not be liable.

## 'COMMON LAW' RIGHTS

**13.25**

EP(C) Act 1978 s.48(1)

Sometimes an employee has terms in her contract of employment that are more favourable to her than those provided by statute. For instance, she may be entitled to have nine months off work following the birth of her child (compared to the statutory 29 weeks).

She is entitled to rely upon those terms, but within the frame-work of the statutory provisions, to exercise her right to return to work.

**13.26**

*EP(C) Act 1978 ss.48(2), 56
& sch.2 para.6(2)
Dowuona v. John Lewis
plc
[1987] ICR 788, CA*

Thus, she still has to comply with the formalities before going on maternity leave. She is required to give the necessary 21 days' written notice of her intention to return within that extended period. Failure to give that final notice will be fatal. The statute provides that a refusal to allow the woman back to her job amounts to a 'deemed dismissal' *only* where the notice has been given. Without a 'dismissal' no claim can be brought.

**13.27**

*Kolfer Plant Ltd. v. Wright
[1982] IRLR 311, EAT*

Further, even though her contract of employment subsists at 'common law' (see Chapter 8), a claim for unfair dismissal under the ordinary rules based on a refusal to allow her to return to work cannot be made.

> "If she had no right [under the Act] to return to work she can no longer regard herself as being employed from the date when she lost that right and cannot therefore claim to have been dismissed thereafter" (per Lord McDonald).

**13.28**

*Lucas v. Norton of London
Ltd.
[1984] IRLR 86, EAT*

On the other hand, if she is given maternity leave, and does not seek to exercise any rights under the Act, but the employer refuses to allow her to return to work on the agreed date or at the implied time, then that will be a 'dismissal' by them under s.55 (see para. 3.37). The ordinary rules regarding the reason (para. 5.20), and whether it is fair and equitable (para. 5.44–45) will then apply.

**13.29**

*Kelly v. Liverpool Maritime
Terminals Ltd
[1988] IRLR 310, CA
Institute of Motor Industry
v. Harvey
The Times, Jan. 16, 1992,
EAT*

A woman sought to extend her *statutory rights* beyond the permitted times because she was not well enough to return to work within the 33 (extended) weeks. The employer had not assented to it and later refused to take her back. There was no dismissal. The position would be different if he had *agreed*, either expressly or impliedly, that she could take sick leave immediately following her maternity absence.

## MATERNITY PAY

**13.30**

The Social Security Act, 1986 now governs the new statutory maternity pay scheme. The Act only sets out the basic framework, but the details are prescribed by statutory instruments.

# CHAPTER FOURTEEN

# Race relations

## GENERAL INFORMATION

**14.1** The Race Relations Act 1976 is almost identical in scope to the Sex Discrimination Act (see Chapter 11) and indeed many of the provisions are worded similarly except for the substitution of the word 'race' or 'racial' for 'sex'.

**14.2**
*RR Act 1976 ss.43–52*

This Act also deals with various criminal offences which are rarely invoked; and provides for various civil causes of action. The latter are dealt with in the County Court (in England) or Sheriff's Court (in Scotland).

**14.3** The Commission for Racial Equality was set up by this Act. Like the Equal Opportunities Commission, it is charged with the duty of eliminating discrimination at all levels and in every field. For these purposes, it is given various powers (see para. 14.46).

## WHAT IS DISCRIMINATION?

**14.4**
*RR Act 1976 s.1(1)(a)*

There are two kinds of discrimination, *direct* and *indirect*. *Direct* discrimination arises where an employer (or other person), on racial grounds, treats a person (and this includes a company) less favourably than he treats or would treat other persons (including a company)

**14.5**
*RR Act 1976 s.3(4)*
*Dhatt & anr. v. McDonalds Hamburger Ltd. [1991] ICR 238, CA*

But it is always necessary to compare like with like. So where two Indian nationals were refused employment when they declined to produce evidence of a right to work (which they had), it was not discriminatory. The same requirements were put to all other non-British and non-EEC subjects.

**14.6** *Indirect* discrimination occurs where a condition or requirement regarding employment is made, and that if not satisfied is as an *absolute* bar to selection; and

*RR Act 1976 s. 1(1)(1b)*
*Perera v. Civil Service Commission [1983] ICR 428, CA*

(a) the ability of persons in a racial group to which the applicant belongs to comply with it is considerably smaller in proportion to others not of that group; and

(b) it is not justified on non-racial grounds;

(c) it is to the applicant's detriment because he/she cannot comply with it:

but, where there is discrimination affecting a racial group, *only* the Commission for Racial Equality (see para. 14.46) can bring proceedings.

**14.7** To establish whether the condition or requirement has a disparate effect on the applicant, it is necessary

*Tower Hamlets LBC v. Qayyum The Times, May 2, 1988, EAT*

(a) to identify the ethnic group to which he belongs,

(b) the extent of the geographic area to take into account in considering the relative proportions, and

(c) to establish what was the condition or requirement which *that* group in that area could not comply with.

**14.8** There may be several conditions or requirements and the importance attached to each by their prospective employers will also be relevant in deciding whether there has been discrimination.

*Meer v. London Borough of Tower Hamlets [1988] IRLR 399, CA*

**14.9** A company can escape liability for a discriminatory condition or requirement by proving (on balance of probabilities: see paras. 2.14–19) that it is justifiable for non-racial reasons, e.g., that it is necessary for the safety of employees, or another nonracial reason.

*Gurmit Singh Kambo v. Vaulkhard, The Times, Dec 7, 1984, CA*

**14.10** It was in the interests of hygiene that operatives should have short hair. It was held to be justified that a Sikh should be refused a job on the grounds that he insisted on having long hair.

*Panesar v. Nestle Co. Ltd. [1980] ICR 144, CA*

**14.11** A genuine belief in the justification is not enough. An objective test must be applied and a balance should be struck between the reasonable needs of the party applying the condition or requirement compared to the discriminatory effect on the complainant. It has to be

*Orphanos v. Queen Mary College [1985] IRLR 349, HL*

"capable of being justified' . . . 'without regard to' the colour, race, etc. of the applicant" (and see paras. 11.71–74).

**14.12** The phrase 'cannot comply' means that an applicant has to proved that in practice persons of his racial group cannot accept the requirement, consistent with their customs and cultural conditions.

*Mandla & anr. v. Lee & ors [1983] IRLR 209, HL*

**14.13** Thus a Sikh who is required by his religion to wear a turban and is prevented from taking a job as a bus conductor by a company rule that all conductors must wear caps could take action against the company on the grounds of racial discrimination.

**14.14**

*RR Act 1976 s.3(4)*
*Reg. v. Birmingham City*
*Council*
*ex.p. Equal Opportunities*
*Commission*
*[1989] IRLR 173, HL*

There must be a comparison with persons where the relevant circumstances are the same, or are not materially different. It does not matter whether there is no intention to discriminate; it is unlawful if the effect is to discriminate.

## Victimisation

**14.15**

*RR Act 1976*
*s.2(1) s.2(2)*

There can also be discrimination by way of victimisation. This arises where a person is treated less favourably because he has brought proceedings or given evidence or information under the Race Relations Act, or done anything connected with this Act. This does not apply where the alleged victim makes a false allegation or one not in good faith (see paras. 11.81–82).

# WHEN IS IT UNLAWFUL?

**14.16**

*RR Act 1976 s.4(1)*

It is unlawful for an employer in relation to employment by him at an establishment in Great Britain to discriminate against a person:

(a) regarding recruitment for jobs, e.g., where an employment officer is directed to take no coloured men;

(b) in the terms on which he offers him that employment, e.g., offering a white person 4 weeks holiday per year and a coloured person only 2 weeks holiday;

(c) by refusing or deliberately omitting to offer him that employment. This might occur, for instance, where an employer requires a written application on company forms but refuses to provide them for coloured people. Or he does provide them, but screens out all those with Asian names.

**14.17**

*RR Act 1976 s.4(2)*

It is similarly (as in the preceding paragraph) unlawful to discriminate against an employee:

(a) in the terms of contract or in the way in which he is

afforded access to promotion, transfer or training, or to any other benefits, facilities or services;

*de Souza v. Automobile Association, [1986] ICR 514, CA*

(b) by dismissing the person, or subjecting him to any other detriment. The latter provision does not cover the position where racially offensive words are spoken to one person relating to a coloured employee who overhears them.

**14.18**

*RR Act 1976 s.4(3)*

Except in the case of victimisation, the provisions in paras. 14.16–17 above do not apply to employment in a private household. It would seem that this may be found to run foul of the Community law.

**14.19**

*Commission of European Communities v. U.K. [1984] ICR 192, ECJ*

The European Court of Justice (see paras. 1.81–85) has made a declaration that a similar express provision in the Sex Discrimination Act 1975 was contrary to Community law, and in particular to Council Directive 207 of February 9, 1976. That Directive required member States to put into effect the principle of equal treatment for men and women, whatever their number, on access to employment, including promotion, vocational training and working conditions.

**14.20**

*SD Act 1986 s.2*

The Sex Discrimination Act 1986 has now remedied the position so far as sex discrimination is concerned. Whether it will be extended to racial discrimination is conjectural.

## GENUINE OCCUPATIONAL QUALIFICATION

**14.21**

*RR Act 1976 s.5*

There are some jobs where it is necessary to have a person of a special race or colour, and in those circumstances the provisions do not apply.

**14.22**

Thus where a job involves participation in a dramatic performance or entertainment, or as a model, or where food or drink is provided and a racial group is required to provide authenticity, or where personal services promoting welfare are provided, then the discrimination is not unlawful (but see paras. 11.90–92).

**14.23**

*London Borough of Lambeth v. Commission for Racial Equality [1990] IRLR 231, CA*

A Local Authority sought to restrict two appointments to Afro-Caribbean or Asian applicants to perform functions that were essentially managerial or administrative. It was held that the work was too remote from the provision of 'personal services', to be protected by the Act. That envisaged direct contact or where language or cultural understanding was important.

**14.24**

*Greenwich Homeworkers
Project v. Marroll
(Case A)
Oct. 19, 1990, EAT
(unreported)*

A person was required for the post of nursery worker to deal with children of primarily AfroCaribbean origin. A white man was rejected because it was thought that a person from the same ethnic background as the children would be more suitable. It was held that as personal services were involved, then the employers were not in breach of the Act. They were entitled to take in 'account the type of person who would *most effectively provide the services* required.

## TO WHOM DOES IT APPLY?

**14.25**

*RR Act 1976
ss.8 & 78*

The Act applies to a person of any age, whether an employee (see paras. 2.1–13), an applicant for a job, or a person under a contract personally to execute any work or labour. There is no requirement as to length of service, but any person whose work is wholly or mainly outside Great Britain (see paras. 3.93–100) is excluded.

**14.26**

*Wood v. Cunard Line Ltd.
[1990] IRLR 281, CA*

Persons employed on ships registered in Great Britain, or on aircraft or hovercraft registered in the United Kingdom and operated from Great Britain, are also protected unless their work is *wholly* outside the territorial waters (and see para. 3.94).

**14.27**

*Deria v. General Council of
British Shipping
[1986] ICR 172, CA*

In determining whether a person works 'wholly outside Great Britain', it is necessary to consider what was contemplated by the parties at the time of making the contract of employment. Subsequent unforeseen events are not relevant.

**14.28**

*RR Act 1976
ss.7, 10, 11, 12,
13, 14, 15, 16*

It also applies to contract labour, e.g., those who are supplied by some third party, to partnerships where there are six or more partners (but see paras. 14.18–19), to trade unions and employers' organisations, to professional and trade bodies, to qualifying and vocational training bodies, to the Employment Service Agency, the Training Service Agency and to the police.

**14.29**

*RR Act, 1976
ss.30, 31, 32 & 33*

Those who give instructions to discriminate unlawfully are caught by the Act, as are those who similarly pressurise others. Employers and principals are liable for the unlawful acts of their employees or agents unless they can prove that they took such steps as were reasonably practical to avoid the discrimination. Aiders of others who breach the Act are also liable provided it is done knowingly. But it is a defence for them to show that they acted on the statement of that other and that it was reasonable for them to rely on it.

**14.30**

RR Act 1976
ss.28, 29 & 75

It is unlawful to make a requirement or condition that results in an act of discrimination, or to publish an advertisement which indicates an intention to discriminate. Acts done by a Minister of the Crown, or a Government Department, or on behalf of the Crown, by a statutory body or a person holding a statutory office, are all within the scope of the Act.

**14.31**

RR Act 1976
ss.34, 39, 42,
75(2)(c),(8)&(9)

The provisions do not apply to the armed services; disputes can only be dealt with by their internal own disciplinary bodies. Discriminatory provisions in charitable instruments are void but acts done to safeguard national security are exempt.

**14.32**

RR Act 1976 s.41
Hampson v. Department of
Education & Science
[1990] ICR 511, HL

An act done pursuant to a condition or requirement contained in statutory instrument is immune except in respect of *indirect* discrimination. To escape liability for *indirect* discrimination, it must be shown that in the exercise of discretion in performing *public* rights and duties a nondiscriminatory approach had been adopted where this was reasonably possible.

**14.33**

RR Act 1976
ss.6 & 36

The Act does not apply where the employment is intended to provide training in skills to be exercised outside Great Britain. Seamen recruited from abroad, and any acts done in providing persons of a particular racial group access to facilities to meet their special needs are excluded.

## POSITIVE DISCRIMINATION

**14.34**

RR Act 1976 s.37

In certain limited instances, positive discrimination is allowed by a training body in affording a racial group access to facilities for training. This must be in order to redress an imbalance that has existed during the previous 12 months.

**14.35**

RR Act 1976 s.38

The same rules apply to employers and trade unions in respect of access to training.

## INSTANCES OF SUCCESSFUL RACE DISCRIMINATION CASES

**14.36**

A white barmaid was instructed by her employer, a

Zarczynske v. Levy
[1979] ICR 184, EAT

licensee, not to serve coloured people and, when she objected, she was dismissed.

*Held*: by dismissing her for these reasons, the employer had treated her less favourably on racial grounds and this was an act of discrimination.

**14.37**

Johnson v. Timber Taylors
(Midlands)
[1978] IRLR 146 IT

A coloured man applied for a job and was told that he would be told the answer in a couple of days. None came, so he contacted the firm and was informed that the job had been filled. A week later after another advertisement appeared he applied again but received the same answer.

*Held*: discrimination on ground of race was proved.

**14.38**

Bohon-Mitchell v. Council
of Legal Education,
[1978] IRLR 525 IT

A requirement was made that a student would have to undergo a 21-month course, as opposed to a one-year diploma, to complete the academic stage of the Bar, because he did not have a U.K. or Irish Republic university degree.

*Held*: it was discriminatory. The proportion of persons not from the U.K. or Irish Republic who could comply was considerably smaller than those from other countries who could, and it was not otherwise justifiable.

**14.39**

Kirszak v. Swinnerton
& Son Ltd
[1979] COIT 851 IT

A Job Centre put forward a man with a foreign name for a job as a driver, but were told by prospective employers that it would be no use sending him round.

*Held*: even though there were other grounds for properly rejecting him, e.g., his bad driving record, nevertheless it was still discrimination.

## INSTANCES OF CASES THAT FAILED

**14.40**

Aziz v. Trinity Street
Taxis Ltd. & ors.
[1988] ICR 534, CA

An Asian was one of a group of taxi drivers who operated as an Association to promote their interests. He brought a claim against the Association in the tribunal alleging discrimination but it was dismissed. During the hearing he disclosed that he had made secret tape recordings of conversations with some members but the contents were never revealed. Later, the Association expelled him on the grounds that his underhand activities amounted to a breach of trust.

*Held*: that he had received less favourable treatment

contrary to the Act but it was not that which caused the Association to expel him.

**14.41**

*Panesar v. Nestle Co. Ltd. [1980] ICR 144, CA*

An orthodox Sikh, wore a beard, which was required by his religion, sought a job in a chocolate factory. He was refused because the prospective employer applied a strict rule of no beards or excessively long hair, on the grounds of hygiene. On a complaint of indirect discrimination, it was asserted that the rule was justified.

*Held*: as there was scientific evidence to support the employer's contention, there was no unlawful discrimination.

**14.42**

*Pel v. Modgill: FTATU . Modgill [1980] IRLR 142, EAT*

Workers employed in the paint shop of a firm were all African Asians who had gone there as a result of introductions from those already working there. This resulted in a de facto segregation. It was not the intention of the employers that this would be so.

*Held*: there was no evidence that the employers (or the union) treated them less favourably merely by reason of the fact that they were concentrated in a unit and had the worst job.

**14.43**

*Bains v. Avon County Council June 7, 1978, EAT (unreported)*

A 45-year-old Indian complained of direct and indirect discrimination. The latter was on the grounds of an upper age limit in respect of his application for the post of lecturer in a college. Although his qualifications were suitable, he was not short-listed. The College applied an upper age limit of 35 years, although with some exceptions. It was claimed that the proportion of immigrants who could comply with this limit was smaller than native born lecturers.

*Held*: both allegations failed because there was nothing to show that the person selected was less well qualified and the number of immigrants who could not comply was not considerably lower.

## PROVING DISCRIMINATION

**14.44**

*Owen & Briggs v. James [1982] IRLR 502, CA*

All that has to be proved, in order to found a case, is that the racial factor was an *important part* in a person's decision or action.

**14.45**

*RR Act 1976 s.65*

It is difficult to prove discrimination. A great deal depends on information that is not readily available to

*RR (Q & R) Order 1977*
*para.5*

the aggrieved. A special questionnaire has been prepared for serving on the employer. The same procedure and consequences follow as are set out in paras. 11.112–117.

## THE COMMISSION FOR RACIAL EQUALITY ("CRE")

**14.46**
*RR Act 1976*
*ss.43–52 & 58–65*

This body has identical duties and powers to the Equal Opportunities Commission, which are dealt with in paras. 11.118–122.

## CODE OF PRACTICE

**14.47** The CRE have issued a Code of Practice to help eliminate discrimination and the promotion of equality of opportunity in employment.

**14.48** The main recommendations are that employers should state that they are committed to equal opportunity and that there is a senior manager responsible for carrying it out. There will be discussions with employees about their programme, together with training, and guidance will be given on the law. The criteria used to select staff should be examined to ensure that it is not discriminatory, and progress should be monitored. The composition of the staff should be analyzed according to ethnic origin and positive steps should be taken to encourage racial groups to train in areas where they are underrepresented.

**14.49** The Code also suggests that deliberate acts of discrimination should be treated as a disciplinary offence.

## REMEDIES AND TIME LIMITS

**14.50**
*RR Act 1976*
*ss.56 & 68*

The remedies available are the same as for sex discrimination and are dealt with in paras. 11.124–127. The time limits are also the same and are set out in paras. 11.130–134.

# CHAPTER FIFTEEN

# Miscellaneous statutory rights

## SUSPENSION ON MEDICAL GROUNDS

**15.1**

*EP(C) Act 1978 s.19 & sch.1*
*Indiarubber Reg. 1922*
*Chemical Works Reg. 1922*
*Ionising Radiations*
*(U.R.S.) Reg. 1968*
*Ionising Radiations (S.S.)*
*Reg. 1969*

Provision is made in various regulations to protect those who are employed in industries where they are liable to come into contact with injurious substances. These include inter alia radio-active articles, certain dangerous chemicals and lead. In such a case where an employee's health is in danger, then he must be suspended from work.

**15.2**

*Radioactive Substances*
*(Road*
*Transport Workers (G.B.)*
*(Amendment)) Reg. 1975*
*Control of Lead at Work*
*Reg. 1980*

If the monitored radiation dose limit of the employee has been exceeded, or if a specially appointed doctor certifies that the employee's health is being endangered because of continued exposure to the dangerous chemical or lead, then he must be suspended.

**15.3**

*EP(C) Act 1978*
*(as amended by E Act 1982*
*sch.2, para.2)*
*s.20*

An employee, who has been continuously employed (see paras. 3.22–36) for 1 month or more and who is suspended in these circumstances, is entitled to be paid his normal week's pay until the doctor declares that it is safe for him to return. This is up to a maximum of 26 weeks.

**15.4**

*EP(C) Act 1978 s.20(1)*
*White v. Holbrook*
*Precision*
*Castings Ltd.*
*[1985] IRLR 215, CA*

The entitlement to pay does not arise where the employee 'is incapable of work by reason of disease or bodily or mental disablement' but only where he is sent home as a result *of a risk* of it.

**15.5**

*EP(C) Act 1978*
*ss.141(2), 144(2),*
*145(2) & 146(2)*

Those not eligible for this right include those who work outside Great Britain (see paras. 3.93–100), share fishermen, dockers, police, and some casual workers. A temporary replacement can be taken on during the employee's absence (see paras. 5.146).

**15.6**

*EP(C) Act 1978*
*s.22*

An employee who has been suspended under the regulations and who is not paid the normal week's pay may apply to a tribunal not later than 3 months after the first day for which the payment, or an under-payment, is claimed. There is power to extend the time limit where it is shown that it was not reasonably practical to have made a claim in time and it is made as soon as reasonable thereafter (see paras. 3.79–88).

## TIME OFF WORK

**15.7**  There are now statutory provisions that oblige an employer to allow an employee (see paras. 2.1–3) to have time off work to attend to the following:

*EP(C) Act 1978 s.27*  (a) to carry out trade union duties or undergo any training in industrial relations;

*s.28*  (b) to participate in union activities;

*s.29*  (c) to perform certain public duties;

*s.31*  (d) to look for other work, where he is under notice of dismissal for redundancy;

*s.19(1)(b)*  (e) to carry out the duties of a safety representative;

*EP(C) Act 1978 (as amended by E Act 1980 s.13) s.31A*  (f) to receive ante-natal care.

**15.8**  The amount of time allowed off has to be 'reasonable', but Parliament has laid down different tests to be applied. Inevitably, there is often a conflict of views between the parties over what is 'reasonable', and this has resulted in some litigation.

**15.9**  In deciding whether an employer has unreasonably refused time off, the test to be applied is whether his decision is within the reasonable band of response, viz. the same test as has to be applied in unfair dismissal claims (see paras. 5.119–122). It is not what the tribunals would do. If an employee declines to disclose his reasons for wanting time off, then an employer cannot be said to be acting unreasonably in refusing it.

*Ministry of Defence v. Crook & Irving [1972] IRLR 488, EAT Ratcliffe v. Dorset C.C. [1978] IRLR 191, EAT*

**15.10**  Some employees (see paras. 2.1–13) are excluded from these rights. They include those who work outside Great Britain (see paras. 3.93–100) share fishermen, and the police. Merchant seamen are excluded from those in paras. 15.7(c) and (d).

*EP(C) Act 1978 ss.141(2) & 146(2)*

### (a) Carrying out Union Activities

**15.11**  Most of the arguments have related to whether an employee comes under this heading or under the next (b) below. Under this heading, the time off can be taken during working hours and with pay, whereas different rules apply under (b).

**15.12**  In order to be eligible under this head, the employee

*EP(C) Act 1978
s.27(1)
Ashley v. Ministry of
Defence
[1984] ICR 299 EAT*

must be an official of an independent trade union (see para. 1.106) which is recognised by the employer for the purpose of collective bargaining (see para. 15.113), and the employer must 'permit' the employee to take the time off under the statute. So if the time off is taken under private internal machinery, then no pay is due.

**15.13**  The statute provides that:

*EP(C) Act 1978
s.27(2)*

'the amount of time [allowed off] . . . and the purposes for which, the occasions on which and any conditions subject to which time off may be so taken are those that are reasonable in all the circumstances having regard to [paras. 8–20 of the] Code of Practice [3] issued by ACAS . . .'.

*Wignall v. British
Gas Corpn.
[1984] IRLR 493, EAT*

and the words 'reasonably in the circumstances' covers the nature, extent and purposes of the time *already being* taken off.

**15.14**  What duties or actions qualify for a right *to be paid*

*E Act 1989 s.14*

during time off to carry out union duties, and what do not, may be difficult to determine. The 1989 Act *restricts* them to matters covered in para. 7.24(a)-(g) or those specifically agreed with the employers.

**15.15** Prior to the limitations placed on it by the 1989 Act, the ACAS Code of Practice sets out extensive guide-lines; but the way that the tribunals approach these provisions was summarised, by Slynn, J.:

*Sood v. G.E.C. Elliott Process Automation Ltd. [1980] ICR 1, EAT*

"It seems to us that when questions involving industrial relations arise, a union official may well be entitled, as part of his duties, to take part in the planning of strategy and in discussing with other workers who are at the time negotiating with their employers, so long as the latter employers are associated with a particular trade union official's own employees. Nor do we accept the argument that a trade union official is only entitled to take time off for the purpose of negotiating where the employers have laid down the particular industrial relations structure . . . the test is whether the time off is required to enable the official to carry out his duties in relation to a matter which arises in relations between employees and management. We do not consider that the mere exchange of information between the trade union officials themselves necessarily qualifies, even if those officials represent workers in a particular group of companies".

**15.16** If the employee is on shift work, and his union duties occur outside that time, then he is not entitled to be paid, nor may he take time off in lieu. But if he was working nights and the duties were during the day, it probably would be reasonable to grant him the night off and pay him, to enable him to attend.

*Hairsine v. Hull City Council The Times, Dec. 5, 1991, EAT*

**15.17** If there has been a breach, then a complaint may be made to the tribunal within three months of the failure complained about, or if that is not reasonably practical, then as soon as reasonable thereafter (see paras. 3.79–90).

*EP(C) Act 1978 s.30(1)*

**15.18** If the tribunal finds the complaint proved (see paras. 2.14–19) it will make a declaration to that effect, and will award such compensation as is 'just and equitable in all the circumstances'.

*EP(C) Act 1978 s.30(2) & (3)*

**15.19** This will consist of:

(a) the wages that have been wrongly withheld; and

(b) compensation for any other injury sustained (e.g., hurt feelings);

*Corner v. Buckinghamshire
County Council
[1978] IRLR 320, EAT*

but it cannot *order* an employer to allow time off for a special occasion or at a specified level, nor can it impose conditions. But any observations made of what it considers to be reasonable time off are likely to be taken into consideration at any hearing of a later complaint.

**15.20**

*McCormack v. Shell
Chemical
UK Ltd
(1979) IRLR 40, EAT
Davies & Alderton v. Head
Wrightson Teesdale Ltd.
[1979] IRLR 170 EAT*

In assessing the amount of lost wages, the tribunal will include premiums for duties that he was *contractually* bound to perform, e.g., for shift work. But any extra payment for non-compulsory overtime, even if he regularly undertook it, would not be recoverable (see para. 3.105).

## (b) Participating in Union Activities

**15.21**

*EP(C) Act 1978
s.28(1) & (2)
E Act 1989 s.14*

This provision covers any member (as opposed to an official) of the union which is recognised by the employer in respect of that description of employee. It enables him to take time off to take part in trade union activities relating to matters covered in para. 7.24(a)–(f) during working hours, provided it is in accordance with arrangements agreed with or consent given by his employer. He is not entitled to be paid for the time off. If he takes time off and is dismissed, then provided he comes within the criteria agreed then the dismissal is automatically unfair (see para. 5.7).

**15.22**

The crucial question usually is, was the time off agreed? If permission ought to have been given, but was not, and the employee has been dismissed, then the ordinary provisions relating to unfair dismissal would apply. It would not be automatically unfair (see paras. 5.44–45).

**15.23**

*EP(C) Act 1978
s.28(3)*

The principles to be applied in ascertaining what is a 'reasonable' amount of time off are set out in para. 15.13 and that are subject to paragraphs 21 and 22 of the ACAS Code of Practice, which state:

"A member should . . . be permitted to take reasonable time off during working hours for union activities such as taking part . . . in meetings of the official policy-making bodies . . . such as the executive committees of industrial training boards . . . [or for the purpose of] voting . . . in union elections. Also there may be occasions when it is reasonable for unions to hold meetingss of members during working hours because of the urgency of the matter . . ."

**15.24**

EP (C) Act 1978 s.28(2)
Oxford & County
Newspapers &
anr. v. McIntyre & Shipton
July 29, 1986, EAT
(unreported)

The refusal by an employer must be unreasonable before a member has a remedy. Thus, if the purpose of the time off is to plan industrial action, or foment unrest, then an employer can refuse to allow it. Indeed he may be able to dismiss without it being held to be unfair (see paras. 5.6(e) & 5.145).

**15.25**

EP(C) Act 1978
ss.29(6) & 30(1)

Complaint in respect of a breach may be made by any employee (except those listed in para. 15.10) to the tribunal. If well founded, the tribunal will:

(a) make a decision to this effect, and

(b) award compensation for any injury sustained, e.g., hurt feelings.

**15.26**

EP(C) Act 1978
s.30(1)

The complaint must be made within 3 months, or if this is not reasonably practical, then within such further period as is reasonable in the circumstances (see paras. 3.79–90).

### (c) Performing Public Duties

**15.27**

EP(C) Act (as amended
by HS Act 1980
ss.1 & 2, & sch.1,
para 84) s.29(1)

Employers are required to allow members of their staff who hold certain public positions to have reasonable time off work to carry out those functions. The positions covered are magistrates, members of local authorities, statutory tribunals, and certain education, health and water authorities.

**15.28**

EP(C) Act 1978
s.29(4)

In deciding whether the time off is reasonable (see paras. 15.8–9) the following have to be taken into account:

(a) how much time is required for the duty;

(b) how much time the employee is allowed off in respect of carrying out union activities and training, and participating in union activities;

(c) the circumstances of the employer's business and the effect of the absence on it.

**15.29**

Ratcliffe v. Dorset
C.C.
(1978) IRLR 191, EAT

A balancing act has to be carried out, and each case has to be decided on its own particular facts. However, there is no obligation on the employer to enable him to make up for lost time.

**15.30**

*EP(C) Act 1978*
*ss.29(6) & 30(1)*
*& (2)*

Complaint for a breach of this duty is made to a tribunal. If it is found proved (see paras. 2.14–19) then the remedy is the same as is set out in para. 15.25 above, which is also subject to the three months rule set out in para. 15.26.

### (d) Where Notice of Redundancy has been given

**15.31**

*EP(C) Act 1978*
*s.31(1) & (2)*

To qualify for this right, the employee must have been employed for not less than two years when the dismissal takes effect (but see paras. 3.64–73). During the period of notice the employee is entitled to take reasonable time off (see paras. 15.13–16) to seek alternate work, or to arrange for training.

**15.32**

*EP(C) Act 1978*
*s.31(1)*

Curiously, although the statute specifies that 'reasonable time off [may be taken off] during . . . working hours', it does not state what matters must be taken into account. The tribunal therefore has to consider every aspect.

**15.33**

*EP(C) Act 1978*
*s.31(6)-(9)*

Complaint for a breach lies to the tribunals which has the same powers as are set out in paras. 15.19–20 above, but which are subject to an total maximum of 2/5ths of a week's pay in respect of the whole period of notice. The same time limits as in para. 15.17 apply.

### (e) Carrying out duties of A Safety Representative

**15.34**

*SRSC Reg. 1977*
*reg. 4(2)*

The subject of the Health and Safety at Work Act is considered in Chapter 16. Safety representatives (see para. 16.5), have certain statutory functions to perform. They should be allowed to take such time off, with pay,as is necessary to enable them to carry out those duties, as well as undergo reasonable training for that purpose.

**15.35**

The Health and Safety Commission have issued a Code of Practice that is intended to give practical guidance to help both sides.

**15.36**

The way that tribunals approach this requirement was summarized by Slynn, J.:

*White v. Pressed Steel*
*[1980] IRLR 176 EAT*

"The question whether time off is necessary to undergo such training as is reasonable in all the circumstances is to be decided not merely by looking at the Code but by looking at all the circumstances having regard to the provisions of the Code of Practice . . . the right approach is to look at the need of the man . . . to have training to enable him to carry out his function."

**15.37**

*SRSC Reg. 1977, reg. 11*

Complaint of a breach lies to the tribunal which has the same powers as are set out in paras. 15.19–20 above. Again the same time limits apply (see para. 15.17).

### (f) To Receive Ante-Natal Care

**15.38**

*EP(C) Act 1978 (as amended by E Act 1980 s.13), s.31A(1) & (4)*

An expectant mother is entitled to have reasonable time off in order to get ante-natal care, and to be paid during her absence. She must have an appointment, and if necessary she can be required to produce a letter of confirmation that she is pregnant and has/had an appointment.

**15.39**

Part time employees are entitled to this benefit, and it matters not how many hours they work each week.

**15.40**

*EP(C) Act 1978 (as amended by E Act 1980 s.13) s.31A(6)*

If an employer unreasonably refuses an employee time off, then she may make a complaint to the tribunal. If the allegation is found proved (see paras. 2.14–19), then the employer can be ordered to make a payment to the employee of a sum equivalent to her loss or the value of her time during the period when she was refused time off. The claim must be made within the time limits set out in para. 15.17.

## INTERIM RELIEF

**15.41**

*EP(C) Act 1978 (as amended by E Act 1982 s.8(1)) s.77(1)*

Where an employee presents a complaint of unfair dismissal on the grounds that the dismissal related to union membership or to the non-membership of a union (as set out in para. 5.7 (A)-(C)) then he may apply to the tribunal for an (interlocutory) order that he be reinstatedor re-engaged pending the hearing of the case.

**15.42**

*EP(C) Act 1978 (as amended by E Act 1982 sch.3 para.24) s.77(2)*

An application for 'interim relief' must be made before the end of seven days from the effective date of dismissal (see paras. 3.64–73). Where the employee relies on a reason connected with union membership or activity (see para. 5.7 (A) and (B)) then there must be a certificate from the union enclosed with the application.

**15.43**

That certificate must be signed by an authorised official of the union, of which the employee was a member of or that he had proposed to join. It must state that there appears to be reasonable grounds for supposing that the reason for the dismissal is that alleged in the complaint.

**15.44**

*EP(C) Act 1978 (as amended by E Act 1982, s. 8(2)) s. 77(3), (3A) & (4)*

A hearing has to be heard as soon as practicable, but not less than seven days after the employer has been served with the application and certificate. Once a date is fixed, it cannot be postponed unless there are special circumstances.

**15.45**

*EP(C) Act 1978 (as amended by E Act 1982 sch.3 para.24(3)) s.77 (5)-(9)*

If the tribunal, in considering whether to grant 'interim relief', is satisfied that when the claim is finally heard it is *likely* to succeed, then it will make a declaration to that effect. The employer will be invited to reinstate or re-engage (see para. 5.149) upon terms that are acceptable to the employee until the final adjudication. If no consent is given, or if the employer does not attend the proceedings, then the tribunal will make an order for the continuation of the contract of employment until the proceedings are completed.

**15.46**

*Initial Textile Services v. Rendell July 23, 1991, EAT (unreported)*

The employer who does not require the employee to work will have to pay him his wages from the date of dismissal up to the final hearing. If the employee loses his case at the main hearing, the total sum paid will be irrecoverable. Although there is a duty on the tribunal to ensure a speedy trial, the employer must also take energetic steps to arrange for an early hearing.

## ITEMISED PAY STATEMENT

**15.47**

Every employee (see paras. 2.1–13) is entitled to receive a detailed written pay statement at the time of or before receiving his pay. This must set out:

*EP(C) Act 1978 s.8*

(a) the gross amount,

(b) the amount of each fixed deduction such as national insurance contributions, subscriptions to unions, pension contribution and so forth,

(c) the amount of any variable deductions and what they are in respect of,

(d) the net amount,

(e) details of how it is paid, e.g., the amount contained in the pay packet or credited to a bank account.

**15.48**  The pay statement need not contain separate particu-

EP(C) Act 1978 s.9 lars of a fixed deduction provided it contains the aggregate. The employee must have been given a written statement of fixed deductions, and the intervals when made.

**15.49**

EP(C) Act 1978 s.11(8) Where an employer defaults then the employee can apply to a tribunal for a declaration to that effect. If the tribunal finds any unnotified deductions have been made during the period of 13 weeks immediately preceding the presenting of the application (e.g., when the Originating Application is received at the Tribunal office), then it may order the employer to pay a sum not exceeding those unnotified deductions.

**15.50**

EP(C) Act 1978 s.11(8) & (9) The tribunal cannot adjudicate unless the application is made before the end of three months beginning with the date on which the employment ceased. There is *no* power to extend time.

## 'GUARANTEED PAYMENTS'

**15.51** If an employer fails to provide an employee with work throughout a whole day on which he is normally required to work under his contract of employment, then that employee is entitled to be paid a 'guaranteed payment' provided that the failure:

EP(C) Act 1978 s.12(1)

(a) is caused by a reduction in the requirement of the business for work of the kind that the employee is required to do, e.g., there is a shortage of work; or

(b) there is some other occurrence that has affected normal working, e.g., a breakdown in power supplies causing a factory to close for the day; and

(c) there has been compliance by the employee with any reasonable requirements that have been made to ensure that his services are available; and

(d) the absence from work is not caused by a strike, lock-out or other industrial action (see paras. 5.6(e) & 5.145); and

(e) he must not have unreasonably refused suitable alternative employment.

**15.52**

EP(C) Act 1978 s.12(2) Where the work of the employee spans two days, e.g., he is on night duty, then the day on which he works longest is the day that counts for these purposes.

**15.53**

*EP(C) Act 1978 (as amended by E Act 1982 sch.2 para.1 & sch.3 para.15) s.13*

The following are not eligible. Those with less than one month's continuous service (see paras. 3.22–36) or those who normally work outside Great Britain (see paras. 3.93–100), and those on fixed term contracts of 3 months or less or on specific tasks which are expected to last less than 3 months unless the day on which the guaranteed payment falls due occurs beyond the three months and they has been continuously employed for three months or more. Employees who do not have any normal working hours (e.g., salesmen), masters and crew engaged in share fishing, registered dock workers and members of the police and armed forces are also excluded.

**15.54**

*EP(C) Act 1978 (as amended by E Act 1980 and EP(V of L) Order 1992) ss.14 & 15*

An employee is only entitled to five payments during any period of 3 months. The maximum amount he can recover is £13.65 per day or such lesser amount as represents his normal day's pay for the period up to April 1, 1992. Thereafter the figure is raised to £14.10.

## DAMAGES

**15.55** Sometimes a tribunal is empowered to award compensation of an amount that corresponds to damages that could be given in the County Court.

**15.56** Damages can generally be divided into three types:

(a) *Ordinary* damages that will compensate the aggrieved for the loss he has sustained, e.g., the amount of wages, holiday entitlement and so forth;

(b) *Aggravated* damages that consist of injury to feelings but are compensatory in nature, although difficult to evaluate;

(c) *Exemplary* damages that are punitive, which are intended to deter a defendant rather than compensate a plaintiff.

**15.57**

*Broome v. Cassel & Co. [1972] AC 1029, HL Bradford City Metropolitan Council v. Arora [1991] ICR 226, CA*

It matters not whether the behaviour of the defendantis high-handed, malicious, insulting or oppressive; exemplary damages may *only* be awarded where:

(a) the defendant was motivated by a search for profit; or

(b) where they are specifically authorised by statute; or

(c) where the defendants are exercising some form of

governmental function, and this extends in appropriate circumstances to the acts of Local Authorities.

**15.58**

*Bradley & ors. v. National & Local Government Officers Association [1991] ICR 359, EAT*

Where a statute directs that an award should be made, inter alia, for injury to feelings, such as in claims for unjustified disciplinary action (see para. 15.80), then generally the amount should be modest. If there is a minimum figure specified in the Act, then that would be appropriate amount provided there are no other aggravating features. Damages should be akin to those in claims for defamation.

## INSOLVENCY OF EMPLOYER

**15.59**

*Companies' Act 1985 s.525*

If a compulsory winding up order is made against an employer, then an employee is precluded from taking any action against that employer in the tribunal, except by leave of the High Court. This will involve some expense that may not be recovered. There is also no certainty that there will be funds available at the end of the day to pay any monies owing or compensation payable to an employee.

**15.60** An insolvency usually brings about the dismissal of the employee, whether it is formally done or not because the company must then cease trading and go into liquidation.

**15.61** On a bankruptcy an employee is entitled to recover the following amounts from the Secretary of State for Employment:

*EP(C) Act 1978 (as amended by E Act 1982, sch.3 paras.3, 4(2) & (3)) s.122*

(a) arrears of pay in respect of one or more weeks, but not exceeding eight weeks;

(b) payment for any statutory period of notice (see para. 3.10) that the employee was entitled to at the time of dismissal;

(c) any holiday pay in respect of a period not exceeding six weeks to which the employee is entitled during the period of 12 months before the dismissal or insolvency;

(d) any 'basic award' (see para. 5.159(a)) of compensation outstanding from an award ordered by a tribunal;

(e) any reasonable sum by way of reimbursement of a

fee or premium paid by an apprentice or articled clerk.

**15.62**

*EP(C) Act 1978 (as amended by EP(V of L) Order 1992) s.122(5) Westwood v. Secretary of State for Employment [1985] ICR 209, HL*

There is a maximum of £198 for any week, or pro-rata for that week, in respect of dismissals (see paras. 3.67–73) that occurred up to April 1, 1992, and thereafter £205. The sum must represent the actual loss to the employee during the weeks in question, e.g., with tax and N.I. deducted.

**15.63**

*EP(C) Act 1978 (as amended by I (E) Reg. 1983) ss. 141(2)(A), 144(2) & (4), 145(2)*

The following employees are excluded. Registered dock workers, share fishermen paid by a share in the catch, employees who normally work outside the territory of the Member States of the European Communities, and merchant seamen.

**15.64**

*Westwood v. Secretary of State for Employment [1985] ICR 209 HL*

The Secretary of State is entitled to make a deduction from the payment of any social security payments that the employee received during the relevant period

**15.65**

*EP(C) Act 1978 s.124*

A person who has applied for a payment to the Secretary of State and is either refused, or, a smaller sum is paid to him than is alleged to be due, may make a complaint to a tribunal. It must be done within three months of the refusal or under-payment. The tribunals, if it finds the complaint proved, will make a declaration that the Secretary of State is in default and determine what amount ought to have been paid. There is power to extend the period of three months where it was not reasonably practical to bring the claim in time and it is made within a reasonable period thereafter (see paras. 3.79–90).

## WRITTEN REASONS FOR DISMISSAL

**15.66**

*EP(C) Act, 1978 s.53(1) & (2) E. Act, 1989 s.15*

An employee with not less than two years of continuous service who is dismissed (see para. 3.62–73), whether with notice or not, is entitled to require his employer to provide him with a *written* statement giving the reasons for his dismissal. That statement must be supplied within 14 days of the request.

**15.67**

*McBrearty v. Thompson t/a Highfield Mini-Market Apr. 9, 1991, EAT (unreported)*

It does not matter that the employee knows perfectly well why he has been dismissed: he has the right to have documentary proof of the reasons. He can rely on the written statement if he decides to bring proceedings.

**15.68** The employee does not need to use any particular form of request, nor does it need to be in writing. It is obviously better that a letter should be sent by recorded delivery post because it will provide documentary proof that the reasons have been sought.

**15.69**

*Gilham v. Kent County Council [1985] ICR 233, CA Harvard Securities plc v. Younghusband [1990] IRLR 16, EAT*

The employer should inform the employee, in broad terms, what were the *true* reasons. If they wish to rely on the contents of a letter previously sent to him setting out the reasons, they are entitled to do so, provided they enclose a copy of it with the written statement. There will be a technical breach if they fail to do so. It matters not whether the reason is good or wholly misconceived; provided it was the *true* reason operating on the employer's mind.

**15.70** So, if the employer tells an employee that the reason was redundancy, whereas in truth he was dismissed for being a trouble-maker (and could have been validly dismissed on this ground), then the employee will be entitled to compensation.

**15.71**

*Walls v. The City Bakeries Feb. 24, 1987, EAT (unreported)*

But there is no obligation to provide detailed reasons; only sufficient to enable the employee to know the basis of the dismissal. Particular events on which reliance is placed should be identified, e.g., "You were dismissed for misconduct arising out of the events of March 3, when you punched the Manager on the nose."

**15.72**

*Broomsgrove v. Eagle Alexander Ltd. [1981] IRLR 127, EAT Banks v. Lavin Oct. 20, 1989, EAT (unreported)*

Where there is a genuine dispute over whether an employee had been dismissed or resigned, and the employer reasonably believes that there had been no dismissal by him, then a failure to supply written reasons will generally not attract any remedy.

**15.73**

*EP(C) Act 1978 s.53(4)*

If an employer un reasonably refuses to provide a written statement, the employee is entitled to receive a *penal* statement of two weeks gross pay, without limit as to the amount.

**15.74**

*EP(C) Act 1978 s.53(5)*

A claim must be made to the Tribunal within three months of the dismissal (see paras. 3.64–73). There is power to extend the time where it was not reasonably practical to have presented it in time and it was done within a reasonable time thereafter (see paras. 3.79–90.).

## UNJUSTIFIED DISCIPLINARY ACTION BY UNION

**15.75**  A statutory safeguard is given to workers against any form of disciplinary action being taken against them for:

*E Act 1988 s.3*

(a) failing to support a strike or other industrial action, or indicating an intention to do so; or encouraging or helping others in ignoring a majority decision in favour of a strike or industrial action;

(b) refusing to engage in conduct that would result in a breach of contract of employment or other agreement;

(c) making a bona fide allegation that a union or a union official has contravened union rules or had acted unlawfully, or because he had sought or was seeking outside advice;

(d) contravening any requirement imposed by a union that has the effect of infringing members' rights in respect of the above, e.g., by imposing a fine for failing to support a strike;

and it matters not that the action has been properly supported by a union ballot or complies with the union rule-book.

**15.76**  A *recommendation* from a branch to the central committee that a member should be expelled from a union does not come within its provisions. There must be a final decision taken to expel him.

*Transport & General Workers Union v. Webber [1990] ICR 711, EAT*

**15.77**  Disciplinary action covers a wide range of matters including expulsions from a union denying a member access to benefits, treating a payment of dues as a payment for fines, or subjecting him or her to any other detriment.

*E Act 1988 s.3(5)*

### Time limits and remedies

**15.78**  A claim must be brought in the tribunal within three months of the matter complained about, or if that is not reasonably practical, then within such further period as is reasonable (see para. 3.79–90).

*E Act 1988 s.4*

**15.79**  An attempt to pursue an internal appeal or otherwise attempt to have the union decision reversed or reconsidered is a valid ground for delay.

**15.80**

E Act 1988 s.4(5)

The tribunal will make a declaration that there has been unlawful disciplinary action, and

UD (I of CL) Order 1991
EP (V of L) Order 1992

(a) provided the union will withdraw the disciplinary action, then the tribunal will make an award of compensation up to a maximum of £15,940 up to April 1, 1992 and thereafter £16,150 on the basis of what is just and equitable:

UD (I of CL) Order 1991
EP (V of L) Order 1992

(b) where the union refuses to withdraw the action, then the matter has to go to the EAT (see para. 19.3) who will decide on the amount of the award up to a maximum of £26,236 up to April 1, 1992 and thereafter £26,810 on the basis of what is 'just and equitable' which will include injury to feelings; and there must be a minimum basic award of £2,520 (e.g., the same as in an automatically unfair dismissal – see para 159(a)(ii)).

E Act 1980
s.5(5) & (6)

but, in both instances, it will be subject to reduction for contributory fault (see paras. 3.123–135) or failure to mitigate the loss (see paras. 2.76–84).

**15.81**

The tribunal only has jurisdiction to determine compensation where the union:

(a) has revoked the disciplinary action, and

(b) has taken all such steps as are necessary to reverse any measures used to give effect to that disciplinary action,

otherwise only the EAT is empowered to make an award.

**15.82**

Leese v. Food From Britain
Mar. 4, 1991, EAT
(unreported)

There has to be full compliance with these requirements. A union wrote to the applicant's employers notifying them that he had been expelled and no further deductions should be made from his pay and sent to them. The expulsion of the applicant was reversed, but no action was taken on the notification, and this resulted in the award having to be made by the EAT.

**15.83**

Bradley & ors v. National & Local Government Officers Association [1991] ICR 359, EAT

A union had expelled some members who had refused to take part in industrial action. Thereafter members of the local branch had wrote objectional articles about them to frighten them. It was held that the appropriate measure of damages for injury to feelings (see para. 11.113) was £2,520, (i.e., the minimum at that time). The remedy had to relate to the expulsion, and not to subsequent conduct.

**15.84** An appeal lies to the EAT on a point of law alone (see paras. 19.1–19).

## UNLAWFUL REFUSAL OF ACCESS TO EMPLOYMENT

**15.85**

*E Act 1990 s.1*

Since January 1, 1991 it has been unlawful for a prospective employer to refuse a person employment because he is, or is not, a member of a union or because he will not accept a requirement to become or remain one. It also applies where he declines to make a payment in lieu of being a member.

**15.86**

*E Act 1990 ss.2 & 3(3)(b)*

The same also applies where an employment agency which refuses to provide its services because of union or non-union membership. But where a trade union supplies workers to an employer, it is not to be regarded as an 'employment agency'.

**15.87**

*E Act 1990 s.1 & 2*

Where an advertisement (or an arrangement or condition) might reasonably be understood to indicate that such restrictions on access to employment apply, then a refusal of employment is deemed to be for that reason.

**15.88** These provisions do not apply to those in police service, employment outside the United Kingdom, those on U.K. ships registered outside Great Britain, share fishermen, members of the armed forces, or where a Minister has certified that internal security has to be safeguarded.

**15.89** Complaints of refusal of employment lie to the tribunals. If proved, the tribunal must make a declaration to that effect, and order the payment of 'such amount as [it] may determine'. The compensation will include injury to feelings, subject to a limitation £10,000. It may also recommend remedial action be taken within a specified period to obviate the effect of the conduct in respect of which complaint is made.

**15.90** There is a three month time limit on complaints, but power is given to tribunals to extend time where it was not reasonably practical to present the claim in time and it was done as soon as reasonable thereafter (see paras. 3.79–90).

**15.91**

*E Act 1990 sch.1 para.6*

Where a complaint can be brought against an employer or an employment agency, then either of those two parties can join the other. Where a complaint is upheld against both, then any compensation ordered must be apportioned according to what is just and equitable (see also paras. 3.178–183).

**15.92** Similarly a trade union or other person, e.g., a shop steward, can be joined where a respondent was induced to act in the manner complained of because of industrial action (see paras. 3.179–182).

## EMPLOYMENT OF DISABLED PERSONS

**15.93**
*DP (E) Act 1944*
*s.6(1) & (2)*

The Disabled Persons (Employment) Acts of 1944 and 1958 enable a disabled person to obtain employment or work on his own account with assistance. The Secretary of State for Employment maintains a register of disabled persons.

**15.94**
*DP (E) Act 1944*
*s.1(1)*

A disabled person means a person who, on account of injury, disease or congenital deformity, is substantially handicapped in obtaining or keeping employment, or in undertaking work on his own account, of a kind that, apart from that injury, disease or deformity, would be suited to his age, experience or qualifications.

**15.95**
*DP (E) Act 1944*
*s.12(1)*
*DP (DE) Order 1946*

The Secretary of State, after consulting with employers' and workers' organisations, may by statutory order designate certain classes of employment as especially suitable for disabled persons. Lift and car park attendants have been so designated. No person who is not a registered disabled may be taken on for such a job except where a permit has been issued by the Secretary of State.

**15.96**
*DP (E) Act 1944*
*s.10(2)(a) & (b)*

Those employers who employ more than 20 staff are expected to employ the appropriate quota of disabled persons unless otherwise excused. They are classified as 'standard' in which case 3% of the workforce should consist of registered disabled, or 'special' when the percentage is 0.1.

**15.97**
*DP (E) Act 1944*
*s.10(2)(a) & (b)*

For the purposes of these requirements, employment means any relationship entered into whether for business or other purposes, which has the character of there being an employer and employee.

**15.98**
*Seymour v. British*
*Airways Board*
*[1983] ICR 148, EAT*

The ordinary law in respect of contracts of employment apply. In considering whether a dismissal is unfair a tribunal will take into account the personal circumstances of a disabled employee, but *not* the fact that the dismissal may result in a drop in the percentage of disabled persons to a figure below that permitted.

### Code of Practice

**15.99** A Code of Practice has been produced by the Manpower Services Commission which suggest objectives to which an employer should aim. In particular, they should ensure that the disabled receive fair treatment and should have been given consideration as to their ability to do a job.

**15.100** There should be an explicit policy aimed at assisting them. They should be helped in integration into jobs and their skills should be developed. Promotion opportunities according to their abilities should be offered to them.

# REHABILITATION OF OFFENDERS

**15.101** Some people break the law, and consequently have convictions recorded against them. Some of the offences are of no consequence, but others might have a serious effect on a person seeking employment.

**15.102** A man with three serious convictions for fraud would be unlikely to get a job in a finance house. A woman with four convictions for shop-lifting would probably have difficulty in securing employment in a departmental store.

**15.103** If a person has shown by his conduct that he has put the more disreputable side of his past behind him, then it would be unfair that he should be virtually precluded from obtaining employment in a field of his choice. Many employers might be sympathetic, but might be prevented from helping. The terms of their insurance cover or other bona fide restrictions may make it very difficult.

**15.104**
*RO Act 1974 s.4* The Rehabilitation of Offenders Act 1974 provides that if those convicted of certain crimes do not commit further offences during a specified period, they become 'rehabilitated'. Their convictions become 'spent'. There is no need for a person to disclose to an

employer any 'spent' convictions, and a failure to do so is not a proper ground for dismissing.

**15.105**

*RO Act 1974*
*RO Act 1974 (Exemption)*
*Order 1975*
*RO Act 1974 (Exemption)*
*(Amendment) Order 1986*

There are exceptions. Lawyers, medical persons, persons connected with the courts, constables, probation officers, some teachers and some employments which are concerned with social services are outside its scope. It has now been extended to cover persons seeking work concerned with the provision of accommodation, and dealing with the care, the leisure and recreational facilities, schooling and training of persons under 18 years.

## DEATH OF EMPLOYEE OR EMPLOYER

**15.106**

*EP(C) Act 1978*
*sch.12 para.2*

Where a worker or an employer (who is in business on his own account) dies before or after proceedings have been started in the tribunal for any rights or obligations, arising out of any of the statutory provisions, then the personal representatives may institute or continue the action, or defend it.

**15.107**

*EP(C) Act 1978*
*sch.12 para.3*

If no personal representative for the deceased employee has been appointed, then the tribunal may allow someone to take his place, whether the action has commenced or not. That person may be anybody who is already acting for him in the proceedings, or, it may be the widow(er), a child, parent, or brother or sister.

**15.108**

*EP(C) Act 1978*
*sch.12 para.4*

The same rights and obligations fall on the personal representative or the person appointed by the tribunal as they would have upon the deceased. There must be compliance with time limits (see paras. 3.74–90), and where there is no discretion to extend time, as for instance in an application for particulars of employment (see para. 9.55), or for a claim for a redundancy payment beyond 12 months (see paras. 4.50–51), then a default by the personal representative – who may be wholly unaware of the position, and whatever the merits – will bring about a cessation of the action.

**15.109**

*EP(C) Act 1978*
*sch.12 paras. 5 & 6*

An employer's personal representative will be liable to discharge (out of the estate of the deceased) any liability that had not accrued at the date of his death, but arose before the date of the termination of employment. Thus, if an employee has been employed for one week short of two years at the time of the employer's death, (which brings about the termination of employment), and so is entitled to a week's notice (see para. 3.10) he will be entitled to redundancy pay.

**15.110**

EP(C) Act 1978
sch.12 para.7
EP(C) Act 1978
(as amended by
E Act 1982
sch.3 para.28)
sch.12 para.9

Where an employee has been given notice of dismissal but before it takes effect either he or the employer dies, then the provisions relating to unfair dismissal (see Chapter 5) apply as if the notice expired at the date of death. However, when computing the period of continuous employment, or calculating a 'basic award' (see para. 5.159(a)), the 'deeming' provisions apply (as explained in para. 3.71).

**15.111**

EP(C) Act 1978
sch.12 para.11

Where, before the death, there have been proceedings in the tribunal resulting in a finding of unfair dismissal, and the employer was ordered to reinstate or re-engage the employee, but refused to do so and was unable to show that it was not practical at the time of the refusal to comply (see paras. 5.147–156), then the employee will be entitled to an 'Additional Award' (see para. 5.159(c)). If he shows that it was not practical to comply then the ordinary rules regarding compensation apply (see para. 5.159(b)).

**15.112**

EP(c) Act 1978
sch.12
paras.14–16

Where an employer dies and the contract of employment is brought to an end, but his personal representative renews the contract not later than 8 weeks after the death, then the employee is not entitled to leave and claim redundancy pay. But where the employer has given notice terminating an employee's contract, but before it expires, he (the employer) dies, then the ordinary provisions in regard to an entitlement to redundancy pay apply (see Chapter 4). The date of termination becomes the date of death unless the deeming provisions apply (see paras. 3.9–13).

## TRADE UNION RECOGNITION

**15.113**

EP Act 1975 (as amended
by E Act 1980 sch.1 para.6)
s.126(1)
EP Act 1975 s.99(1) & (2)
EP(C) Act 1975 (as
amended by
E Act 1980, sch.1 para.9 &
sch.2) s.32(1) & (2)

If an employer recognises an independent trade union (see para. 1.106) to any extent, for the purpose of collective bargaining, then that union acquires certain rights, like the right to be consulted on redundancy dismissals (see para. 4.53), for member of its union to be allowed time off for certain specified duties and in certain other areas (see paras. 15.12 & 15.34).

**15.114**

*TULR Act 1974 (as amended by E Act 1982 s.18(2)(a),(b) & (c)) s.29(1)*

Collective bargaining means negotiations relating to or connected with one or more of the matters specified in paras. 7.24 (a)-(g). The agreement to recognise a union does not have to be in writing or formally agreed.

**15.115**

*NUGSAT v. Albury Brothers Ltd. [1978] ICR 62 EAT (affirmed on appeal [1979] ICR 86, CA)*

It is a question of fact and degree whether there is 'recognition'. It requires "mutuality, that is to say, that the employer acknowledges the role of union" which "may be . . . express or implied". The course of conduct must be "clear and unequivocal . . . over a period", and "there may be partial recognition, that is recognition in certain respects but not in others."

**15.116**

Mere discussion with a union over matters specified in paras. 7.24 (a)-(g) is not sufficientl it must be established that an employer is willing to negotiate with a view to reaching an agreement in *one* of those areas.

**15.117**

*Peart & Co. Ltd. v. TASS Craft Section Dec. 16, 1988, EAT (unreported)*

An employer was member of a trade association. The latter had effected agreements with a trade union relating to the terms and conditions for those working in the trade. The employer used it as a basis of an agreement with his own work-force. It was held that that alone was sufficient to establish 'recognition'.

**15.118**

*Cleveland C.C. v. Springett & Ors. [1985] IRLR 131, EAT*

Recognition cannot be imposed on an employer by a third party or by an extraneous event where it is against his will. Only the acts of the employer are relevant for the purposes of deciding whether he has (whether intentionally or not) recognised a union.

**15.119**

There is now no statutory procedure by which a union can complain that an employer has failed to 'recognise' it, nor any remedy where an employer has withdrawn recognition from a union.

## TRANSFER OF AN UNDERTAKING

**15.120**

*TU (P of E) Reg. 1981 reg. 10*

There is an obligation on an employer (i) to inform a recognised union about any employees who might be affected by a proposed transfer of a business, and (ii) provide the following information in sufficient time to enable consultations to take place:

(a) the date and reasons for the transfer;

(b) the implications for affected employees;

(c) any measures it is envisaged will take place in respect of any employees; and

(c) if the transferee is proposing to carry out any measures then he must inform the seller of them in good time to enable the information to be passed over.

**15.121**
*TU (P of E) Reg. 1981 reg. 10*
The defence of 'not reasonably practical' is available. If there is a breach, then 'appropriate compensation' of up to a maximum of two weeks' pay must be awarded to the affected employees.

## PAYMENT OF WAGES BY CHEQUE/CREDIT TRANSFER

**15.122**
*W Act 1986 s.11*
The Wages Act 1986 entitles employers to pay their workmen by means other than cash. They may now pay by cheque or credit transfer, but the actual method of payment will be a matter of negotiation.

**15.123**
If the employer is insistent upon making payment by cheque then it would seem that the employee cannot refuse to accept it. There must be means by which it can be cashed reasonably easily. An employer might make it a term of the contract with all new employees that wages would be made by credit transfer. Perhaps he might offer existing employees a once-and-for-all sum to accept their wages in future by a non cash means.

## DEDUCTIONS FROM WAGES

**15.124**
An employer is entitled to make a deduction from the wages of his employee where:

*W Act 1986 s.1*

(a) it is authorised by statute (e.g., tax, national insurance contributions, an attachment of earnings order etc.);

(b) it is deducted pursuant to a contract made in writing by the employee with the employer before any deduction;

(c) it is a sum that the employee has agreed in writing to repay (e.g., a loan from the employer);

(d) it arises from an over-payment of wages or expenses;

(e) payment is to be made to a third party pursuant to written instructions given by the employee (for instance, to his union);

(f) deductions are made because the employee has taken part in a strike or other industrial action.

**15.125**

*W Act 1986 s.7*

Wages cover all emoluments, however classified. They include fees, bonuses, holiday pay, commissions, but not advances, loans, expenses, pensions or redundancy payments or any other payments made other than in the employee's capacity as a worker.

**15.126**

*Smith & ors. v. London Borough of Bromley, Apr. 5, 1991, Cty.Ct. (unreported)*

Where deductions are made for absences on strike, the correct way of assessing the amount is to approach it on a breach of contract basis. For how many days' work annually were the employers paying their employee his salary? If he was contracted to work 200 days p.a., and was on strike for 10 days, then the appropriate reduction would be 1/20th. of his annual salary.

**15.127**

*W Act 1986 s.8*

An independent contractor who is performing acts of personal service is also protected by the Act. An employer may only make deductions from his gross paywhere he has agreed in advance to this in writing.

**15.128**

*Delaney v. Staples (t/a De Montfort Recruitment) [1991] ICR 331, CA*

If an employer fails to pay a sum that is due, then that would be deemed to be a 'deduction' and recoverable under the Wages Act 1986. To escape liability the employer would have to prove that the non-payment was as a result of a matter set out in para. 15.124 above.

**15.129**

*Home Office v. Ayres The Times, Oct. 22, 1991, EAT County Council of Avon v. Howlett [1983] IRLR 171, CA*

A person may seek recovery of a deduction made in respect of an over-payment (which can normally be deducted from wages). This may occur where the employer had made an over-payment under:

(a) a mistake of law, or

(b) a mistake of fact, *provided* the recipient was led to believe the money was his and he has changed his position to the worse, e.g., he has spent it: additionally he must not be at fault;

because the employer cannot *lawfully* recover the over-payment.

**15.130**

Often the employer, in failing to pay a sum due, will be in breach of contract as well. The employee can sue him for damages in the ordinary civil courts (see paras. 1.55–58).

**15.131**    Only the industrial tribunal has jurisdiction to entertain a claim under the Wages Act 1986. Where it finds a complaint well founded it will make a declaration to that effect and order the repayment of the unlawful deduction. There is *no* limit to the amount. Claims for non payment of commission can be very high on occasions.

**15.132**    A complaint to the tribunal must be made within three months of the deduction complained about or where it consists of a series, then the last of them, or if that is not reasonably practical, then within a reasonable period thereafter (see paras. 3.79–90).

**15.133**    The tribunal has no power to deal with claims for money in lieu of notice. Strictly speaking this is a claim for damages arising out of a breach of contract and the Wages Act 1986 does not deem it to be a 'deduction'. It has to be recovered in the County Court (but see para. 1.11).

**15.134**

*Delaney v. Staples (t/a De Montfort Recruitment) [1991] ICR 331, CA*

The wording of the Act can cause a curious result. If a tribunal has ruled that an employer has *unlawfully* made an deduction of a loan made to an employee because hedoes not have authorization *in writing* to do so, then, the employer will not only be obliged to pay it back but he will also be debarred from recovering the deducted amount in any other proceedings in the civil courts. It effectively becomes a gift.

**15.135**

*E. Act 1988 s.7*

If an employee has certified to his employer that he has resigned from membership of a union, the employer must cease making deductions from his wages as from the date of notification. If it is not reasonably practical for the employer to modify his pay-roll in time, then liability would be avoided. A breach by the employer results in a deemed contravention of the Wages Act, entitling the employee to apply to the tribunal for reimbursement of the amount.

## CASH SHORTAGES AND STOCK DEFICIENCIES

**15.136**

*W Act 1986 s.2*

The right to recover cash shortages and stock deficiencies is restricted to workers in *retail* employment. This is defined as relating to those involved in the sale and supply of goods or services. It need not be the employee's regular or main employment, e.g., a fitter in a garage might help out to sell petrol.

**15.137**   There is no statutory restriction on making deductions from a worker in the retail field:

W Act 1986
ss.3 & 4

(a) where he has agreed to it in writing in advance; and

(b) before it is done, a demand in writing for the payment of a sum due must have been made by handing him a letter personally or sending it to his last known address; and

(c) any deduction must *not* be more than 10% of the wages made on one pay day, except on the last one before he leaves the employment; and

(d) it must be made within 12 months of the detection of the shortage or deficiency.

**15.138**   If the total amount exceeds the 10% ceiling, then the deductions may be spread over subsequent pay days until fully recovered. If there is still a sum outstanding after the termination of the employment, then the employer can recover the balance by taking proceedings in the county court.

### Complaints to Tribunals

**15.139**   Where an employer has made an unauthorised deduction, any employee may apply to the tribunal for reimbursement. He must do so within three months of the date of the allegation or if there are a series, then the last date on which it occurred. The time limit may be extended where it was not reasonably practical to make the complaint in time and it was done as soon as reasonable thereafter (see paras. 3.78–86).

W Act 1986 s.5

**15.140**   Where a complaint is *also* made under the 'itemised pay statement' provisions (see paras. 15.47–50) the aggregate of an award from the tribunal cannot exceed the amount of any particular deduction.

# CHAPTER SIXTEEN

# Health and safety at work

## GENERAL INFORMATION

**16.1**
*HSW Act 1974 ss.2 & 3*
The Health & Safety at Work etc., Act, 1974 provides that it is the duty of every employer to ensure, so far as is 'reasonably practical' (see paras. 16.19–20), the health and safety at work of all his employees. This same duty extends other persons who are on his premises or who may be affected by his operations.

**16.2**
At the present moment, there are extensive obligations imposed on an employer. They are found in many statutes: Factories Act 1961, Offices, Shops and Railway Premises Act 1963, Agriculture (Safety, Health and Welfare Provisions) Act 1956, Mines and Quarries Act 1954 and others, together with a mass of statutory instruments.

**16.3**
*HSW Act 1974 s.1*
Under this 1974 Act, it was intended that a new system of regulations and codes of practice (see para. 3.153) should be made and they would progressively replace all other Acts. This has not come to fruition. It was also proposed that the standards laid down by the existing legislation will be maintained or improved and that there should be a unified inspectorate.

**16.4**
The Act also established a Health and Safety Commission together with a Health and Safety Executive. The former is charged with the duty of monitoring matters relating to health and safety, and the latter has to exercise functions delegated to it.

**16.5**
*Cleveland C.C. v. Springett & Ors. [1985] IRLR 131, EAT SRSC Reg. 1977*
Powers are conferred on the Secretary of State to pass regulations providing for Safety Representatives to be appointed by *recognised* trade unions (see paras. 15.113–119) at places of work, to ensure the health and safety of employees at places of work.

### Code of Practice

**16.6**
A Code of Practice gives guidance on what information should be disclosed by employers. They include those relating to proposed changes that affect health and

safety, technical information about hazards, consultants reports, manufacturers' instructions, records of accidents, dangerous occurrences, notifiable industrial diseases and results of routine tests.

## AN INSPECTION

**16.7** Inspectors, who are very often local authority environmental health officers, are appointed to carry out the duties specified in the various Acts. They visit premises from time to time to check that there is compliance with the Acts. Sometimes they attend as a result of complaints made to them, or because of an accident.

**16.8** If upon an inspection, the inspector finds that there has been a contravention of the Act, he can take any one of the following courses.

*HSW Act 1974*

(a) He can give the employer an oral run-down of what is defective and tell him to put it right, and then later ensure that it has been done. For instance, if a thermometer is broken, then that could be replaced almost immediately.

(b) He could serve an Improvement Notice under s.21 or a Prohibition Notice under s.22.

(c) He can take proceedings in the Magistrates' Court under s.33 and allege that the employer has committed an offence.

**16.9** The last mentioned course (c) will not generally be taken unless the matter is very serious and obvious. If there is no fencing on a guillotine machine, or where an employer has been flouting the law for over a period, then they may face penal proceedings.

## AN IMPROVEMENT NOTICE

**16.10** An Improvement Notice is a document which states
*HSW Act 1974 s.21* that in the opinion of the inspector the employer is contravening one or more of the relevant Acts (see paras. 16.1–2), or has done so and it is likely that it will continue or be repeated. He must give his reasons, and require the employer to remedy the contravention

within a period of not less than 21 days or such further period as he specifies.

**16.11** The notice may be withdrawn by an inspector at any time before the end of the period specified. The period may be extended more than once, provided no appeal against it has been lodged.

**16.12**
*HSW Act 1974 s.24*
*IT (IPNA) Reg. 1974*
*reg. 2(1) & (2)*

An employer can appeal to a tribunal on the grounds that it is not 'reasonably practical' (see paras. 16.19–20) to comply with the notice. He must do so within 21 days of the service of the notice on him, or within such further period as is reasonable in the circumstances (see paras. 3.79–90).

**16.13**
*HSW Act, 1974*
*ss.23(5) &*
*24(3)(a)*

The lodging of an appeal has the effect of suspending the operation of the notice until the appeal is disposed of finally. It may be by way of a hearing or a withdrawal of the appeal.

## A PROHIBITION NOTICE

**16.14**
*HSW Act 1974 s.22*

Where an employer is carrying on any activities, which in the opinion of the inspector involve, or will involve, the risk of serious personal injury, the inspector may serve on him a Prohibition Notice.

**16.15** That notice has to state that the inspector is of that opinion, specifying the matters giving rise to that risk, and identifying the relevant statutory provisions that are or would be contravened.

**16.16** It will also state that the activities must cease within the time specified in the notice and until the matters specified in the notice have been remedied. Where the inspector states in the notice that he believes that the risk to serious personal injury is *imminent*, then the activities must cease immediately.

**16.17** Where the notice does not take immediate effect, the inspector may withdraw it at any time before the period specified. He may extend, or further extend the period provided no appeal has been lodged.

**16.18**
*HSW Act 1974 s.24(3)(b)*

An appeal to the tribunal may be made on the same grounds as are set out in para. 16.12, but the lodging of an appeal does not automatically suspend the operation of the notice. A separate application to do so has to be made to the tribunal.

## DEFENCE OF NOT 'REASONABLY PRACTICAL'

**16.19** In deciding whether it is 'reasonably practical' to comply it is necessary that:

*Edwards v. National Coal Board*
*[1949] 1 KB 704, CA*

"a computation must be made by the owner, in which the quantum of risk is placed on one scale and the sacrifice involved in the measure necessary for averting the risk (whether in money, time or trouble) is placed on the other: and that if it be shown that there is a gross disproportion between them – the risk being insignificant in relation to the sacrifice – the [employers] discharge the onus on them" (per Asquith, L.J.).

**16.20** Thus, an employer would have to show that the risks were small compared to the cost of carrying out the remedial work. For instance, an inspector might serve a notice on an employer requiring him to put in some proper banisters. Because of the difficult position they might cost £10,000. If evidence adduced showed that the stairs were practically never used and the risk of injury was small, then it would be likely that a tribunal would cancel the Notice.

*West Bromwich Building Society v. Townsend*
*[1983] ICR 257, DC*

## PROCEDURE ON APPEAL

**16.21** The manner in which proceedings are conducted is dealt with at paras. 18.1–108. The onus will lie on the employer (see paras. 2.14–19), to show that it is not 'reasonably practical' to comply with the order.

**16.22** The tribunal may either cancel or affirm the notice. If it decides to affirm it, then it may make any modifications it thinks fit.

*HSW Act 1974 s.24(2)*

## COSTS

**16.23** The tribunal has power to award costs against the loser. It will only generally exercise this power against the inspector where it is shown that the notice should never have been issued on the material known at the time.

*IT (IPNA) Reg. 1974 reg. 13(1)*

**16.24**   It is likely to make an order against an employer where he brings an appeal that is lacking merit or is otherwise hopeless.

## PROCEEDINGS IN THE MAGISTRATES' COURT

**16.25**

*HSW Act 1974 s.33(1)*

If proceedings are taken against an employer in the Magistrates' Court on the grounds that he has failed to comply with a notice, or with a notice that has been modified on appeal by the tribunal, then he cannot raise the defence of not 'reasonably practical' (see paras. 16.19–20). It does not matter that there are valid grounds for resisting the allegation.

**16.26**

*Dearey v. Mansion Hide Upholstery Ltd.*
*[1983]*
*ICR 610, DC*

If a notice is served on him, he must either appeal to the tribunal, and avail himself of the defence, or comply: the offence lies in his failing to comply.

**16.27**

*HSW Act 1974 s.40*

If proceedings are brought against him in a Magistrates' Court for a breach of an Act, then the defence of not 'reasonably practical' is available, but the employer must prove it, on a balance of probabilities (paras. 2.14–19).

## APPEAL TO HIGH COURT

**16.28**   An appeal from the tribunal or from the magistrates court lies to the divisional court of the High Court (see paras. 19.36–37). Its powers are very similar to the Employment Appeal Tribunal (see paras. 19.1–22).

# CHAPTER SEVENTEEN

# Levies

## GENERAL INFORMATION

**17.1** In order to make better provision for the training of persons for employment in industry or commerce, the Secretary of State is empowered under the Industrial Training Act, 1982 (which replaced the Industrial Training Act, 1964) to establish Training Boards. Since 1964, many Boards have been set up. He can wind up Boards as well.

**17.2** The Boards are charged with the duty of encouraging adequate training of those employed or seeking employment in industry or commerce by the provision of courses, arranging research, publishing recommendations and certain other functions.

**17.3** It may make payments to those who avail themselves of the facilities, either by paying the costs or loss of income and so forth. The funds for carrying out its duties are derived from levies, which are imposed on employers in the industries concerned.

## LEVY ORDERS

**17.4** A Board puts forward proposals for the raising and collecting a levy to the Manpower Services Commission, who, if they approve of them, submit them to the Secretary of State. The proposals have to include several matters.

**17.5** If the Secretary of State is satisfied that the proposals are necessary to encourage adequate training, then he may make an order for a levy to be raised. Since 1964, levy orders have been made for each industry and in respect of different periods.

**17.6** An employer in the industry concerned at the material time is liable for the levy. The Act defines an 'employees' as including:

*IT Act 1982 ss.1(1) & (7) & 12(6)*

"a person engaged under a contract for services, and 'employer' shall be construed accordingly";

and 'employment' as:

> "employment under a contract of service or apprenticeship or a contract for services or otherwise than under a contract, and 'employed' shall be construed accordingly."

**17.7** Thus person who uses sub-contractors (apart of any of his own staff) is caught by the provision.

**17.8** The statutory orders made by the Secretary of State set out the formula to be used to determine the extent of the liability. Thus in the Industrial Training (Construction Board) Order, 1982, liability (with exceptions) to pay the levy is assessed on the basis of employment at the relevant time at a 'construction establishment'. This is defined as:

*Art 2*

> ". . . an establishment in Great Britain engaged wholly or mainly in the construction industry for a total of 27 or more weeks in the period of twelve months that commenced on 6th April 1981 . . ."

**17.9** This means that if the turnover in terms of manpower or turnover in a business that is partly concerned with the construction industry (which, again, is given a very wide definition) is greater than the rest, then the employer will be liable to pay the levy. A shop, selling flooring materials using outside contractors to lay them, that earns more from that activity than from the retailing side, or it has more persons engaged on that activity than retailing, will be liable.

## DUTIES OF BOARDS

**17.10**
*IT Act 1982 s.6*
Each Board is charged with the duty of maintaining a list of 'employers' in the industry. For this purpose, they are empowered to require an 'employer' in the industry to provide information about themselves, which is usually done by means of a questionnaire.

**17.11**
*IT Act 1982 s.11*
If it is found that the 'employer' comes within the statutory definition, then he will be required to supply full details of his financial and man-power position. His liability can then be assessed. A 'Levy Assessment Notice' is served on the employer who is obliged to pay unless he appeals.

## HOW THE LEVY IS ASSESSED

**17.12**  The statutory orders set out the formula for assessingthe levy; and it varies for each industry. The extent of the liability is based on a head count with a higher rate for more skilled employees.

**17.13**  Thus, in the Construction Industry Order (see para. 17.8), under the formula (which is not easy to understand) the amount to be levied:

"shall be the aggregate . . . by which [(a)] 2 per cent of labour-only payments exceeds [(b)] 2 per cent labour-only receipts and the amount of [(c)] the occupational levy".

(a) 'Labour-only payment' relates to payments made to sub-contractors.

(b) 'Labour-only receipts' means payments received from other employers in the industry.

(c) 'The occupational levy' is the sum produced by multiplying the amount specified in the Appendix to the Order by the average number of employees less the amount by which 2 per cent of labour-only payments, subject to a ceiling of 1 per cent of payments made to persons in the industry in the 12 months from April 6, 1981.

**17.14**  The amount specified in the Appendix varies from nil for most trainees to £85 for a mechanical engineering craftsman. Persons in managerial or administrative positions are rated at £39, and specialist building operatives (which includes floor-layers) at £45.

**17.15**  In practical terms, this would mean, in the example given in para. 17.9, that if the shop-keeper had one full time employee in the shop but he spent some of his time on the carpet fitting side of the business and he paid the two sub-contractors a total of £20,000 a year, his liability would be £400 for them, and £39 for himself.

## APPEALS TO TRIBUNALS

**17.16**  An appeal lies to the tribunal. Each levy order prescribes the time within which it must be made. For instance, the current Construction Order (see para. 17.8) provides it must be within one month from the

*IT Act 1982 s.12(4)*

date of the assessment notice 'or within any further period . . . that may be allowed by the Board or an industrial tribunal'. The discretion to extend time is much less rigorous than under the employment legislation (see paras. 3.79–90). The tribunal will look at the reason for the delay and probably at the merits of the case.

**17.17**   On an appeal, the tribunal has power to:

*IT Act 1982 s.12(5)*

(a) rescind the levy assessment,
(b) reduce the amount,
(c) confirm it,
(d) increase the amount.

**17.18**   If an employer decides to appeal, then he must set out his grounds in his notice of appeal.

## PROCEDURE ON APPEAL

**17.19**   The manner in which proceedings are conducted in the tribunal is dealt with at paras. 18.1–108. It is very important that as much evidence is presented by way of documentation. The onus lies on the employer to prove (see paras. 2.14–19) that the Board have made a mistake. Documents will speak for themselves whereas evidence given by a witness may or may not be believed.

**17.20**   The evidence should be directed to the point in dispute, e.g., that more of the man-power is spent on the retailing side than construction work, or whatever the complaint is about. The argument generally tends to be over whether various staff come within different definitions.

## COSTS

**17.21**   The tribunal has power to award costs against the loser of an appeal. It will only generally do so against the Board if it can be shown that they are wholly at fault. This might arise where they should never have made a levy assessment notice, or the amount they sought to impose was wholly wrong on the information that had been supplied to them.

*IT (E&W) Reg. 1965 (as amended by IT (E&W) (Amendment) Reg. 1967)*

**17.22**   An order may be made against an employer if it is shown that there is no merit in the appeal. Before one is made the Board must attend the hearing and seek an order. Very often they make written representations only (see para. 18.72).

## APPEALS TO HIGH COURT

**17.23** Appeals lie to the Divisional Court of the High Court from the Tribunal (see para. 19.36).

# CHAPTER EIGHTEEN

# Tribunals and Courts in action

## TRIBUNALS – GENERAL INFORMATION

**18.1** Tribunals, of which about 60 sit each day in various parts of the country, are independent courts presided over by a legally qualified Chairman. Two lay members sit with him (or her). The former are specialists in the field of industrial relations, one being drawn from the employer's side of the industry and the other from the unions'.

**18.2**

*University of Swansea v. Cornelius [1988] ICR 735, EAT*

The Members (and Chairman) must have no connection with the case before them. This includes knowing any witnesses or being related to them or having a financial interest in a firm that is before the tribunal.

**18.3**

*Reg. v. Mulvihill The Times, July 13, 1989, CA*

If he/she does, then it must be disclosed. Failure to do so will result in the findings of the Tribunal being set aside and a retrial ordered. It matters not that there was no bias by the individual: justice must *seem* to be done.

**18.4**

*IT (E&W) Reg. 1965 (as amended by IT (E&W) (Amendment) Reg. 1867 reg.4(1)) reg. 5(1)*

There is power, with the consent of both parties, for the tribunal to adjudicate with the Chairman and one member only sitting. This might arise if one of the two members were to become ill shortly before a case was scheduled to commence.

**18.5**

*IT (R of P) Reg. 1985 rule 9(1)*

When all three are sitting, the majority view prevails but, where there are two, the Chairman has a casting vote in the event of a disagreement. Surprisingly, there is unanimity in about 96 per cent of cases. This shows the degree of objectivity applied in this sensitive area.

**18.6** The intention is that the proceedings should be as informal as possible. All the parties should feel at ease. Tribunals do follow, in substance, the ordinary procedure applicable in the courts in the presentation of evidence.

**18.7**

*Murphy v. Epsom College [1985] ICR 80 CA*

Parties are not expected to know the law (although they may do so). It is up to the Chairman to fit the facts (as they are found by the tribunal) into the law. For instance, a party may think that he is entitled to compensation for unfair dismissal, whereas, in law, he is entitled to a redundancy payment.

**18.8**     If one side is not represented and does not appear to be able to present their case properly, then the Chairman will generally ask many questions. It is the duty of the tribunal to find out all the relevant facts and seek, if possible, the truth. Members generally ask questions as well, although it is usually done at the end of the evidence of a witness.

**18.9**     There is no duty on Chairmen to raise points on behalf of a party, especially where represented albeit incompetently, although in practice they generally do. It is up to each side to ensure that they are aware of any technicalities that might be fatal or do serious damage to their cases (see paras. 1.56).

*Dimtsu v. Westminster City Council [1991] IRLR 50, EAT*

## COMMENCEMENT OF A CASE

**18.10**     A case starts off with an 'applicant', generally an employee but it can be others, e.g., a union, or, a firm (but called an 'appellant') appealing against a levy order, filing an Originating Application. This is done at the Central Office of the Industrial Tribunal, now at Bury St. Edmunds, although it can be received at Ebury Bridge Road, London.

*IT (R of P) Reg. 1985 rule 1*

**18.11**     In order to be valid the Originating Application *must* identify

*IT (R of P) Regs. 1985, rule 1*
*Dodd v. British Telecommunications plc [1988] ICR 116, EAT*

(a) the applicant,
(b) the employer (or the person or body against whom the proceedings are being brought), and
(c) give an outline of the nature of the claim or the relief sought.

**18.12**     When it is received at the tribunal, it is said to be 'presented'. The time limits no longer runs against an applicant. An application can be made by letter but it is better to complete an Originating Application form. The latter sets out all the questions that have to be answered. A copy of the document is obtainable at unemployment offices, or Citizens' Advice Bureaux.

**18.13**     The employer (called 'the respondent') receives a copy of the Originating Application and a blank Notice of

*IT (R of P) Reg. 1985*

*rule 3* Appearance. He sets out his defence in the latter and returns it to the tribunal. When received he is on the record and may take part in the proceedings.

**18.14** There is no obligation to set down in detail the nature of the case. Nevertheless, if a party is relying on one-substantial ground in his Originating Application or Notice of Appearance, then he is unlikely to be allowed to change it during a hearing if in reality he relies on another ground.

**18.15**

*Hotson v. Wiesbech Conservative Club [1984] IRLR 422, EAT Nelson v. BBC [1977] ITR 273, CA*

An employer sought to resist an allegation of unfair dismissal on the grounds that the employee was sacked for 'inefficiency'. They were debarred from alleging in the course of the hearing that the true reason was suspected dishonesty. So too where an employer relied on redundancy as his defence. At an appeal hearing he wished to change it to other grounds, but was not permitted to do so.

**18.16**

*Leffen v. Bexley London B.C. The Times, Nov. 14, 1985, EAT*

An employee alleged in her Originating Application that her employer refused to allow her to go back to work after maternity leave. She sought an order that she should be allowed to do so under her contract of employment. It was held that her 'pleadings' should be widely construed and so include, by inference, a claim for unfair dismissal.

**18.17**

*William Muir (Bond 9) Ltd v. Wood Aug. 21, 1986, EAT (unreported) Smith v. City of Glasgow D.C. [1987] ICR 796, HL*

Where an employer 'pleads' one ground, e.g., capability, and brings evidence in support of it, but the tribunal decides that it should truly be described as conduct, he will not be debarred from a finding that the dismissal was fair despite his failure to put the correct label on it. But where he relies on an important matter to dismiss but fails to prove it, then the dismissal is likely to be unfair.

**18.18**

*Bradford City Metropolitan Council v. Arora [1989] IRLR 442, EAT (but overturned on another point [1991] ICR 226, CA)*

If an important point is to be taken in a case, then there *must* be some reference to it in the pleadings. Otherwise, except in the case of jurisdiction (see para. 18.51), it cannot be dealt with by the tribunal. A tribunal has power to enable a party to add the matter to his Originating Application or Notice of Appearance where this is appropriate.

**18.19** An application to amend the Originating Application or Notice of Appearance can always be made during the course of the proceedings to enable the tribunal to adjudicate on the point. This will generally be granted subject to the other side not being prejudiced.

**18.20**

*Interpretation Act, 1978*
*s.15*

Any Notice, or other document or letter posted to the address specified by the parties in the Originating Application or Notice of Appearance (or to any notified change of address) is deemed, without further proof, to have been properly served upon that party. If he disputes that he has received it, then the onus of disproving receipt will be on him. It is important to keep the tribunal informed of any changes of address.

## 'FURTHER PARTICULARS'

**18.21**

*International Computers*
*Ltd.*
*v. Whitley*
*[1978] IRLR 318, EAT*

Each side will then be able to see the nature of the other's case in the pleadings. One side may want to know more about the allegations made against him, and he is entitled to ask for 'Further Particulars'. What is the exact nature of the incompetence alleged? Whether it is alleged that the discrimination is *direct* or *indirect*? The tribunal may ask for particulars to clarify the issues or assist in some other way.

**18.22**

*Byrne & ors. v. The*
*Financial Times Ltd.*
*[1991] IRLR 417, EAT*

What a party cannot do is to use the procedure to try to find out the evidence to be adduced by the other side or the names of their witnesses. It is only available to do justice in a case, by identifying matters in issue, i.e., to know the case that has to be met.

**18.23**

*P & O European Ferries*
*(Dover) Ltd. v. Byrne*
*[1989] IRLR 245, CA*

A dismissed employee who had been taking part in industrial action claimed that another person, who had also been participating in it, had not been sacked. If this was correct the tribunal had power to adjudicate (see para. 5.6 (e)). It was held that the former employers were entitled to know the *identity* of that person so as to be able to meet the case against them. It mattered not that the provision of the information would enable them to dismiss that employee and thereby defeat the claim.

**18.24**

If a party refuses or fails to supply particulars voluntarily then provided they:

(a) are relevant,
(b) are not oppressive, and
(c) will help in fairly disposing of the case or in the saving of costs

the tribunal will order them to be given. But complicated pleading battles are discouraged by the tribunals. The line can sometimes be a fine one.

**18.25**

*IT (R of P) Reg. 1985*
*rule 4(1)(b)(i)*

If a party refuses or fails to comply with an order, then an applicant's Originating Application will be struck out. If it is the respondent who is in default, then his Notice of Appearance will be struck out and he will be debarred from defending, or the (relevant) part of it will be struck out. In both cases they must be given the opportunity of showing cause why an order should not be made. When an order against the respondent has been made the applicant is not entitled to an automatic judgment in his favour. He still has to prove his case before the tribunal.

## DISCOVERY AND INSPECTION OF DOCUMENTS

**18.26**

*IT (R of P) Reg. 1985*
*rule 4(1)(b)(ii)*
*West Midlands Passenger*
*Transport Executive v.*
*Singh*
*[1988] ICR 614, CA*

There is power vested in the tribunals to order Discovery and Inspection of Documents where this is necessary for 'fairly disposing of the proceedings or for saving costs'. An order must not be oppressive in the sense of being too demanding financially or physically.

**18.27**

*Leyland Cars (B.L. Cars)*
*Ltd. v. Vyas*
*[1979] ICR 921, HL*

In certain instances, a document may be highly confidential and the employers might wish that no-one should see it. Before a case comes on for hearing, it will have to be shown to the Chairman, who having seen it, will decide whether it should be disclosed. If it must, then he will rule on whether any parts of it should be covered up.

**18.28**

*The Captain Gregos*
*The Times, Dec. 22,*
*1990, EAT*
*Rowley v. Liverpool*
*City Council*
*Oct. 24, 1989, CA*
*(unreported)*

The test of whether a document should be disclosed is not its probative value, but whether it might be expected to lead to a line of enquiry that would be of assistance to a party. The information sought can relate to details of other employees that would normally be protected from disclosure by the Data Protection Act, 1984. That can be over-ridden by a Court or Tribunal Order.

**18.29**

*West Midlands PTE v.*
*Singh*
*[1988] ICR 614, CA*
*Carrington v. Helix*
*Lighting Ltd.*
*[1990] ICR 125, EAT*
*Demmel v. YKK Fasteners*
*(UK) Ltd*
*March 17, 1987, EAT*
*(unreported)*

An order can be sought for the production of relevant statistics, but *only* where they exist or the information is available and does not involve great difficulty or expense in producing the data. Thus, they were ordered where they showed the relative success rates of white and black applicants for a senior post. They were 'logically probative' on the issue of discrimination. But where written statements had been obtained from fellow employees on the pledge of confidentiality, an order to disclose them was not made.

**18.30**

*Leverton v. Clywd C.C. [1989] ICR 33, HL*

A party may not use the procedure as a 'fishing expedition' to find evidence upon which to mount a case. But he may seek an order to improve a *prima facie* case that, on its own, may not be very strong.

**18.31**

*Birds Eye Walls Ltd. v. Harrison [1985] ICR 278, EAT*

There is no general obligation on a party to disclose what relevant documents they have in their possession. If they produced some, there is a duty not to withhold others that might mislead the other side to misconstrue the effect of those disclosed.

**18.32**

Not all documents have to be produced for inspection. Some may be 'privileged', that is to say, they form part of a special type of document that have come into existence for the purpose of litigation. Examples are briefs to counsel, opinions from counsel, solicitor's letters to their clients, and matters of that kind. Such documents do have to be disclosed though so that the other side can in appropriate cases dispute whether privilege should be attached to them.

**18.33**

*Sharples v. Halford & ors. The Times, Oct. 9, 1991, EAT*

Other documents belonging to public bodies such as a Police Authority are subject to 'public interest immunity'. However, a Chairman has power to order disclosure after inspection of them by him. He has to balance the public interest in non-disclosure against that of justice to the other party and the importance of any document to the issue to be decided.

## APPLICATIONS TO AMEND

**18.34**

*British Newspapers Printing Corporation (North) Ltd. v. Kelly & ors. [1989] IRLR 222, CA*

Where a claim is made on one ground, but after the close of pleadings and when all the documents have been inspected, it is thought that the claim would be better placed on another basis, an application to add the additional ground should be made to the tribunal. If the time for preferring that other allegation is outside the time limits (see paras. 3.74–88), the Tribunal has discretion to allow the amendment having

*Clocking v. Sandhurst Ltd. [1974] ICR 650, NIRC*

"regard to all the circumstances of the case. In particular, they should consider any injustice or hardship which may be caused to any of the parties . . ."

## IMPORTANCE OF DOCUMENTS

**18.35** If a party is going to use documents at the tribunal hearing, he ought to supply copies to the other side well before the hearing. Failure may result in the other side asking for an adjournment to study them, especially if they are bulky or complicated. An order that the costs thrown away may be made against him (see para. 18.96). Remember that documents are usually the *most important part* of any case. Often they are self-explanatory and usually provide very compelling evidence.

**18.36** If an employer has given evidence that he had received many complaints from customers about the workmanship of goods made by the 'applicant', his former employee, then whether allegation is accepted as a fact will depend upon whether the tribunal believes him. This must depend on his demeanour in the witness box, which may be good or poor. If the employer produces six written complaints from customers, those documents will speak for themselves. He did produce defective goods. The only question then will be, why?

**18.37** Three bundles of exhibits, preferably set out in date order, numbered consecutively and simply bound (which can be done very cheaply at most 'copying shops'), should be sent to the tribunal a week in advance. The Chairman and Members will have an opportunity of reading them ahead of the hearing. It will greatly help the case being put forward.

## CONSOLIDATION

**18.38**
*T (R of P) Reg. 1985 r.15*
If two or more employee have common matters of fact or law to be decided against the same employer, either side may apply for the cases to be consolidated. Very often the tribunal of its own motion will raise the matter with the parties. There will be a saving of time and costs if there is consolidation.

**18.39** Although both, or all, the cases will be heard together, nevertheless the tribunal will give its decision for each employee separately. Each party is entitled to be separately represented.

**18.40**
*Courage Ltd. v. Welsh*
If either party objects, then usually no order for consolidation will be made, unless the case for it is over-

& ors
Mar. 18, 1991, EAT
(unreported)

whelming. There may have to be a preliminary hearing (see para. 18.49–53) to decide the point.

## STRIKING OUT

**18.41**   A Chairman (or a full Tribunal) is empowered (in addition to the circumstances set out in para. 18.25) to strike out a pleading if he finds:

*IT (R of P) Regs. 1985*
*r.12(2)(e)*

*O'Keefe v. Southampton*
*City Council*
*[1988] ICR 419, EAT*

(a) the *contents* of an Originating Application or a Notice of Appearance is 'scandalous, frivolous or vexatious'. 'Scandalous' relates to such matters as allegations of dishonesty, or degrading or outrageous conduct that are not related to the issues to be decided. 'Frivolous' applies where the claim is bound to fail; and 'vexatious' where the proceedings are brought for the wrong motive.

The term 'frivolous and vexatious' generally connotes that the claim is unsustainable and constitutes an 'abuse of process'. This power to strike out does not extend to the *conduct* of a party, e.g., writing in abusive letters to the other side or even to the staff of the tribunal; or

*IT (R of P) Regs. 1985*
*r.12(2)(f)*

(b) there has been 'want of prosecution', e.g., where an applicant (or his representative) does not press home his case. This includes a failure to answer letters from the Tribunal;

but in both cases, before an order can be made, the defaulter must be given written notice of an intention to make the order. A time limit will be imposed on him to show cause why an order should not be made. If no representations are made before the expiry, it will be struck out.

**18.42**   The fact that an employer offers to pay the employee the maximum that a tribunal can award on a claim is not enough to obtain an order striking out the Originating Applications (see para. 18.10). It would not be vexatious to allow the proceedings to continue. There would need to be an admission that the claim was well founded.

*Telephone Information*
*Services Ltd. v.*
*Wilkinson*
*[1991] IRLR 148, EAT*

## WITNESSES

**18.43**   Sometimes a witness is hesitant to appear for one side, and it may be essential that he or she attends. A party can apply for an order from the tribunal for the person to be directed to appear. Provided the tribunal is satisfied that efforts made to persuade the person to give evidence voluntarily have failed *and* the evidence to be given is relevant, then an order will be made.

**18.44** The full name and address of the person will have to be provided. The order, when made, will be sent to the party applying for it. He will have to serve it on the witness.

## ADJOURNMENTS

**18.45**

*Jacobs v. Norsalta Ltd.*
*[1977] ICR 189, EAT*

If proceedings on the same subject matter are taking place in both the High Court and the tribunal, then a party may apply by letter to the tribunal for the case not to be listed for hearing before the decision in the High Court is given. If the other side does not oppose it, then the case will generally be adjourned *sine die*. A finding of fact in proceedings in either forum is binding on the other (see para. 18.90–94).

**18.46**

*Mavity Gilmore Jaume Hill*
*Brook FCA Ltd. v. Brooks*
*Feb. 7, 1991, EAT*
*(unreported)*
*First Castle Electronics*
*Ltd. v. West*
*[1989] ICR 72, EAT*

There is generally a very long delay before proceedings are heard in the High Court whereas they are disposed of in a short period in the tribunals. It is sometimes in the interests of justice to proceed in the latter, where this is feasible. If an application to adjourn is resisted, a Hearing for Directions will normally be convened to decide what course to follow. Only a Chairman will sit at such a hearing.

**18.47**

*IT (R of P) Reg. 1985*
*rule 11(2)*

If an application for an adjournment is made at the commencement of a hearing in the tribunal, or during it, and is opposed by the other party, then in the event of it being successful an order for costs (see paras. 18.95–100) is likely to be made against the person seeking the order. This could arise, for instance, if an a witness fails to attend, through not having been told of date of hearing.

**18.48** Adjournments sought on the grounds that proceedings are currently taking place in the criminal Courts will be granted if overall justice demands such a course. However, consideration will be given to the delay, the costs involved, the prejudice to the applicant and whether the same issue will have to be decided in both forums.

## PRELIMINARY TRIAL

**18.49**  Sometimes the Originating Application (see para. 18.10) shows that, on the face of it, the claim will fail. For instance, the worker may not have the necessary qualifying period of employment to bring the claim (see paras. 3.11–14). The tribunal will generally write to him to seek clarification of the basis upon which he alleges there is jurisdiction. It may be that he is able to show that he has worked for an 'associated employer' (see paras. 3.153–161) previously and consequently has the required length of service.

**18.50**  If the employer disputes any facts put forward by the employee, or he is able to show that there are other grounds that prevent an employee from pursuing his claim, then the tribunal would list the case for consideration of the preliminary point. The hearing would deal with that matter alone, and if the applicant was successful then the case would proceed (probably later) to a hearing on merits.

**18.51**  The procedure is very frequently used when an applicant did not present his Originating Application in time. He would have to prove (see paras. 2.14–19) on claim for unfair dismissal that it was not reasonably practical for him to do so and he did so within a reasonable period thereafter. If he can establish this then the tribunal would have jurisdiction to adjudicate.

**18.52**  If it is found that the applicant cannot succeed, a Decision (see paras. 18.83) will be given, dismissing the claim. That will be the end of the case. If shown that the tribunal does have jurisdiction, perhaps as a result of further information coming to light, then it will be listed for a full hearing on the merits.

**18.53**  A preliminary hearing may take place to consider whether a claim for equal pay for work of equal value should be dismissed on the basis 'that there are no reasonable grounds for determining that the work is of equal value'. Or it may adjudicate on which persons should be included in a 'pool' for the purposes of comparing the sexes in considering whether there has been indirect discrimination.

*EqP Act 1970 (as amended by SD Act 1975 & EqP (A) Regs. 1983) s.2(A)(1) Bromley & ors. v. H & J Quick Ltd [1988] ICR 623, CA*

## PRE-HEARING ASSESSMENT

**18.54**  Some claims, on the face of them, are bound to fail. For instance, if a manager is sacked for secretly setting up a competitive company and using his employer's secrets, then a claim for unfairly dismissal would almost certainly founder.

**18.55**
*E Act 1989 s.20*
If he takes proceedings, and he cannot normally be prevented from doing so (see paras. 3.1–9), there would be an enormous waste of money, not only to the employer, but also to the public purse.

**18.56**
*IT (R of P) Reg. 1985 rule 6*
Tribunals are empowered to have a 'pre-hearing assessment'. This is a hearing at which no evidence is called but the parties may make submissions on their cases as presented in the documents, or on the agreed facts.

**18.57**  For instance, does the applicant agree that he was sent to prison for six months for the offence of burglary of his employer's premises? Does he agree with the employer's record of his sickness absence or with a medical report which states that he cannot lift heavy weights?

**18.58**  If the tribunal forms the view that the claim will fail, it will warn the employee that if he insists on going on to a full hearing, an order for costs may be made against him at that hearing.

**18.59**  The same applies to a hopeless defence, e.g., where a dismissal has been manifestly unfair. The employer will be similarly warned.

**18.60**  The disadvantage of these hearings is that sometimes litigious parties, who are warned, still insist on continuing, thus putting the other side to the costs of two actions instead of one. An order for costs apart from one of a nominal amount would be inappropriate if a party is unemployed and without any capital.

### Pre-Hearing Reviews

**18.61**  Regulations may be introduced which will empower a Chairman (or a tribunal) to order a party, at a Pre-hearing Review, to put down a deposit of up to £150 as a condition of continuing proceedings.

## CONSENT ORDERS

**18.62**   Sometimes in the course of a case, either at the interlocutory stage, or at a preliminary or full hearing, the parties come to a compromise. The claim is formally dismissed on agreed terms.

**18.63**
*House of Fraser (Stores) Ltd. v. Davies Feb. 15, 1990, EAT (unreported)*
Generally, a consent order, especially where made by a party who was legally represented, cannot be later withdrawn and the claim reopened. It does not matter that on further consideration of the terms a party feels aggrieved (but see para. 2.97).

## ACKNOWLEDGEMENT OF LIABILITY

**18.64**   Sometimes an employer realises that he is liable to pay some compensation to an employee but the latter will not settle the claim. The latter either wants the matter disposed of in the tribunal, or alternatively he makes quite unreasonable demands.

**18.65**   Unlike the High or County Court (see paras. 18.116–117 & 18.124) there is no provision for a payment into court. The only procedure available in tribunals is to make a 'without prejudice' offer in a letter (see paras. 2.55–5).

## THE FULL HEARING

**18.66**   Usually the parties at the hearing are the employee 'applicant' and the 'respondent' employer. Where thereare several employees claiming against the same employer in respect of the same matter and the claims have been consolidated (see paras. 18.38–40) they all appear together, but may be separately represented. In practice, usually one person will speak for all of them.

**18.67**
*IT (R of P) Regs. 1985 rule 7(1)*
The proceedings are always heard in public unless there are particular grounds for not doing so. Examples are matters of national security, or there would be a contravention of a requirement imposed under a statute. There might be a most serious effect upon the employers' business.

**18.68**
*Kennedy v. Commissioner*
The tribunal is empowered to conduct the proceedings with a view to the 'just handling' of the case. It can take

*of Police for the Metropole The Times, Nov. 8, 1990, EAT*

some of the evidence in private and the rest in public. Further, being the master of its own procedure, it can take any reasonable course to enable the relevant facts to be elicited.

**18.69**

*IT (R of P) Reg. 1985 rule 7(6)*

Each party may be represented by whoever they wish (see paras. 1.48–50). If represented by a lay-person, it is as well to ensure that not only is he or she familiar with the law and procedure but also knows how to conduct the case in the tribunal. Bad representation can turn out to be a disaster.

**18.70**

It is important to remember that very often a case put forward by a litigant in person can be won or lost in the manner of presentation. Possibly he or she feel strongly about it. Tribunals are on their guard against being unduly influenced by appearances and feelings. But if a litigant is antagonistic, or keeps repeating matters that have no relevance, he may do his case a lot of harm. An agreeable, reasonable and objective litigant always gets the 'ear' of the tribunal and very often their sympathy as well.

**18.71**

What can be seen by the tribunal is also important. If an employer alleges, for instance, that a typist was very slovenly, and she denies it, but she appears with her dress crumpled and her hair in a mess, the tribunal will be bound to be influenced. Seeing is believing. A smartly turned out person can make a lot of difference.

**18.72**

*IT (R of P) Reg. 1985 rule 7(3) Showmaster Ltd. v. Lawson July 25, 1990, EAT (unreported)*

It is permissible for a party not to attend but to make written representations. A copy of the statement (with exhibits attached) has to be supplied to the other side at least *seven days* before the hearing. Such a course is often fraught with danger because a tribunal can only come to a decision based on the evidence adduced. Some unforeseen point may have been overlooked.

**18.73**

The person on whom the burden of proof lies (see paras. 2.14–19) has the right to present his case first. If he opens it, he should outline the principle events and their dates in a summary form, going through the relevant exhibits where this is helpful. It must be borne in mind that the documents will generally speak for themselves. Opinions should be avoided as they tend to carry little weight.

**18.74**

For instance, it is one thing to say, "This applicant was always very late arriving for work", which may mean many things, and depend on a subjective view. The time sheets *will show* how often and how late he actually was and there is nothing more to be said.

**18.75** The litigant should call his witnesses, and get each to deal with the relevant events. It is best to obtain from each a 'proof of evidence'. This will enable a party to concentrate on the points that matter and remind him of what the witness should say.

**18.76** The other side will cross-examine each witness and should put to them any matters in dispute or elicit any other material facts. It is their duty to cross-examine

*Batley plc v. Jones*
*July 18, 1988, EAT*
*(unreported)*

"a witness, on material parts of his evidence, if it is to be challenged, . . . so that not only the witness, [but also the other side may] have the chance to deal with it";

and failure to do so may result in a decision being overturned on appeal, and a rehearing ordered, perhaps at the expense of the party in default.

**18.77** When a party has finished calling all his evidence, the other side will call their witnesses in the same way and they too will be subject to cross-examination.

## Bias

**18.78** A party at a hearing who believes a tribunal in the course of a hearing is biased against him is entitled to apply to the tribunal that it should disqualify itself from hearing the case further. If granted the tribunal would order that it be tried by another tribunal.

**18.79** Before such an order can be made, the other side must

*Kennedy v. Commissioner*
*of Police for the Metropolis*
*Oct. 25, 1990, EAT*
*(unreported)*

be given the opportunity of making representations. The test of bias is whether a reasonable fair-minded observer who has heard all the relevant facts would have thought that a party was not having a fair trial. A party may notrealise that the way he is presenting a case is bound to cause annoyance, or that there is almost no basis upon which it can succeed.

## 'Hearsay Evidence'

**18.80** When presenting evidence, it should be borne in mind

*IT (R of P) Reg. 1985*
*rule 8(i)*
*Coral Squash Clubs Ltd.*

that the strict rules about 'hearsay evidence' are not applied in the tribunals. Most of such evidence is *v. Matthews & Arm [1979] ICR 607, EAT*

admitted (except sometimes on a crucial point) and the tribunal will decide what weight to attach to it. It is obviously better to get as much 'primary evidence' as possible, i.e., the person who saw some events or heard some conversation. It carries vastly more weight.

### Summing-Up

**18.81**    Finally, after all the evidence is completed, each side is usually allowed to sum up its case to the tribunal. They should deal not only with the facts but also with the law, if any arises. If legal authorities are to be cited, it is better to give a list to the tribunal clerk ahead of the hearing. They can be obtained and considered in advance if necessary. The observations of Waite J. at para. 19.21 should be borne in mind.

**18.82**    In applying the law, Waite J. said that tribunals have to seek to

*Surrey C.C. v. Lewis [1986] ICR 404, EAT*

> "penetrate [any] superficial disguise, to look to the form and not to the substances of the arrangements"

*Surrey County Council v. Lewis [1987] ICR 982, HL*

in determining the true position between the parties. Unscrupulous persons should be discouraged from trying to circumvent the intention behind the legislation or express provisions contained in it. This approach was approved by Lord Ackner on a final appeal to the House of Lords.

### Decision

**18.83**    After completion of the final speeches, the tribunal will reflect on the matter and give its Decision. Sometimes the Decision will be reserved for further consideration. In the latter case the parties will be notified later of the result.

**18.84**    Usually the Decision will be given orally after a short break. Sometimes will be in full (and recorded on a tape) but normally it will consist of a precis of the facts and the result. Later the Decision will be set out in aformal document. Again this may either be a full one or it may be in summary form setting out the result and a few other details. Where the allegation relates to

*IT (R of P Reg. 1985 rule 9(1)-(5)*

equal pay, discrimination and in certain other cases, it will be a full Decision.

**18.85**

IT (R of P) Reg. 1985
rule 9(5)
Spring Grove Service
Group plc v. Hickinbottom
The Times, Oct. 25, 1989,
EAT

I T (R of P) Reg. 1985,
rule 9(9)

Once an oral Decision has been given, or where a reserved Decision has been sent to the parties (e.g., 'promulgated'), it becomes binding. The Tribunal has no power to reconsider it even if it subsequently realises that it has made an error, unless it relates to some nominal matter or clerical error. If, for instance, the figures for the award have been added up incorrectly, then an amendment by a Certificate of Correction may be made.

**18.86**

Hanks v. Ace High
Productions Ltd.
[1978] ICR 1155, EAT

If the mistake is one of substance, it could point it out to the parties and ask them whether either would wish for a Review (see paras. 18.101).

**18.87**

IT (R of P) Reg. 1985
rule 9(5)
Meek v. City of
Birmingham DC
[1987] IRLR 250, CA
Palmer v. British Railways
Board
Dec. 14, 1990, EAT
(unreported)

If a summary Decision is given, then within 21 days of its receipt either party may request a full one. The full Decision does not have to be the product of fine legal draftsmanship, but it must be sufficiently informative to enable each side to know why they have won or lost. It will normally outline the facts leading to the complaint, and where there is a conflict on a basic point it will state which story it prefers. It will lay out the reasons why it has come to the conclusion it has reached.

**18.88**

Neale v. Hereford &
Worcester C.C.
[1986] ICR 471, CA

In coming to their Decision, the tribunal is entitled to consider matters that they feel are important, even though the parties had not placed much significance on them. It is also entitled to pay attention to the extent to which a point has or has not been relied on by a party during a hearing.

**18.89**

But this is subject to the overriding consideration that each side must be given the opportunity of arguing any point that has not been raised at all, and that the tribunal considers to be important.

### Effect of a Decision

**18.90**

Munir & Farooqi v. Jang
Publications Ltd.
[1989] ICR 1, CA
Crawford & Crawford
v. Salveson
May 14, 1990, EAT
(unreported)

Generally once a tribunal has decided an issue in the proceedings, e.g., that a person was an employee, or his summary dismissal was justified by his conduct, it is binding on every tribunal and court. But the other proceedings must be between the same parties. It is said to be 'res judicata' or there is an 'issue estoppel'. It cannot be rescinded except on appeal.

**18.91**

*O'Laoire v. Jackel International Ltd. (No.2) [1991] ICR 718, CA Arnold & ors. v. National Westminster Bank plc. The Times, Apr. 26, 1991, HL*

It does not matter that the tribunal was wrong in their interpretation of the law, or that an order made was improper in the circumstances. All other courts and tribunals are bound by that decision, except where there are special circumstances. This could arise, for instance, where a judge or chairman has made a mistake on the material in front of him. For instance, if he misread the date on a document that was vital to the proceedings.

**18.92**

*Secretary of State for Employment v. Cheltenham Computers Bureau Ltd. [1985] ICR 381, EAT*

The recording of *an agreement* between the parties by a Tribunal in a Decision for a redundancy payment does not imply *per se* that it is a statutory redundancy payment.

**18.93**

On the other hand a finding of fact, for instance, that an employee was late arriving for work on six occasions, and not 10 as alleged by one party, may be different. It will be based on the evidence laid before a tribunal. If there are further proceedings before another tribunal, other evidence may be produced that will irrefutably show that the finding was wrong.

**18.94**

*Ashmore v. British Coal Corporation [1990] ICR 485, CA*

A finding of fact made in a test case that the wages of a (comparator) employee were 'red circled' (see para. 11.44) may be used in a related case to determine whether that case would be bound to fail. A decision to strike out such a claim on the basis that it was vexatious (see para. 18.41) was upheld on appeal.

## COSTS

**18.95**

*IT (R of P) Reg. 1985 rule 11(i)*

This has been a ticklish subject for a long time because a lot of undeserving claims are brought and some unmeritorious defences to claims are made. If it is shown that they are 'frivolous and vexatious', e.g., there never was a valid claim but it is brought out of spite, then an order for costs is likely to be made.

**18.96**

*IT (R of P) Reg. 1985 rule 11(1)*

An order for costs can also be made on the grounds that the proceedings have been *brought* or *conducted* unreasonably. A party who is unduly prolix in the presentation of his case is at risk. If an adjournment is sought in the middle of proceedings because of some failure then that would be likely to attract an order for costs.

**18.97**

*Carr v. Allen Bradley Electronics Ltd. [1980] ICR 603, EAT*

Generally, the mere fact that a claim fails is not in itself grounds for saying that it has been brought unreasonably. There has to be some degree of 'pig-headedness' about the prosecuting of the case before an order is made. Even where an order is made it has to be tailored to meet the ability of a party to pay it.

**18.98**

*Colin Johnson v. Baxter, [1985] IRLR 96, EAT*

Thus if a former employee is out of work, has no capital and is living on social security, it would be unlikely that an award exceeding £100 would be made. If it is not paid, then its recovery has to be done through the county court. This may turn out to be more expensive than the sum that is ultimately recovered. An application for costs must be made either at the hearing, or within a reasonable time after it. If the Decision is reserved, then a party seeking costs must do so reasonably promptly after receipt of the result.

## EXPENSES

**18.99**

The tribunal pays litigants and their witnesses an allowance for the loss of their pay, up to a certain amount, and costs of attending a tribunal, again with a limit. A tribunal can order that payment should be withheld against a party, if a claim should not have been brought or for some similar reason.

**18.100**

Professional advisers, representatives for employers' organisations and union officials are not entitled to be paid for their attendance.

## REVIEW OF DECISION

**18.101**

There is a procedure under which a Decision can be challenged and that is by way of 'Review'. This course can be taken where:

*IT (R of P) Reg. 1985 rule 10(1)*

(a) the Decision was in error as a result of a mistake by the tribunal staff; or

(b) a party did not receive a notice telling them of the date of the proceedings; or

(c) the Decision was made in the absence of a party

entitled to be heard; or

(d) new evidence has turned up that could not have reasonably been known or foreseen; or

(e) the interests of justice require such a review.

**18.102** Thus, if the tribunal failed to give compensation for an item that had been claimed, e.g., the loss of pension-rights, then the tribunal can be reconvened to put the matter right. Or there might have been a judgment in the Employment Appeal Tribunal that has been over-looked and that would have affected the outcome of the proceedings.

**18.103** What a disabused party cannot do is to use the pro-cedure to try to have another 'bite at the cherry'. There has to be an end to litigation.

**18.104** If a party claims that there is new evidence that he could not have known about at the time of the proceed-ings, or that he could not have unearthed with reason-able diligence or have reasonably foreseen to be important, then he must send a copy of the written statement of the person who is to give further evidence to the tribunal. The Chairman can decide whether to order that the full tribunal should be reconvened to consider the application for a Review.

*Borden (U.K.) Ltd.*
*v. Potter*
*[1986] ICR 647, EAT*

*Vauxhall Motors Ltd.*
*v. Henry*
*[1978] ITR 332, EAT*

**18.105** The fact that the matter raises an issue of widespread public importance is not a proper ground under the 'interests of justice' provision.

*Deria v. General Council*
*of British Shipping*
*[1986] ICR 172, CA*

**18.106** The Chairman has power to refuse an application for a 'Review' where he thinks that it has no reasonable chance of success. He has no power to institute a review of his own motion. Where appropriate he may cause the parties to be informed that he feels the tribunal has made a mistake and ask whether either wishes to apply for a review.

*IT (R of P) Reg. 1985*
*rule 10(3)*
*Casella London Ltd.*
*v. Banai*
*[1990] ICR 215, EAT*

**18.107** An application for a review must be made within 14 days of the promulgation of the Decision (see para. 18.83–87), although there is power to extend time in an appropriate case.

*IT (R of P) Reg. 1985*
*rule 10(3)*

**18.108** There can be no review of an interlocutory order, and it matters not whether it is described as a 'Decision'. In determining whether a ruling is interlocutory,

*Nikitas v.Metropolitan*
*Borough of Solihull*
*[1986] ICR 291, EAT*

*Salter Rex & Co.*

". . . regard must be had to the nature of the

*v. Ghosh*
*[1971] 2 QB 597, HC*

application made . . . An order is not final unless it would have finally determined the proceedings which ever way the application . . . had been decided. Thus . . . an order striking out . . . is interlocutory, because, had the court below decided the matter the other way, the action would have continued".

## ENFORCEMENT OF AWARDS

**18.109**

*EP(C) Act 1978*
*sch.9 para.7(1)*

All monetary awards from the Tribunal are enforced in the County Court. If a party fails to make payment then a plaint may be taken out in the County Court, lodging with it a copy of the Decision. If the party still does not pay, then judgment can be obtained and if necessary the bailiffs can be sent to seize assets to the appropriate value.

**18.110** Any other declaration or order cannot be enforced save as is provided under the statutory provisions. An order for reinstatement cannot be specifically enforced. The only remedy for a refusal to comply open to an aggrieved is then to apply to the tribunal for an order of compensation for breach of its order. If the award is not paid, party can take proceedings in the County Court.

## THE COUNTY COURT

### General Information

**18.111** This court and its powers are derived from statute. It is presided over by a Circuit Judge who sits on his own, although assessors can sit with him in special cases. A District Judge, formerly known as the Registrar, also sits there and deals with the smaller claims and with interlocutory work. All civil actions start there where the claim does not exceed £50,000, although some may be transferred to the High Court if they are particularly difficult.

**18.112** The proceedings are conducted in a formal way, although there are many litigants who are not represented. The Judge has to try to unravel the relevant facts before applying the law. A considerable amount of the workload relates to property 'possession actions'.

**18.113**  Unlike the tribunals the rule concerning the admissibility of 'hearsay' evidence (see paras. 18.88) is strictly applied. It is necessary to have the witnesses in court to prove a case. There are also strict rules regarding discovery and inspection of documents.

**18.114**  Also unlike the tribunals, the loser generally has to pay the costs of the proceedings, irrespective of his means unless he is protected by a legal aid certificate. In that case his liability is generally restricted to his maximum contribution to his legal aid certificate (see para. 18.119).

### Representation

**18.115**  This is dealt with at paras. 1.57–58.

### Payment into Court

**18.116**  Sometimes a party acknowledges that he is liable to make some payment to the other side. He cannot reach a settlement because his opponent is being unreasonable. There is a procedure by which he can make a payment into court up to the amount that he feels that he is liable. If he does so the other side have to make up their minds whether to accept or reject the money paid in.

**18.117**  If the other side accept the money they are entitled to their costs up to that stage. If they decline, and in the subsequent action they recover less than the amount paid in, then they will have to pay all the costs incurred after the payment into court.

**18.118**  It is also possible sometimes to make a 'without prejudice' offer to settle a case. This is dealt with at paras. 2.58–65.

### Legal Aid

**18.119**  This is available, not only for advice but also for representation in court. A party's means have to be assessed first, and if they come within the range then he or she will be granted a legal aid certificate, subject to a contribution that will be assessed.

**18.120**  The court has no power to deal with claims over £50,000 (but see para. 1.56) unless both parties agree that the jurisdiction of the court should be enlarged. Otherwise, if a party is found to be entitled to a judgement over this amount, he will be unable to recover the difference.

**18.121**    The court enforces its own judgments as well as those of the tribunals. It matters not that the amount being recovered in respect of an action in the tribunal is more than its jurisdiction.

# HIGH COURT

## General Information

**18.122**    The High Court is presided over by a High Court Judge who sits on his own. The rules in the court regarding 'hearsay evidence', discovery of documents and so forth are strictly applied. They otherwise follow, in the main,those applicable in the County Court.

**18.123**    There is no restriction on its jurisdiction. Furthermore, unlike the County Court, the powers of a High Court Judge are derived not only from statutes but also from its 'inherent' jurisdiction, that is to say, from the Sovereign.

**18.124**    The procedure for making payment into court is the same as in the County Court (see paras. 18.116–118).

**18.125**    This is no place for the uninitiated to get involved without professional help. There are not only difficulties of conducting a case in the correct way but great risks regarding costs. Costs are awarded against the loser, and they can be extremely high on occasions (but see para. 18.114).

## Legal Aid

**18.126**    Legal Aid is available, not only for advice but also for representation. If a party loses, he will generally only have to pay costs limited to the amount of his legal aid contribution. It is strongly recommended that it is used.

# CHAPTER NINETEEN

# Appeal Courts and procedure

## EMPLOYMENT APPEAL TRIBUNAL ['E.A.T.']

### General Information

**19.1** If either side feel that a decision of the Industrial Tribunal is wrong, or a Certification Officer has come to an erroneous conclusion (see para. 1.107) then they have the right of appeal to the Employment Appeal Tribunal ['E.A.T.'] on any '*point of law*'.

**19.2**
*Medallion Holidays Ltd. v. Birch [1985] ICR 578, EAT*

This right extends to appeals against interlocutory orders, e.g., an order for Discovery of documents. But in this case it must be shown that a tribunal (or chairman) has exercised its discretion on wrong principles.

**19.3** The E.A.T. is presided over by a specially assigned High Court Judge who, like the Chairman of the tribunal, sits with two lay members, each drawn from one side of industry. One division of the E.A.T. sits in London and the other in Glasgow. There is no reason why they should not sit at other centres should the need arise.

**19.4** As to what is '*law*' and '*fact*' so as to enable an appeal court to intervene has been the subject of much judicial debate. Lord Radcliffe put it this way:

*Edwards (Inspector of Taxes) v. Bairstow & Anr. [1956] A.C. 14, HL*

". . . I think that it is a question of law what meaning it to be given to the words of the Income Tax Act 'trade, manufacture, adventure or concern in the nature of trade' and for that matter what constitutes 'profits or gains' arising from it. Here we have a statutory phrase involving a charge of tax, and it is for the courts to interpret its meaning, having regard to the context in which it occurs and to the principles which they bring to bear upon the meaning of income . . . In effect it lays down the limits within which it would be permissible to say a 'trade' as interpreted . . . does or does not exist. But the field so marked out is a wide one and there are many combinations of circumstances in which it could not be said to be wrong to arrive at a conclusion one way or the other.

All these cases in which the facts warrant adetermination either way can be described as questions of degree and therefore as questions of fact.

**19.5**

O'Kelly v. Trusthouse Forte plc [1983] ICR 708, CA Four Seasons (Inns on the Park) Ltd. v. Hamaret April 17, 1985, EAT (unreported)

The consequence is that where there are two cases with very similar facts, then two differently constituted tribunals can reach different decisions, and neither can be over-turned on appeal. This sort of situation frequently arises in disputes over whether a person is an 'employee' or is self-employed.

**19.6**

A '*point of law*' generally arises in the following sort of circumstances:

(a) where the tribunal has made an error in law. This could arise, for instance, where it has ruled that it has power to make a redundancy award when the employee made a claim after 12 months after his dismissal. There is no power to make an award where the claim is this length out of time (see paras. 4.50–51);

(b) where there is no evidence to support an important finding of fact that forms the basis of a decision. For instance, if a tribunal was to make a finding that an employee had been warned on five occasions about his conduct before being dismissed and that consequently it was fair in the circumstances, whereas the evidence given was that it was another worker who received the warnings, and the employee who was dismissed had never been warned before, then a decision based on erroneous facts would be palpably wrong;

Chiu v. British Aerospace plc [1982] IRLR 56, EAT Neale v. Hereford & Worcester C.C. [1986] ICR 471, CA

(c) where the result is 'perverse', that is to say, no reasonable tribunal could have reached that decision. In effect, the decision would raise the reaction "My goodness, that was certainly wrong", because the agreed evidence pointed in the opposite direction;

Walker, Laird, Heron & Harper v. Marshall June 2, 1989, EAT (unreported)

(d) where there is evidence of bias by the tribunal or any of its members. This is difficult to prove. An aggrieved party with a particularly bad or unmeritorious case is unlikely to get far on an appeal. But if a view has been expressed during the hearing indicative of bias, then a fresh hearing will be ordered.

**19.7**

*Piggott Brother & Co Ltd v. Jackson & ors [1991] IRLR 309, CA*

In deciding whether a decision is perverse, it is *not* sufficient that the appeal court would have certainly-reached a different conclusion. They must be left in the position of ruling that *no* reasonable tribunal could have reached that decision. This is because there are many factors that affect the minds of those adjudicating. Using their industrial experience they will have assessed the relative value of events outlined before them, noted any failures by either party and considered what further action could have been taken.

**19.8**

*Clifford v. Union of Democratic Workers [1991] IRLR 518, CA*

Where all the relevant information is derived from documents *alone*, then the decision is one purely of law. The appeal court can intervene if the tribunal or a lower court have got it wrong. But where it depends partly on documents and partly on evidence, then it is a mixed one of law and fact. There can only be intervention if there has been some mis-direction.

**19.9**

It is concerning (c) above that most confusion generally occurs. Many litigants feel that their story is right, and they find it difficult to understand how a reasonable tribunal could have believed the other side.

**19.10**

*Piggott Brother & Co. Ltd. v. Jackson & ors. [1991] IRLR 309, CA*

If there was credible evidence to support the tribunal's findings then the E.A.T. will (or should) not interfere. An appellate court must be able to identify a finding of fact made by the tribunal that was unsupported by *any* evidence or unless there had been a clear misdirection in law.

**19.11**

The fact that a tribunal's evaluation of the relevant materials leads to different conclusion to that of another one is not *in itself* grounds for interfering. This point is particularly pertinent where, for instance, a tribunal has to decide whether a casual worker is an employee, or who is the correct employer.

**19.12**

*Duncan & Ors. v. Wallace-town Engineering Ltd., May 6, 1986, EAT (unreported) Jones v. R M Douglas Construction Ltd. [1979] ICR 278, EAT*

Except in very rare circumstances, an issue must have been raised in the tribunal before it can be reargued on appeal. The complaint before the tribunal was that an employee had been unfairly selected for redundancy because of his work performance and experience. He was not allowed to argue on appeal that it was unfair because of a failure to consult him or warn him about the impending redundancy.

**19.13**

House v. Emerson Electric
Industrial Controls
[1980] ICR 795, EAT
Sheikh v. Anderton
Mar. 21. 1989, CA
(unreported)

But a well known exception to the rule exists regarding whether there is jurisdiction. This can be raised at any stage of the proceedings. Indeed an appellate court can not only take the point itself, but are bound to do so once they become aware of it. They will then act on it.

**19.14**

Barber v. Thames TV plc.
[1991] ICR 253, EAT

Where jurisdiction had not been raised in the tribunal-below but there is a *chance* of establishing lack of jurisdiction by calling fresh evidence that had always been available, the position is more difficult. Generally, where the employer had put their case on one basis that failed and wished to change tack by alleging lack of jurisdiction, the E.A.T. will not remit the case back to the tribunal to hear the evidence to enable the employer to have "a second bite at the cherry".

**19.15**

If the tribunal makes a finding of fact based on their assessment of the credibility of witnesses, e.g., they say that they 'prefer' the evidence given by 'A' rather than that given by 'B', or they rely on their industrial experience, it is extremely rare that the E.A.T. will reverse the decision. Stephenson L.J. in an appeal on a contributory fault point (see paras. 5.123–135) said:

Hollier v. Plysu Ltd.
[1983] IRLR 260 CA

"In a question which is obviously a matter of impression, opinion and discretion as is this kind of apportionment of responsibility, there must be either a plain error of law, or something like perversity, to entitle an appellate tribunal to interfere . . ."

**19.16**

Martin v. Glynwood
Distributors Ltd.
[1983] ICR 511, CA

Sir John Donaldson, M.R., put it this way:

"It was very important to remember that where a right of appeal was confined to questions of law, the appellate tribunal has loyally to accept the findings of fact with which it was presented and, where it was convinced that it would have reached a different conclusion of fact, it has to resist the strong temptation to treat findings of fact as holdings of law or mixed findings of fact and law. The correct approach involved a recognition that Parliament had constituted the industrial tribunal the only tribunal of fact and that conclusions of fact had to be accepted unless it was apparent that, on the evidence, no reasonable tribunal could have reached them."

**19.17**

*Retarded Children Aid Society v. Day [1978] ICR 437, CA Kearney & Trecker Marwin Ltd. v. Varndell & ors. [1983] IRLR 335, CA*

The appeal courts discourage litigants from searching around in a Decision with a fine tooth comb to find grounds of appeal. A Decision is not expected to record all the findings of fact or to contain a detailed analyses of the evidence but merely to give the findings in broad terms.

**19.18**

*Ellis v. Ministry of Defence [1985] ICR 257, EAT*

It is permissible for a tribunal in mid-hearing to give a preliminary view of the case. This must be for the purpose of saving time or promoting a settlement, but such a course has to be exercised with care. It shouldbe made clear that no concluded view has or would be taken until all the evidence is heard and until the parties have made their submissions. A failure to do so is likely to result in the Decision being set aside, on the grounds that not only must justice be done but it must *seem* to be done.

**19.19**

*United Counties Omnibus Ltd. v. Amin Jan. 20, 1986, CA (unreported)*

Certain evidence was unchallenged and was crucial in that it provided a proper and adequate reason for the dismissal of a member of staff. A failure by the tribunal to record in their Decision that the evidence had been considered, when they made a finding that the dismissal was unfair, was held to be indicative that they had either overlooked the matter. Or, if they did consider it, then their decision was perverse. The decision was reversed on appeal.

**19.20**

*Dobie v. Burns International Security [1984] IRLR 329, EAT*

Furthermore, even where the tribunal has misdirected itself on the law but has nevertheless reached the correct decision, E.A.T. will not overturn the ruling provided they are satisfied that 'the verdict was plainly and unarguably right'.

**19.21**

The E.A.T. is generally bound by precedent, even when a decision is given by another division of the E.A.T. There are several exceptions, but usually it can find distinguishing features in an appeal to enable it to come to another view. Hence, it is unwise to rely on other cases too much. They may hold the day, but a party can come unstuck. Waite J. succinctly put the point in this way:

*Anandaraja v. Lord Chancellors Dept. [1984] IRLR 131, EAT*

"Sometimes the judgment in a particular case will be found to express in concise and helpful language some concept which was regularly found in this field of inquiry and it becomes of great illustrative value. But reference to such a case could never be a substitute for taking the explicit directions of the statute as the guiding principle."

## Bias

**19.22**

*Kennedy v. Commissioner of Police for the Metropolis Oct. 25, 1991, EAT (unreported)*

Many a litigant who has lost their case feel that a tribunal was biased against him or her. To overturn a Decision on this ground it is not sufficient to rely on perceptions. Anyone who is aggrieved at the result could then appeal seeking a rehearing before a fresh tribunal. They could perhaps present their case in a better way. The test of bias is set out at para. 18.79; and this is very difficult to prove on an appeal.

## When Further Evidence May Be Given

**19.23**

*Howard v. N.G.A. [1985] ICR 101, CA*

*Ladd v. Marshall [1954] 1 WLR 1489 CA*

The general rule is that on every appeal no further evidence may be placed before the E.A.T. An exception lies

(a) where it was not known that some evidence existed at the time of the hearing before the tribunal, and
(b) that is credible and likely to have an important influence on the result and
(c) that could not have been reasonably unearthed at the time.

**19.24**

*Saunders v. Bakers Food & Allied Workers Union [1986] ICR 28, EAT*

But the E.A.T. will not permit a disaffected party to take advantage of its discretion by allowing him to re-litigate his case again. The power is exercised in *only* the most exceptional circumstances (see para. 18.103).

**19.25**

*Bagga v. Heavy Electricals (India) Ltd. [1972] ICR 118, NIRC*

An employee claimed that he had not worked since his dismissal, and was awarded compensation on that basis. The employer later learnt that in fact he had had a job. It was held that further evidence on it could be adduced.

**19.26**

*Trimble v. Supertravel Ltd. [1982] ICR 240 EAT*

It should be borne in mind that in the instance above, it would be possible to apply to the tribunal for a Review (see para. 18.101–108). The tribunal may be persuaded to alter the terms of compensation. This would be a better and cheaper course to follow in many instances.

## Desirability of Representation

**19.27**

The rules regarding who may appear are dealt with in para. 1.61. It should be borne in mind that legal representation is likely to be essential not only to explain how it is alleged that the tribunal is wrong in law, which in itself may require a considerable amount of research, but it is very important to have the technique of 'putting a case over'. Both often require years of experience, together with much knowledge. The law is no longer simple, and the 'common law' (see Chapter 8) often bears on a problem affecting the statutory provisions.

**19.28**   Legal Aid is available for representation as well as advice, and litigants are strongly advised to make use of it, if they are eligible. Alternatively, a lawyer should be instructed privately where possible. Only about 25% of appeals are wholly or partly successful, and there is no point in embarking on an appeal, with all the consequent expense, unless there is a reasonable chance of success.

## Costs

**19.29**
*EAT Rules 1980*
*rule 27*

Costs can be, and are, awarded by the E.A.T. where it finds that the proceedings were 'unnecessary, improper or vexatious, or . . . there has been . . . other unreasonable conduct . . .'

**19.30**   Strong feelings in the justice of a litigant's case are not enough. There has to be valid grounds upon which the E.A.T. can intervene. A suggestion that a tribunal was biased will not find a sympathetic ear, if the evidence shows that their decision could be right.

**19.31**
*Rock plc. v. Fairbrother*
*Feb. 11, 1986, EAT*
*(unreported)*

An employer appealed against a finding by the tribunal of unfair dismissal of an employee who had been dismissed for alleged misconduct, and against an order for costs. The tribunal had found that there was no evidence to support the employer's contentions. E.A.T., in dismissing their appeal, made an order for a further £500 costs on the basis that the appeal raised issues of fact rather than law.

## Time Limits

**19.32**
*EAT Rules 1980 rule 3(1A)*
*(& as amended by EAT (A)*
*Rules 1985) rule 32(3)*

Appeals have to be lodged within 42 days of the Decision (or an Order) being sent to the parties.

**19.33**   The time limits still apply where a party has applied for a Review (see paras. 18.101–108). A party is entitled to apply for both at the same time, and should do so if he wants to preserve his rights in respect of each. Before being given leave by the tribunal to have a Review he will have to bring his case within one of the matters set out in para. 18.101 (a)-(e), otherwise it will be refused.

**19.34** Once he has lodged his appeal to the E.A.T., he can always add to them later, with leave. He would have to set out some valid points of law before in the first instance, or it may be dismissed under a special procedure.

**19.35**

*EAT Rules 1980 rule 30*

Although the E.A.T. has power to extend the time for lodging an appeal, it is only rarely exercised.

# HIGH COURT

## General Information

**19.36** The High Court, when it sits as the 'Divisional Court' has an appellate jurisdiction. It hears appeals from the tribunals and magistrates' courts relating to decisions given on Health and Safety at Work cases (see para.16.28) and also those concerning levies (see Chapter 17 & paras. 1.64–76).

**19.37** Like the E.A.T., it can only interfere where the tribunal or court has gone wrong on a point of law (see paras. 19.1–6).

# COURT OF APPEAL

## General Information

**19.38** A further appeal is possible from the E.A.T. to the Court of Appeal on a 'point of law' (see paras. 19.1–13) only. This could arise in two ways. Firstly, the E.A.T. might have gone wrong in interpreting a section of an Act. Secondly, they might have reversed a tribunal on a 'point of law' that was in fact one of 'fact', and where they have no power to intervene.

**19.39**

*Adlington & ors. v. British Bakeries (Northern) Ltd. [1989] IRLR 218, CA*

The approach of the Court of Appeal is to consider, not so much whether the E.A.T. went wrong, but whether the original tribunal was right.

**19.40** The Court of Appeal is generally composed of three Lord Justices of Appeal, although, on occasions there will only be two sitting. Before they will adjudicate in any case, leave to appeal must have been granted by the E.A.T. The Court of Appeal themselves will sometimes give leave where this has been refused by the E.A.T.

### Desirability of Representation

**19.41** It is important that a litigant should be represented by counsel and solicitors, although an individual is entitled to appear on his own behalf. He may not do so on behalf of a company or others (see para. 1.79).

**19.42** It goes without saying that a litigant has to be extremely knowledgeable and be able to present his case with great skill, otherwise his appearance is likely to be a disaster. Not only may he lose the case but also be ordered to pay the other side's costs.

**19.43** The Lord Justices are extremely busy and mostly deal with points of great principle. Generally they do not suffer fools gladly.

### Costs

**19.44** Contrary to the position in the tribunals below, costs are always awarded against the loser, except in rare circumstances. If a litigant has a legal aid certificate, then his liability for an order for costs is generally limited to the maximum amount of his contribution to legal aid.

## HOUSE OF LORDS

### General Information

**19.45** A final appeal is possible from the Court of Appeal to the House of Lords in respect of any matter of great public importance. Only the Court of Appeal can certify that the matter is of such importance and grant leave to appeal. If it is refused, an application can be made to the Judicial Committee of the House of Lords who can decree that the case may proceed.

**19.46** This is no place for amateurs and great learning is required to present an appeal. A litigant can appear in person where he is acting on his own behalf. It is generally strongly discouraged because great expertise, which is acquired after years of experience, is necessary.

**19.47** Legal Aid is available for representation, and as in the Court of Appeal, the loser pays the costs (but see para. 19.44).

## COURT OF JUSTICE FOR THE EUROPEAN COMMUNITIES [E.C.J.]

### General Information

**19.48** This Court can only entertain claims that are referred to it by one of our own judicial bodies, or where one member of the Community takes proceedings against another. After certain formalities, the Commission (see paras. 1.80–83) may allow a claim by an individual to proceed there.

**19.49**

*Article 177*
*Article 177 (3)*

A reference *may* be made by a Judge where he considers that the interpretation of the Treaty is necessary to enable him to give a judgment in a case before him. He *must* refer it where a question of the community law is raised and there is no appeal against his decision under the national law.

**19.50** There is an elaborate procedure, which is contained in 'Protocols', for presenting claims. Written proceedings are followed by oral hearings, after which an 'Advocate General' will state his opinion. Months later, the court's verdict will be given, which will usually follow the views expressed by the Advocate General.

**19.51**

*Worringham & anr. v.*
*Lloyds Bank plc*
*[1981] ICR 558, ECJ*
*[1982] ICR 299, CA*

It only adjudicates on the interpretation of the Treaty and gives general guidance, leaving it to the domestic courts to apply that interpretation to the particular case before it. It tends to follow its own previous decisions, although it is not bound to do so.

## EUROPEAN COURT OF HUMAN RIGHTS

### General Information

**19.52** This Court sits at Strasbourg. It adjudicates in disputes between an individual litigant and a country that is a signatory to the European Convention on Human Rights and Fundamental Freedoms. That include all western European countries except Finland.

**19.53** A litigant does have direct access to the Court, but before any claim is accepted, it has to be lodged with the Commission that is set up by the Council of Europe who vet it to ensure that it is admissible, that is to say:

(a) all domestic remedies have been exhausted,

(b) that the proceedings before it have been taken within six months of the final domestic adjudication,

(c) that they relate to a right guaranteed by the Convention.

19.54  If the Commission finds that the complaint is admissible, then they will try to bring about a 'friendly settlement' between the litigant and the State concerned. If it fails to do so, it will draft a report setting out the facts and its opinion whether there has been a violation of the Convention.

19.55  The case is then referred to the Committee of Ministers of the Council of Europe. They can make a decision on it, unless the Commission or the State concerned refer it to the Court.

19.56  The Court consists of a judge from each member State. Each give their decisions.

19.57  Litigants can present their own cases, but it is more usual for a lawyer to conduct the proceedings because of the complexities involved. There is a fair volume of case law beginning to build up, not dissimilar to our own 'common law' (see Chapter 8).

# CHART FOR CALCULATING REDUNDANCY

This chart can be used for calculating the **Basic Award** (see para. 5.159(a)) but, if the employee started work below the age of 18, an additional ½ week's pay will have to be added on for each full year of service.

**Age of employee on date of dismissal**

(*Warning: see paras. 3.62–71 and 4.44–46*)

To calculate how many week's pay the employee is entitled to, run across table from age of employee on date of dismissal (see para. 3.71) until it meets the vertical line of reckonable years of service, and read off figure.

For employees approaching their 65th birthday, see para. 4.49(a) in redundancy claims and para. 5.159(a) in unfair dismissal claims.

## Reckonable years of service (see paras 3.23–36)

| Age | 2 | 3 | 4 | 5 | 6 | 7 | 8 | 9 | 10 | 11 | 12 | 13 | 14 | 15 | 16 | 17 | 18 | 19 | 20 |
|---|---|---|---|---|---|---|---|---|---|---|---|---|---|---|---|---|---|---|---|
| 20 | 1 | — | — | — | — | — | — | — | — | — | — | — | — | — | — | — | — | — | — |
| 21 | 1 | 1½ | — | — | — | — | — | — | — | — | — | — | — | — | — | — | — | — | — |
| 22 | 1 | 1½ | 2 | — | — | — | — | — | — | — | — | — | — | — | — | — | — | — | — |
| 23 | 1½ | 2 | 2½ | 3 | — | — | — | — | — | — | — | — | — | — | — | — | — | — | — |
| 24 | 2 | 2½ | 3 | 3½ | 4 | — | — | — | — | — | — | — | — | — | — | — | — | — | — |
| 25 | 2 | 3 | 3½ | 4 | 4½ | 5 | — | — | — | — | — | — | — | — | — | — | — | — | — |
| 26 | 2 | 3 | 4 | 4½ | 5 | 5½ | 6 | — | — | — | — | — | — | — | — | — | — | — | — |
| 27 | 2 | 3 | 4 | 5 | 5½ | 6 | 6½ | 7 | — | — | — | — | — | — | — | — | — | — | — |
| 28 | 2 | 3 | 4 | 5 | 6 | 6½ | 7 | 7½ | 8 | — | — | — | — | — | — | — | — | — | — |
| 29 | 2 | 3 | 4 | 5 | 6 | 7 | 7½ | 8 | 8½ | 9 | — | — | — | — | — | — | — | — | — |
| 30 | 2 | 3 | 4 | 5 | 6 | 7 | 8 | 8½ | 9 | 9½ | 10 | — | — | — | — | — | — | — | — |
| 31 | 2 | 3 | 4 | 5 | 6 | 7 | 8 | 9 | 9½ | 10 | 10½ | 11 | — | — | — | — | — | — | — |
| 32 | 2 | 3 | 4 | 5 | 6 | 7 | 8 | 9 | 10 | 10½ | 11 | 11½ | 12 | — | — | — | — | — | — |
| 33 | 2 | 3 | 4 | 5 | 6 | 7 | 8 | 9 | 10 | 11 | 11½ | 12 | 12½ | 13 | — | — | — | — | — |
| 34 | 2 | 3 | 4 | 5 | 6 | 7 | 8 | 9 | 10 | 11 | 12 | 12½ | 13 | 13½ | 14 | — | — | — | — |
| 35 | 2 | 3 | 4 | 5 | 6 | 7 | 8 | 9 | 10 | 11 | 12 | 13 | 13½ | 14 | 14½ | 15 | — | — | — |
| 36 | 2 | 3 | 4 | 5 | 6 | 7 | 8 | 9 | 10 | 11 | 12 | 13 | 14 | 14½ | 15 | 15½ | 16 | — | — |
| 37 | 2 | 3 | 4 | 5 | 6 | 7 | 8 | 9 | 10 | 11 | 12 | 13 | 14 | 15 | 15½ | 16 | 16½ | 17 | — |
| 38 | 2 | 3 | 4 | 5 | 6 | 7 | 8 | 9 | 10 | 11 | 12 | 13 | 14 | 15 | 16 | 16½ | 17 | 17½ | 18 |
| 39 | 2 | 3 | 4 | 5 | 6 | 7 | 8 | 9 | 10 | 11 | 12 | 13 | 14 | 15 | 16 | 17 | 17½ | 18 | 18½ |
| 40 | 2 | 3 | 4 | 5 | 6 | 7 | 8 | 9 | 10 | 11 | 12 | 13 | 14 | 15 | 16 | 17 | 18 | 18½ | 19 |
| 41 | 2 | 3 | 4 | 5 | 6 | 7 | 8 | 9 | 10 | 11 | 12 | 13 | 14 | 15 | 16 | 17 | 18 | 19 | 19½ |
| 42 | 2½ | 3½ | 4½ | 5½ | 6½ | 7½ | 8½ | 9½ | 10½ | 11½ | 12½ | 13½ | 14½ | 15½ | 16½ | 17½ | 18½ | 19½ | 20½ |
| 43 | 3 | 4 | 5 | 6 | 7 | 8 | 9 | 10 | 11 | 12 | 13 | 14 | 15 | 16 | 17 | 18 | 19 | 20 | 21 |
| 44 | 3 | 4½ | 5½ | 6½ | 7½ | 8½ | 9½ | 10½ | 11½ | 12½ | 13½ | 14½ | 15½ | 16½ | 17½ | 18½ | 19½ | 20½ | 21½ |
| 45 | 3 | 4½ | 6 | 7 | 8 | 9 | 10 | 11 | 12 | 13 | 14 | 15 | 16 | 17 | 18 | 19 | 20 | 21 | 22 |
| 46 | 3 | 4½ | 6 | 7½ | 8½ | 9½ | 10½ | 11½ | 12½ | 13½ | 14½ | 15½ | 16½ | 17½ | 18½ | 19½ | 20½ | 21½ | 22½ |
| 47 | 3 | 4½ | 6 | 7½ | 9 | 10 | 11 | 12 | 13 | 14 | 15 | 16 | 17 | 18 | 19 | 20 | 21 | 22 | 23 |
| 48 | 3 | 4½ | 6 | 7½ | 9 | 10½ | 11½ | 12½ | 13½ | 14½ | 15½ | 16½ | 17½ | 18½ | 19½ | 20½ | 21½ | 22½ | 23½ |
| 49 | 3 | 4½ | 6 | 7½ | 9 | 10½ | 12 | 13 | 14 | 15 | 16 | 17 | 18 | 19 | 20 | 21 | 22 | 23 | 24 |
| 50 | 3 | 4½ | 6 | 7½ | 9 | 10½ | 12 | 13½ | 14½ | 15½ | 16½ | 17½ | 18½ | 19½ | 20½ | 21½ | 22½ | 23½ | 24½ |
| 51 | 3 | 4½ | 6 | 7½ | 9 | 10½ | 12 | 13½ | 15 | 16 | 17 | 18 | 19 | 20 | 21 | 22 | 23 | 24 | 25 |
| 52 | 3 | 4½ | 6 | 7½ | 9 | 10½ | 12 | 13½ | 15 | 16½ | 17½ | 18½ | 19½ | 20½ | 21½ | 22½ | 23½ | 24½ | 25½ |
| 53 | 3 | 4½ | 6 | 7½ | 9 | 10½ | 12 | 13½ | 15 | 16½ | 18 | 19 | 20 | 21 | 22 | 23 | 24 | 25 | 26 |
| 54 | 3 | 4½ | 6 | 7½ | 9 | 10½ | 12 | 13½ | 15 | 16½ | 18 | 19½ | 20½ | 21½ | 22½ | 23½ | 24½ | 25½ | 26½ |
| 55 | 3 | 4½ | 6 | 7½ | 9 | 10½ | 12 | 13½ | 15 | 16½ | 18 | 19½ | 21 | 22 | 23 | 24 | 25 | 26 | 27 |
| 56 | 3 | 4½ | 6 | 7½ | 9 | 10½ | 12 | 13½ | 15 | 16½ | 18 | 19½ | 21 | 22½ | 23½ | 24½ | 25½ | 26½ | 27½ |
| 57 | 3 | 4½ | 6 | 7½ | 9 | 10½ | 12 | 13½ | 15 | 16½ | 18 | 19½ | 21 | 22½ | 24 | 25 | 26 | 27 | 28 |
| 58 | 3 | 4½ | 6 | 7½ | 9 | 10½ | 12 | 13½ | 15 | 16½ | 18 | 19½ | 21 | 22½ | 24 | 25½ | 26½ | 27½ | 28½ |
| 59 | 3 | 4½ | 6 | 7½ | 9 | 10½ | 12 | 13½ | 15 | 16½ | 18 | 19½ | 21 | 22½ | 24 | 25½ | 27 | 28 | 29 |
| 60 | 3 | 4½ | 6 | 7½ | 9 | 10½ | 12 | 13½ | 15 | 16½ | 18 | 19½ | 21 | 22½ | 24 | 25½ | 27 | 28½ | 29½ |
| 61 | 3 | 4½ | 6 | 7½ | 9 | 10½ | 12 | 13½ | 15 | 16½ | 18 | 19½ | 21 | 22½ | 24 | 25½ | 27 | 28½ | 30 |
| 62 | 3 | 4½ | 6 | 7½ | 9 | 10½ | 12 | 13½ | 15 | 16½ | 18 | 19½ | 21 | 22½ | 24 | 25½ | 27 | 28½ | 30 |
| 63 | 3 | 4½ | 6 | 7½ | 9 | 10½ | 12 | 13½ | 15 | 16½ | 18 | 19½ | 21 | 22½ | 24 | 25½ | 27 | 28½ | 30 |
| 64 | 3 | 4½ | 6 | 7½ | 9 | 10½ | 12 | 13½ | 15 | 16½ | 18 | 19½ | 21 | 22½ | 24 | 25½ | 27 | 28½ | 30 |

# Barristers and Solicitors Offering Their Services in the Field of Employment Law

## Barristers' Directory

**Chambers of Michael Burton QC**
**2 Crown Office Row, Temple, London**
**EC4Y 7HJ**
**Telephone: 071 583 2681**
A chambers with a long established reputation for expertise in all aspects of employment law. Many members from beginners to silks specialize in this area, advising on appearing in court. See our advertisement on page 6.

**Devereux Chambers**
**Devereux Court, London WC2R 3JJ**
**Telephone: 071 353 7534**
A leading set of chambers specialising in employment law with counsel available at all levels of seniority to undertake such work including wrongful and unfair dismissal, trade disputes and discrimination.

**Nicholas P Valios QC (Head of Chambers)**
**Francis Taylor Building, Temple, London**
**EC4Y 7BD**
**Telephone: 071 353 7768/9**
All areas of employment law work undertaken, both advisory and advocacy services offered.

## Solicitors' Directory

**Hancocks Solicitors**
**24 Horsefair, Banbury, Oxon OX16 0YA**
**Telephone: 0295 253211 or 0865 200345**
A progressive firm of solicitors offering independent professional advice through an employment law group for businesses and private individuals. See our advertisement on page 225.

**Davies and Partners**
**Rowan House, Barnett Way, Barnwood,**
**Gloucester GL4 7RT**
**Telephone: 0452 612345**
Commercial firm undertaking all aspects of employment law from its Gloucester and Bristol offices including contract advice, unfair dismissal, wrongful dismissal, Wages Act, transfer of undertakings, discrimination and redundancy.

**Cyril Morris Arkwright**
**Churchgate House, 30 Churchgate,**
**Bolton BL1 1HS**
**Telephone: 0204 35261**
Representation before industrial tribunal, unfair dismissal cases. General advice on employment matters.

**Gales Solicitors**
**188–192 Alma Road, Bournemouth,**
**Dorset BH9 1AH**
**Telephone: 0202 512446**

Unfair dismissal and redundancy tribunal work.

**Gordons Wright & Wright**
**14 Piccadilly, Bradford, West Yorkshire**
**BD1 3LX**
**Telephone: 0274 733771**
Substantial experience in both employee and employer contentious and non-contentious matters.

**Cartwrights**
**PO Box 18, Marsh House, 11 Marsh Street, Bristol BS99 7BB**
**Telephone: 0272 293601**
Advice on contracts of employment, service agreements, transfers of employees, employee benefits and staff procedures, trade union disputes, dismissal and redundancy claims including representation at industrial tribunals.

**Veale Wasbrough**
**Orchard Court, Orchard Lane, Bristol BS1 5DS**
**Telephone: 0272 252020**
All areas of employment law covered throughout U.K. In-house training courses organized for companies on employment and contract law.

**Wm McKenna & Co**
**6 Spencer Street, Carlisle CA1 1BG**
**Telephone: 0228 27615**
Advice and representation in tribunals nationwide and the Employment Appeal Tribunal: also High Court and County Court employment matters. Work undertaken under Legal Aid schemes where available.

**Crosse & Crosse**
**14 Southernhay West, Exeter EX1 1PL**
**Telephone: 0392 58451**
Advice on all aspects of employment law, industrial tribunals, unfair dismissal etc.

**Hawkins Russell Jones**
**7–8 Portmill Lane, Hitchin, Herts SG5 1AS**
**Telephone: 0462 451411**
This firm advises both employers and employees on all matters related to employment law including the formation of employment contracts and the firm's solicitors regularly attend tribunals.

**Rollit Farrell & Bladon**
**Wilberforce Court, High Street, Hull HU1 1YJ**
**Telephone: 0482 23239**
The largest legal firm in Humberside, provides comprehensive advice on all employment matters – terms of employment, redundancies, dismissals, discrimination and health and safety – including representation in courts and tribunals.

**Prettys Solicitors**
**Elm House, 25 Elm Street, Ipswich IP1 2AD**
**Telephone: 0473 232121**
Prettys' employment law unit fields a team of specialist solicitors experienced in providing practical and efficient solutions to industrial relations and employment law problems.

**Read Hind Stewart**
**Trafalgar House, 29 Park Place, Leeds, West Yorkshire LS1 2SP**
**Telephone: 0532 436014**
Specialists in employment and industrial relations law, both contentious and non-contentious, coupled with related commercial fields and specifically, intellectual property law and protection.

**Simpson Curtis**
**41 Park Square, Leeds LS1 2NS**
**Telephone: 0532 433433**
Employment and industrial relations law. A complete service including employment contracts, industrial tribunals, redundancy planning, enforcement of service agreements, severance schemes, discrimination and equal pay, legislation queries and training seminars.

**Fox Williams**
**City Gate House, 39–45 Finsbury Square, London EC2A 1UU**
**Telephone: 071 628 2000**
Recognized as leading employment specialists by major companies and senior executives, Fox Williams advises on every aspect of employment law including golden

handshakes, pension and share schemes, and service agreements.

### Goodman Derrick
9–11 Fulwood Place, Grays Inn, London WC2H 9DL
Telephone: 071 404 0606
The laws relating to employment and industrial relations are becoming increasingly complex. Goodman Derrick's Employment Department offers advice on the full range of contentious and non-contentious issues.

### Howard Kennedy
23 Harcourt House, 19 Cavendish Square, London W1A 2AW
Telephone: 071 636 1616
A commercial solicitors practice giving cost-effective advice on the full range of contentious and non-contentious aspects of employment law. See our advertisement on page 294.

### Ingledew, Brown, Bennison & Garrett
International House, 26 Creechurch Lane, London EC3A 5AL
Telephone: 071 623 8899
Fax: 071 626 3073
This long-established city firm has considerable experience in advising employers and senior employees on all aspects of employment law, both contentious and non-contentious.

### Jaques & Lewis
2 South Square, Grays Inn, London WC1R 5HR
Telephone: 071 242 9755
Jaques and Lewis is well known for employment law. Advises on 'crisis in the boardroom', discrimination, unfair dismissal, pensions and employee benefits. Acts for employers and employees.

### Masons
30 Aylesbury Street, London EC1R 0ER
Telephone: 071 490 4000
Masons Employment Law Group deals with all aspects of non-contentious and contentious employment law. It also has particular expertise in European law.

### Reynolds Porter Chamberlain

Chichester House, 278/282 High Holborn, London WC1V 7HA
Telephone: 071 242 2877
Substantial experience in employment field representing both employers and employees, including work permits, employer's liability, sex and racial discrimination, redundancy, wrongful and unfair dismissals, trade union law, health and safety.

### Richards Butler
Beaufort House, 15 St Botolph Street, London EC3A 7EE
Telephone: 071 247 6555
The firm gives advice on, and legal representation in connection with, employment contracts, pay and benefits, transfers of employment pensions, insolvency, discrimination, trade unions, redundancy, industrial relations and termination of employment.

### Pannone March Pearson
41 Spring Gardens, Manchester M2 2BB
Telephone: 061 832 3000
Pannone March Pearson operates a specialist employment unit with a wealth of experience. The firm advises on the whole range of employment related issues, providing a pro-active as well as reactive all round quality service.

### Jacksons
1/15 Queens Square, Middlesbrough, Cleveland
Telephone: 0642 244154
Jacksons' employment law department can advise on all related matters including representation before High Court, Employment Appeal Tribunal and industrial tribunals and advice on terms and conditions of employment and executive service contracts.

### Short Richardson & Forth
4 Mosley Street, Newcastle Upon Tyne NE1 1SR
Telephone: 091 232 0283
Specialists in employment law with considerable experience of advising on all aspects, and in appearing in industrial tribunals nationwide for both employers and employees.

**Wilkinson Maughn**
**Sun Alliance House, 35 Mosley Street,**
**Newcastle Upon Tyne NE1 1XX**
**Telephone: 091 261 1841**
Advice on all aspects of employment law
including contracts of employment and
service contracts, Trade Union and related
law, EC law including discrimination legislation and transfer of undertaking. Advice
on unfair and wrongful dismissal.

**Toller Hales & Collcutt**
**Castilian Chambers, 2 Castilian Street,**
**Northampton NN1 1JX**
**Telephone: 0604 232105**
Toller Hales & Collcut have offices cover-
ing Northamptonshire and Cambridge-
shire. The firm offers considerable experi-
ence in all aspects of employment law
including representation before Industrial
Tribunals and the Employment Appeals
Tribunal. See our advertisement on page
98.

**Cocks Lloyd & Co**
**Riversley House, Coton Road, Nuneaton,**
**Warwickshire CU11 5TX**
**Telephone: 0203 641642**
Wide experience over many years in advis-
ing both employers and employees.

**Hawkins Russell Jones**
**Town Square Chambers, Town Square,**
**Stevenage, Herts**
**Telephone: 0438 312849**
For many years this firm has advised both
employers and employees on all matters
related to employment law including the
formation of employment contracts, and
the firm's solicitors regularly attend
tribunals.

# INDEX

Figures refer to pages. Read beyond the page as there may be references to the subject on the pages following it.